GLOBALIZATION, TECHNOLOGICAL CHANGE, AND PUBLIC EDUCATION

GLOBALIZATION, TECHNOLOGICAL CHANGE, AND PUBLIC EDUCATION

TORIN MONAHAN

Routledge
Taylor & Francis Group
New York   London

Published in 2005 by
Routledge
Taylor & Francis Group
270 Madison Avenue
New York, NY 10016

Published in Great Britain by
Routledge
Taylor & Francis Group
2 Park Square
Milton Park, Abingdon
Oxon OX14 4RN

Printed in the United States of America on acid-free paper
10 9 8 7 6 5 4 3 2 1

International Standard Book Number-10: 0-415-95102-X (Hardcover) 0-415-95103-8 (Softcover)
International Standard Book Number-13: 978-0-415-95102-9 (Hardcover) 978-0-415-95103-6 (Softcover)

Library of Congress Cataloging-in-Publication Data

Monahan, Torin.
    Globalization, technological change, and public education / Torin Monahan.
        p. cm. -- (Social theory, education, and cultural change)
    Includes bibliographical references and index.
    ISBN 0-415-95102-X (hb : alk. paper) -- ISBN 0-415-95103-8 (pb : alk. paper)
    1. Education--Social aspects. 2. Education and globalization. 3. Educational technology--Social aspects. 4. Education Effect of technological innovations on. I. Title. II. Series.

LC191.M5943 2005
306.43'2--dc22
                                            2005001981

Taylor & Francis Group
is the Academic Division of T&F Informa plc.

Visit the Taylor & Francis Web site at
http://www.taylorandfrancis.com

and the Routledge Web site at
http://www.routledge-ny.com

Contents

Foreword

The Globalization Question

The publication by Nicholas Burbules and Carlos A. Torres, editors, of *Education and Globalization: Critical Perspectives* (New York: Routledge, 2000) opened a line of inquiry asking about the possible implications of globalization in educational systems and policies. The globalization question has been galvanized in the 1980s and '90s, given the growing international discourse and contradictory national debates about globalization from an economic, political, and social perspective. At the turn of the century, the globalization of the politics of culture and the political economy of industrially advanced, emerging, and less developed economies was affecting the nature and operations of perhaps one of the most "national" (and historically conceived) avenues for social mobility and equity of all social services of any country: the educational systems.

The globalization question is on the table and the stakes are indeed high. Public policy during the past three U.S. presidential administrations intensified the discourse of free trade and expansion of new markets. While this process hardly culminated in our contemporary understanding of the phenomenon of globalization — after all, as Burbules, Torres, and their contributors proposed, there are very different and contradictory definitions of globalization, its nature and its history — still very few research projects within the United States and elsewhere have critically examined the ways in which educational systems have been affected by economic and social policies prompted by globalization.

In a broad assessment of international patterns associated with globalization, it seems that public education has been called upon to develop a new labor force to meet the rapidly changing economic demands, which present policy dilemmas on issues concerning privatization and decentralization of schools.[1]

This movement includes raising educational standards and placing stronger emphasis on testing and school accountability. Decisions based on economic changes have given rise to new visions for school reform in universities as well. These reforms, associated with international competitiveness, are also known as "competition-based reforms."[2]

As a past president of the Comparative and International Education Society (CIES), I remember debates years ago about the importance of internationalizing U.S. education. Scholars versed in comparative education complained about the poor understanding of many of our colleagues at schools of education about the processes, systems, pedagogies, and educational histories of other countries, the political economy of the world system, and the regulatory role of the state and international system. Most U.S.-based education scholars seemed — in the view of many comparativists — parochially concerned with their own disciplines and research themes, usually associated with specific local, state, or national problems. While this degree of specialization and concern was commendable as a way to pursue rigorous research agendas, what was also remarkable is that it showed a blatant disregard for international developments or international education, despite the fact, comparativists would argue then and now, that these international developments could affect not only their own profession but also their own lives and the lives of the schools, teachers, administrators, and students that they studied with so much compassion.

I am convinced that this concern of comparativists, anticipating to some extent the changes that have swept the globe in the last two decades, is now only partially valid. Despite the still proverbial parochialism of American education, which in my opinion is part and parcel of "American exceptionalism," many teachers, students, policymakers, legislators, community activists, and parents — in short, people concerned with the educational democratic promise in the United States — now realize that it is getting harder and harder to talk about the connection between education and national labor markets without considering the importance of global markets and, of course, the growing trends toward outsourcing production of goods and services. Few people would question that discussions about testing, accountability, and curriculum — proverbial issues of debate among local, state, and federal jurisdictions in the United States — are no longer merely national or state questions. They now have an international presence; they are part of an international research agenda of bilateral and international organizations like the World Bank or the International Monetary Fund (IMF), and these ideas have saturated educational discourse in most parts of the globe.[3]

Will globalization deeply affect the way each country trains its workforce? Will globalization enhance the ability of countries and educational systems to comply with the growing demands of human rights? Will globalization affect the way our children and youth become socialized in the understanding and practice of the most deeply held cultural and social values, beliefs, and commonsense knowledge of each society? This concern would, were they alive, definitely affect the thinking of great educational sociologists of the past, such as Emile Durkheim or Karl Mannheim.

This book, the first by Torin Monahan, is a welcome addition to the growing bibliography exploring the connections between globalization and education. Yet this is not simply a new book. It is a different book. A most needed contribution to our understanding of this complex and — shall I dare say? — convoluted and contradictory phenomenon.

To the best of my knowledge, this book is the first systematic multi-sited ethnography of one of the largest and most complex educational systems in the United States, the Los Angeles Unified School District. Using a multi-sited ethnography, Monahan questioned how the institutions of L.A. Unified responded and coconstructed global-political forces across its many interconnecting domains. Monahan focused on neoliberal articulations, concepts, and readjustment throughout the many domains of the school system. Using key concepts such as *space, pedagogy, organization, policy, governance,* and *imagination,* Monahan explores particularly the new organizational form of the U.S. unified school system — one that he aptly defines and analyzes as "fragmented centralization," linking it to the overall framework of the No Child Left Behind Act of President Bush.

Yet this is only one of the reasons why this book is so powerful. Unlike previous work, it offers empirical analysis of an ongoing process, showing how globalization affects educational systems. The impact of globalization has been suspected by many scholars, certainly discussed by most, but without much empirical data on actual life in the schools to delve in.

A second, most powerful concept in Monahan's book is the notion of "built pedagogy," which the author uses to explore how technologies are changing school spaces. Like many critical theorists, Monahan does not believe that technologies are neutral. Quite the contrary, our author argues that "Saying that technologies and spaces are political means that they engender certain power relations and that they are infused with the values and ideologies of their creation." One of his conclusions, aptly documented throughout the book, is that "the built pedagogy of technologized schools shuffles traditional relations between students and teachers, but it meanwhile dramatically increases bureaucratic control over both groups while aggravating their institutional vulnerability."

It is evident in the book that adding technology to school sites as the panacea to promote learning is a strategy that is not working as planned. Moreover, the built pedagogy of technologized schools became another way, to use allegoric poker language, to "reshuffle the deck" of power relations in the schools. One of the main points of Monahan is that one cannot think of technology without thinking of pedagogy. I might add, following Monahan's powerful insights, built in the tradition of critical theory, that one cannot think of pedagogy, as Michael Apple and many other critical scholars have taught us for decades, without thinking of the connections between pedagogy, politics, and power.

As a scholar and social activist preoccupied with the impact of the globalization processes on schools and communities, there is no question in my mind that the issues explored by Monahan need to be discussed widely and that his findings should improve not only our understanding of educational policy but also help us to affect policy. Each and every one of the more than 70,000 teachers working in the L.A. Unified School system should read this well-written book. In the context of new and changing social and technological relations, this book will provide them with a fresh view and a powerful critique of their own practices and the power relations they are subject to. Communities should be acquainted with the findings of this book in order to be prepared to challenge some of the most deleterious outcomes of what the author calls "regimented fragmented centralization." If the experience of L.A. Unified is instructive, educational stakeholders — especially graduate students, researchers, and faculty interested in the destiny of education in the United States — should read this book immediately.

Carlos Alberto Torres
Professor, Social Sciences and Comparative Education
Graduate School of Education and Information Studies-UCLA
Director, Paulo Freire Institute
Director, Latin American Center

Acknowledgments

This book represents, for me, a lengthy process full of hope and concern, laughter and frustration. From the beginning to its present form, this process has been one of intense collaboration and growth, and I heartily thank my collaborators for infusing this experience with meaning, emotion, and life.

I must begin by expressing the deepest gratitude to my parents, Ken and Diane, and my brothers, Brendan, Brent, and Sean. It is no exaggeration to say that the many conversations I have had with them, political and otherwise, have shaped who I am, and the examples set by them have powerfully illuminated the somewhat different path I have taken from theirs. I am proud to call them my family.

Next, I must offer warm thanks and sincere appreciation to my close friends outside academia. They, along with my family, have kept me grounded and connected to the world in all its complexity and beauty. Jeff Miller, a long-time companion and personal inspiration, has taught me honesty, trust, and patience. Riccardo Boccanegra, the most charismatic individual I have ever known, has taught me confidence and humility. Christy Sayeg, an indescribably magical person, has taught me through her grace, altruism, and wit. These individuals are my role models, and I count each of them as a lifelong friend.

I must next thank the people who have provided intellectual homes for me at Rensselaer Polytechnic Institute (RPI) and Arizona State University (ASU). Several individuals read multiple drafts of this book and supplied generous comments: David J. Hess, Kim Fortun, Mike Fortun, Ken Warriner, Jason W. Patton, and Jill A. Fisher. Others must be credited for asking hard questions and offering much-needed encouragement and support: David Altheide, Jean-François Blanchette, Steve Breyman,

Nancy D. Campbell, Todd Cherkasky, Ron Eglash, Virginia Eubanks, Patrick Feng, Luis Fernandez, Ken Fleischmann, Rayvon Fouché, Art Fricke, David H. Guston, Edward J. Hackett, Randel D. Hanson, Aaron Kupchik, Linda Layne, Cecilia Menjivar, Kathryn Milun, Michael Musheno, Dean Nieusma, Hector Postigo, Daniel Sarewitz, John Schumacher, Langdon Winner, and Edward J. Woodhouse. Finally, participants in my 2004 graduate seminar entitled "Globalization, Technology, and Justice" at ASU catalyzed articulations that helped hone the general arguments made in this text (special thanks to Christopher Carey and Lisa Stephani).

In the larger academic universe, many colleagues have reoriented my work in meaningful ways. Among these, I must thank Hank Bromley, Bob Chianese, Marianne de Laet, Michael M. J. Fischer, Elizabeth Grosz, Carl Maida, Saskia Sassen, Ernst Schraube, Kaushik Sunderrajan, Carlos Alberto Torres, Sharon Traweek, Sharon Zukin, and an anonymous reviewer of the manuscript. The editorial team at Routledge, Catherine Bernard and Brook Cosby, deserve special mention for their gracious assistance and for immediately "getting" what this book is about. I also thank the following journals for permitting the use of previously published chapters or chapter sections: "Computers and Society," "Critical Sociology," "Globalisation, Societies and Education," and "The Urban Review." A reprinted map of the Sachsenhausen camp appears courtesy of the Sachsenhausen Concentration Camp Museum, Oranienburg, Germany. And while I need to preserve the anonymity of my research informants, I am extremely grateful for their friendship and insights, particularly the technology coordinator at the school that I call "Concrete High."

Finally, I must direct profound thanks to my thrillingly subversive partner, colleague, and chief collaborator, Jill A. Fisher.

Introduction

Progress is destruction with a compass.

Richard Powers 2000, 275

In the shadow of progress, globalization takes root in public education. At first it is difficult to detect because discussions of globalization tend to concentrate on everything but local public institutions: labor outsourcing, international trade agreements, foreign relations, telecommunications networks, individual mobility, immigration concerns, cultural homogenization, antiglobalization protests, and, more recently, terrorism. Public education may not seem like an obvious site for inquiry into the development and implications of globalization, but as perhaps *the* primary location for social reproduction, values cultivation, and identity construction, it is surprising that research on globalization and education is so scarce.

Slowly, glimpses of globalization become visible in the discourses and practices of school accountability, organizational restructuring, and technological literacy. These developments seem justified by the widespread recognition that there are serious problems with public education. Pundits of privatization and other critics recount the woes of this misguided institution, arguing that because "lumbering bureaucracies" are more interested in politics than students, in stasis rather than change, they can never provide students with individual attention or adequate resources. The system, according to this position, invites incompetence and produces inequality, so extreme intervention is the order of the day, lest societies betray and abandon their youth.

The threat of privatization, however, is only one dimension of the globalization of public education. Globalization also manifests itself in neoliberal administrative projects, pedagogical alignment with industry,

1

and technological contracts and commitments. Neoliberalism, which implies a simultaneous retreat from social programs and advancement of social control by the state, serves as the dominant expression of globalization in the public sector. School districts restructure themselves as corporations would, trying to balance bottom lines and to project positive images. Accountability regimes proliferate, demanding myriad tests and audits, placing the labor burden and punishment for inadequate performance on the shoulders of students and teachers. Pedagogy shifts to accommodate industry's needs for a compliant labor force, emphasizing entrepreneurial training, flexible multitasking, mundane skills acquisition, and apolitical acceptance of the status quo. Finally, vast technology projects unfold, drawing funds from every governmental level, supplying contractors and subcontractors with years of work, and enriching hardware and software manufacturers with lucrative equipment orders regardless of the state of the stock market. In these ways, the mission of education increasingly mutates into one of nourishing the private sector while imposing ever more control over the people within the system, especially students and teachers.

More than any other element in this list of changes, technology symbolizes global connectedness and student empowerment. Collectively, school districts invest billions of dollars in computers, telecommunications networks, and media equipment with the goal of correcting social inequalities through technology access. The reasons behind this belief in the corrective powers of technology are complicated, having to do primarily with society's unassailable faith in technological progress but also with political expediency. For instance, in some ways it is easier to demonstrate commitment to students through the purchasing of computers than through other measures, such as reducing class sizes or tackling the deeper social problem of poverty. Nonetheless, technologies alter the very composition of educational institutions. From classroom activities to organizational forms, from policymaking processes to industry contracting, technology integrates into the root structure of public education, hardwiring new power relations that cannot be removed without threatening the viability of the institution itself.

Broad brushstrokes aside, this book is about "globalization on the ground." It is a detailed ethnographic study of globalization and technological change in the Los Angeles public school system, which is the second largest in the United States, behind New York City's. Without denying the specificity of this particular school system or Los Angeles as a city, this book is designed to communicate larger trends in public education and changing relations among the state, industry, and the public. It describes the material and social conditions of equipping classrooms with computers, contentious debates over and resolutions of technology policies, subtle but profound shifts in jurisdiction and accountability within the organization, and the cultivation of myths — some with merit — about the revolutionary potential of technology in education. Because smaller school districts tend to follow the examples set by larger ones, an understanding of changes under way in Los Angeles public schools should provide important insights for those concerned about public education throughout the United States and beyond.

Technological Change across Local/Global Layers

Studying globalization on the ground is a tricky venture. Almost all theories of globalization position it as an assemblage of macrostructural forces, discernible in networks of capital, information, labor, products, and people across nation-state lines. The temptation is to view these powerful abstract forces as somehow natural and evolutionary, operating without much agency yet imposing radical new orders — social, political, or environmental — upon the world. There are several problems with this viewpoint. First, in naturalizing global interconnectedness of this sort, avenues for political intervention — which do exist — are severely restricted, because not only are there no clearly defined responsible parties (for negative repercussions) but state opposition is considered ultimately futile. Second, local sites — whether cities, communities, or school districts — are seen, at best, as only able to mediate these forces, not actually to shape them; this perception imposes a passive role on localities whereby reaction or adaptation are the only sanctioned responses. Finally, viewing globalization as a macrostructural force, and usually in terms of economics, deflects inquiry away from its instantiations and ramifications in the public sector. But when public institutions internalize global competitiveness as a goal, implement neoliberal policies to mold the needs of the public into those of industry, and restructure into organizations run more like corporations than democratic institutions, then this is globalization on the ground, and it deserves to be studied and critiqued as such, which is the task taken up by this book.

Rather than reify globalization as a monolithic macrostructural force that threatens to homogenize cultures, anthropologists demonstrate how people interpret relations of dependency and appropriate images and artifacts to generate new cultural meanings and understandings of the world (Inda & Rosaldo 2002). The same holds true for the many cultures within public school systems, where people do not passively accept the dominant streams of these complex systems in transition but instead tactically resist them and reinterpret them to generate alternative social practices, relations, and meanings. A study of globalization on the ground, then, should attend to the interplay of macrostructural forces, global logics, local material conditions, and cultural agency.

I define globalization as the blurring of boundaries previously held as stable and fixed under conditions of modernity: between local/global, public/private, self/other, nation/world, space/time, and structure/agency, to name a few. This blurring process is characterized by increased flows, exchanges, and interconnections but also by points of resistance, disconnection, and abjection. In other words, asymmetrical power relations are produced through these reconfigurations, seemingly pushing many of the world's populations and ecosystems to the margins of existence, while enmeshing all individuals, cultures, and institutions in a new world order. This is not to say that boundaries were ever as stable or clear as they were discursively constructed to be, which is a point well made by postmodern and postcolonial theorists, but instead that a phase shift has occurred where suddenly fixed categories or conditions are seen as obstacles to economic growth, social progress, and enlightened thinking rather than as necessary structures for stability in an unstable world.

To study globalization and technological change is to recognize both the situated specificity of a place of inquiry and the simultaneous embeddedness of that place within multiple spheres of influence. Because putting technologies into low-income inner-city schools is a politically charged endeavor to begin with, one that carries with it a heroic promise of correcting systemic inequalities (Gell & Cochrane 1996; Starr 1996), it is impossible to read such efforts abstracted from the political, economic, and cultural worlds within which these changes operate. Rather, technology projects occur within and across multiply embedded layers that, like transparencies laid on top of one another, each contribute to the final if never complete visible picture.

Through successive layering, one could perceive the local in the frame of the global just as readily as the global in the local, and the same for all the intervening layers, whether deictic (the nation, the city, the organization) or disciplinary (political, economic, cultural). As with the many global "scapes" presented by Arjun Appadurai (1996) as manifesting with varying intensities in every locality (i.e., ethnoscapes, mediascapes, technoscapes, financescapes, and ideoscapes), this approach does not imply a universalist lens for viewing all local/global conditions. What it does instead is stress the particularity of each locality while compelling investigation into the general crosscurrents that differentially inflect places or identities.

Layer 1: The Nation-State

Opinion was almost universal among my interviewees in attributing the current funding wave for educational technology to the Clinton administration's commitment to overcoming "the digital divide," an effort that was propitiously initiated in the 1990s, when the economy was "good." The federal government's E-Rate program (meaning "education rate"), which grew out of the Telecommunications Act of 1996 and is administered by the Federal Communications Commission under "universal service," was a key force in this national effort and an impetus for complementary state and local grants. The E-Rate program provides discounts between 20 and 90 percent for telecommunications networks in schools, based on school need, which is determined by the number of students eligible for the Federal Lunch Program.

Public funding for telecommunications networks in schools seems to be a politically wise investment, especially and explicitly on the national level, because these networks promise to increase the global competitiveness of the United States by supplying a high-tech skilled labor force that can vie with bourgeoning technology industries in places like India and China. As researchers of globalization and education observe, however, such "technological nationalism" works in concert with dramatic neoliberal and neoconservative reforms in educational and other public institutions

(Apple 2000). The focus on "traditional values" and fear of others (or of difference) adds a neoconservative dimension to the neoliberal changes under way, manifesting as "new managerialism" regimes of decentralization, self-management, performance contracts, and individualized accountability (Peters, Marshall, & Fitzsimons 2000).

In these ways, public education reproduces values and social relations that meet the needs of global capital. Especially ascribed to the terrain of urban metropolises like Los Angeles, the cultivation of technology literacy skills by students can be perceived as supplying a flexible and docile work force for low-end service-sector jobs in the city. The goal of this text, however, is not to argue that industry is literally making demands of school districts (although it may be), but instead to document larger cultural shifts that are acquiring material and institutional presence in public education, thereby becoming both structurally and symbolically reinforced and normalized. The advent of technological change in schools is interlaced with global flows, national agendas, shifting value systems, and local particularities.

Layer 2: The City

Los Angeles as a lived place and a global city is a powerful mediator of structural changes and cultural forces and, as many urban theorists have argued, a prescient indicator of social polarization to come elsewhere.[1] That city is the location for this study, and its contours shape the task and meaning of technological projects in its public schools. Los Angeles has been called a global and a postmodern city because of its advanced internationalization with high-tech industries, foreign investments, media and image production, expansive service sector, decentralized development, and large immigrant populations (Davis 1990; Scott & Soja 1996; Abu-Lughod 1999; Valle & Torres 2000). This city is also home to extreme social inequality and ethnic tension; it is well known for its myriad gated communities, periodic social uprisings, and large homeless population, which exceeds 200,000 people (Wolch 1996; Caldeira 2000).

Layer 3: The Organization

The organization of the Los Angeles Unified School District (hereafter L.A. Unified) reflects and is modulated by each of these city characteristics.

This under-researched yet enormous organization serves 746,610 students from kindergarten through twelfth grade, employs 80,325 workers in 806 schools across 704 square miles, and has an annual budget of $13.35 billion (LAUSD 2004). This is a global organization in the sense that it must contend with the city's immigrant flows, development patterns, and world-city image. As with the city, the organization has shifted in response to privatization pressures, particularly by morphing into a decentralized form to inoculate itself against dissolution or state takeover. Since 2000, it has been divided into eleven local districts, each with its own superintendent, staff, and budget.

Layer 4: The School

The school site offers perhaps the most crucial local/global layer in this study, because it is here that the effects of globalization and technological change become grounded and instantiated. My primary field site was a year-round high school in Central Los Angeles, which I will hereafter refer to as Concrete High. This is a "multi-track" high school, meaning that its population of close to 4,500 students and 180 teachers is split into three groups with two tracks always "on" and one always "off" year-round. This arrangement is designed to maximize space and service within the overpopulated school, which, like the district as a whole, must adapt to the rapidly growing L.A. population while the district's budget struggles to keep pace. The demographics of this school are over 75 percent Latino and less than 1 percent white, with an approximately equal number of black and Asian students making up the remainder. (In order to protect the anonymity of the school, I am not providing precise demographic information here.) These demographics are more or less in keeping with those in the district as a whole, with the exception of white students who comprise 10 percent of the total number in the district (LAUSD 2003). Finally, over 80 percent of students at this school qualify for the Federal Lunch Program, which provides subsidized meals for low-income students while serving as an index of poverty; the connection is meaningful because, as mentioned above, qualification for E-Rate, the federal discount program for technology, is determined by this index.

Argument and Concepts

The main argument advanced in this book is that when public institutions such as education scale back on their social or civic functions in order to accommodate global expectations and industry needs, they concurrently exert greater social control on actors in these systems. Neoliberal mechanisms of control are manifold in public education, including a host of tests, standards, benchmarks, and audits, but foremost technologies, which cut across all educational domains to naturalize disciplinary practices and industry dependencies. Ultimately, these developments shift authority and control away from teachers, parents, and students and into the hands of administrators, outside contractors, and the police (who are acquiring a greater presence on school campuses throughout the United States). While it may be difficult to apprehend the gestalt effects of these new power relations on societies, this book develops several concepts for identifying and analyzing them within the realm of public education.

Built Pedagogy

In looking at the use of information technologies (IT) in public education, whether for instructional or accounting purposes, rather than ask "Do they work?" I ask "What social relations do they produce?" This approach opens up inquiry into the context of technology use, the content of instruction, and the politics of technological change, unlike questions of efficacy, which tend to block out larger issues of power. For instance, if people wonder about the ability of computers to "work" in classrooms, they probably mean do students who use computers score higher on standardized tests than students who do not. This may be an important question, but it reifies dominant educational paradigms, shutting down conversations about the social effects of tests and technologies on student and teachers. Thus, the focus here is on the social life of technologies and their links to the political economy.

Technologies operate as extensions of space. Architects, educational philosophers, and teachers know well the force that spatial configurations exert on people — how they shape what actions are possible, practical, or even conceivable. Because space constrains certain actions and affords others, the design and layout of space teaches us about our proper roles and places in society. A classroom with neat rows of desks bolted to the floor, with the teacher's position front and center, communicates lessons to both students and teachers about the value of discipline, orderliness, standardization, and centralized control. Similarly, depending on how they are deployed, the presence of computers in classrooms can either reinforce or challenge these traditional "lessons." If computers are bolted to linearly arranged desks, they can introduce a climate of discipline while creating further disconnection between students and teachers, because neither can effectively make eye contact over the monitors. If, instead, computers are arranged in clustered patterns throughout a room, they can encourage student group work and autonomy while destabilizing some of the centralized control usually granted to teachers.

Built pedagogy means the lessons taught by technological systems and spaces. It recognizes how technologies are always embodied in material forms, regardless of their potential for catalyzing virtual experiences, and how, like all spatial expressions, they are inherently political. Saying that technologies and spaces are political means that they engender certain power relations and that they are infused with the values and ideologies of their creation. It is no accident, for example, that in the early 1900s, a historical period of mass production and scientific management, where the primary job for working-class laborers was on factory assembly lines, school architecture reproduced the regimentation and standardization of those factory conditions. Additionally, the schools of this period were designed to sort, order, and control students so as to meet compulsory education's goal of socializing new immigrant populations into American society. This is not to say that people have no choice but to follow the dictates of technologies or spaces, only that built pedagogy can offer stiff resistance against efforts of appropriation while lending full support to actions that adhere to dominant value systems. This book shows that, with some exceptions, the built pedagogy of technologized schools does shuffle traditional relations between students and teachers, but it meanwhile dramatically increases bureaucratic control over both groups while aggravating their institutional vulnerability.

Fragmented Centralization

In concert with the implementation of technological networks, which communicate messages of progress, school districts are restructuring to lend themselves the appearance of greater accountability and local responsiveness. Because L.A. Unified is such a large district, it projects an image of responsible government by adopting an organizational form that is "decentralized" in name but not in function. Notwithstanding surface-level modifications, in practice most of the decision-making operations of the district, especially those concerning technology, have become more centralized since the restructuring. At the same time, accountability for centrally made decisions has become more distributed to those along the multiple peripheries of the organization.

I call this new organizational form *fragmented centralization*, indicating the double-movement of increased centralization of power and distribution of responsibility. This is a uniquely neoliberal or "post-Fordist" articulation of power that can be seen readily in the technology policies of L.A. Unified. Examples include centralized policies for the implementation of automated reading software that teachers cannot alter, purchasing decisions about technology that exclude input from expert technologists in the schools, and centrally managed databases for evaluating teacher and student performance from afar. Centralization is not necessarily a bad thing, but the kinds of centralization occurring in schools pretend to be decentralized while advancing social control over those who are most marginalized in the system.

Not only is fragmented centralization apparent in the operations of public institutions, but it can be seen in recent laws such as President Bush's No Child Left Behind Act of 2001. Among other things, this law holds individual schools and/or districts responsible if students do not demonstrate improvement on test scores, while it meanwhile forces unfunded mandates upon districts for meeting the costly needs of specialized student populations. Most decision-making authority is centralized while social control and punishment for failure is decentralized. In this way, politicians can call for more accountability without accepting any responsibility themselves. More importantly, perhaps, the transformation of public institutions to accommodate globalization can occur behind a smokescreen of political sound bites, usually well insulated from public attention or scrutiny.

Structural Flexibility

Flexibility is the catchword of this global era. It is a term used to describe competitive industries, valuable knowledge workers, and new modes of capital accumulation (Harvey 1990; Martin 1994; Bourdieu 1998). Students are told that they must be flexible in order to adapt to changing labor markets, and public institutions are harshly criticized for not being flexible enough to compete with the private sector. As a discursive engine of globalization, flexibility cultivates desire for the rush that instability can bring. The lows following in the wake of that rush include an array of evils: environmental pollution and degradation, decline of the welfare state, neutering of organized labor, and uneven international development, to name a few. Flexibility produces such dire results, I argue, because it is most often a quality demanded of individuals, communities, or organizations so that they can adapt to globalization and its effects.

The discourse of flexibility has serious ramifications for public education as well, justifying organizational restructuring, the outsourcing of technology infrastructure construction, and the alteration of curricula. Ironically, in the name of flexibility, students, teachers, and even administrators must adapt to conditions of increased rigidity, with fewer avenues for innovation, interpretation, or expression. Examples of this pattern are noted throughout this book, but so are rare instances when social or material conditions support the needs of people in more polyvalent ways. It could be that in addition to the trends of disempowerment associated with globalization that institutions are shaken up sufficiently to allow for alternate, enabling articulations of flexibility to emerge. If so, then the challenge lies in quickly identifying and modeling them in some way so that they become the norm rather than the exception.

Rather than demand flexibility of people, what would it look like instead to make the structural conditions of people's lives more flexible? I advance a theory of *structural flexibility* as a conceptual response to systemic conditions of domination in public education. This response focuses not only on creating enabling processes for marginalized groups, as other democratic theories do, but on building semi-durable systems to support the continual reevaluation and re-creation of such enabling processes. I define structural flexibility as contexts that enable (1) alteration and modification; (2) multiple forms of individual action, interaction, and expression; and (3) power equalization among actors in the system. Examples might include wide-open classrooms that decentralize power, invite student mobility and collaboration, and support inquiry-driven learning tasks without imposing formulas or rubrics on students. Another example could be a technology policy that allows personnel at school sites to assess the school's unique needs, decide what equipment should be purchased, and place orders with the vendors or contractors of their choosing. Such examples of structural flexibility are rare, but they do exist, and they could chart an alternative pathway for globalization in public institutions.

Multi-Sited Ethnography of Global Technological Change

I arrived in Los Angeles in the summer of 2000, just a few months before the U.S. Supreme Court would decide the presidential election in favor of George W. Bush, and I concluded my fieldwork in the summer of 2001, just a few months before the terrorist attacks of 9/11 would shake the very foundations of the country. Having grown up and spent most of my adult life in Los Angeles, I knew about the culture of the city, its intricate freeway system, and the reputation of the public school system, which my parents pulled me out of in 1978, when mandatory busing designed to correct segregation would have sent my brothers and me 35 miles away from the school across the street. Over the years, I had witnessed radical transformations in urban development and population politics, the demise of the agriculture and aerospace industries, and the astonishing growth of homelessness and social unrest. My research in Los Angeles was facilitated by preexisting networks of colleagues and friends who were able to locate knowledgeable and willing guides for me within the school system, and especially at individual school sites in the heart of the city, Central Los Angeles.

The task of researching globalization and technological change in one large public institution and of observing and making some sense of the complexity, meaning, and implications of these processes was an incredibly daunting one. Rather than circumscribing this study to one domain, such as pedagogy, and then documenting how teachers use computers in classrooms, my goal instead was to study how the institution of L.A. Unified responds to and co-constructs global-political forces across its many interconnecting domains. The approach I adopted was one of multi-sited ethnography (Marcus 1995), focusing on the production of power relations throughout the many domains of the school system: space, pedagogy, organization, policy, governance, and imagination.

This book relies on many sites and people to add flesh, life, and voice to its body. Throughout my fieldwork, the Central Los Angeles high school that I call Concrete High was my most regular place of inquiry and learning; it was there that I observed the process of wiring classrooms for telecommunications, daily expressions of frustration and humor, local translation of district policies, and student and teacher navigation and appropriation of newly technologized spaces. The many stories recounted by the technology coordinator and his staff at this site added a sense of institutional memory and historicity to my study, and the countless theoretical debates I had with them enhanced my understanding of what technological change means to those living and working within the system.

A second site of research was a largely abstract one: the information technology community in L.A. Unified. Meeting monthly at different schools and daily in an asynchronous online discussion group, this collective of experts includes technology coordinators from elementary, middle, and high schools and a few network administrators and district-level (non-school site) technology administrators. This community has a relatively small and tight-knit core of about twenty individuals who meet monthly, whereas the extended online community is easily double that and is probably well in excess of a hundred members. The principal function of this group is a social one: to provide a sense of cohesion and belonging to the many technologists who otherwise engage in solitary battles to make things work at their schools. The practical purpose is to pose questions, share information, and agitate for change. It was through this group that I gained comprehension of the systemic dimensions of and subtle power negotiations over technology projects. Many members of this group readily invited me to their respective schools, and it was through these dozen or so other site visits that I acquired a comparative perspective on technological infrastructures throughout the district.

The policy arena of L.A. Unified, specifically bimonthly meetings of the Board of Education and monthly technology-related committee meetings, served as a third site of research. By attending these meetings in downtown Los Angeles, I developed an appreciation for the intricate procedural rituals that underlie official decisions about technology. In contrast to the narratives proffered by those at school sites about the misguided, top-down control exercised by board members, it was clear from these meetings that official policymakers were more preoccupied with taming the constant stream of systemic crises and projecting the appearance of competent management than with issuing fiats. It was at these meetings that I began to realize how much policy is shaped by central-level administrators and staff rather than by elected officials.

I intentionally moved between these three sites (school, IT community, policy arena) in order to triangulate perspectives on the evolving meaning of the large-scale technological enterprise at hand — the networking of the entire district. In my conversations and interviews with individuals in L.A. Unified, I would deliberately invoke a dialogue across these spheres, giving voice to the opinions of those occupying different institutional positions and then soliciting responses to those articulations. In this way, playing the nomadic researcher, I was often able to elicit impassioned and candid responses that illustrated worldview patterns that readily mapped onto the organizational addresses of my informants.

There were a host of secondary sites that offered further refinement of the collective picture that, like film being developed in a darkroom, slowly grew more distinct with the passage of time. These sites included administrative offices in downtown Los Angeles, "local district" offices in business districts just outside of downtown, "local district" technology meetings in museums and community centers across Los Angeles, and a large technology conference held in Anaheim, California.

I conducted a total of fifty semi-structured interviews and three focus group interview sessions while in the field. These included interviews with Board of Education members, administrators, teachers, students, technology coordinators, technical staff, contractors, and state policymakers. The primary goals of these interviews were to corroborate (or correct) insights gleaned from participant observation; add personalized meaning to ongoing technology practices in the form of stories, reflections, and concerns; and gain a holistic understanding of infrastructure projects through the juxtaposition and interplay of interview responses. The interview times ranged from 30 minutes to 3 hours, with the exception of one board member who dismissed me after my first question, but the average interview lasted 1 hour. (When interview passages are presented in the text, my voice is indicated by *italicized* type.)

By mobilizing multi-sited ethnography to direct inquiry into globalization and technological change, this research takes up the challenge posed by George Marcus and Michael Fischer (1986, 39) concerning the ethics of contemporary knowledge production: "Ethnography thus must be able to capture more accurately the historic context of its subjects, and to register the constitutive workings of impersonal international political and economic systems on the local level where fieldwork usually takes place." Tracing the implications of the global political economy on the ground, the workings of power in the design of emergent systems, and the processes of manufacturing new forms of life — these are the aspirations of the project at hand. The second dimension of Marcus and Fischer's (1986, 115–117) rally is to engage in "critical ethnography," where researchers self-consciously position themselves in relation to that which they study and pose culturally plausible alternatives to the situations with which they find fault. To this end I purposefully integrate my own voice into the text, through first-person descriptive accounts and analyses. I also recognize, however, that most of the data about the meaning of technological change were collaboratively produced in conversation with others. Thus, there is no discernible boundary between the perspectives of subject and object, because the knowledge did not exist prior to our engagement in dialogue and debate. This co-construction of knowledge was most readily apparent, for example, when conversations about the social effects of classroom layouts and computer placement would inspire technology coordinators to attempt new design configurations; my "research" in cases like this not only enhanced my understanding of constraints and processes but also functioned as an agent of intervention.

On a level of intervention once removed from my research in the field, this text develops specific alternatives (across each domain) to the problems of globalization and technological change that I observed in the field. For instance, structurally flexible designs and interpretable policies tended to generate better conditions for student learning and empowerment. It is my hope that the alternatives I propose, which are largely drawn from existing exemplars within L.A. Unified, will have salience for those in the system and that this text will become a secondary object of intervention and knowledge reevaluation in public school systems.

Book Overview

As public education conforms to global flows and industry needs, further social control is exercised on actors in the school system; in this way, neoliberalism functions as an expression of globalization in the public sector. At the same time, technology serves as an agent of globalization by interlinking all educational domains into asymmetrical relations of dependency and control. This book is organized around the multiple domains of public education (space, pedagogy, organization, policy, governance, and imagination), and each chapter illustrates the emergence of neoliberal relations within each of these domains. For each domain, however, I also introduce countervailing examples of empowering and equalizing conditions latent in the structures of the school system, sometimes made possible by the major institutional changes under way.

My analysis expands outward from the predominately physical realm of infrastructure, to the less solid but similarly constraining realms of pedagogy, organization, policy, and governance, and finally to the more amorphous but perhaps most constraining realm of the imagination. The purpose of this trajectory is not to delimit these domains but instead to argue for strong structural similarities in spite of what outwardly appear to be radically different qualities. The rationale behind this book's organization is that the ramifications of globalization are in some ways much more apparent and less contestable on the material level. By making the argument on this level first and then ratcheting-up to harder investigations of other domains, I encourage a systemic understanding of globalization and technological change in public education.

Chapter 1 ("Politics of Space") addresses infrastructure design and spatial transfiguration in L.A. Unified. It argues that technological infrastructures and their necessary spatial counterparts embody politics and establish social relations by design, and it develops the concept of built pedagogy to explain this relationship between space and practice. Technological spaces in public education reveal ideological overlaps between mass production and flexible production regimes, between institutional histories and current global imperatives. Through readings of classroom spaces and examples of design processes, this chapter presents a spectrum from inflexible structures that control actors to flexible structures that liberate them.

Chapter 2 ("Just Another Tool?") builds on the previous one to analyze pedagogy in technology classrooms. It describes social relations produced in these settings, discusses gender and ethnic inequalities with technology, and documents the kinds of educational technology programs that teachers and administrators find valuable, namely school "academies" and "enterprises." Rather than IT being an apolitical tool, these examples illustrate how technologies operate within larger ideological systems, linking students and public institutions intimately with globalization processes of privatization and commodification. In conclusion, an alternative framework for technology pedagogy is introduced, one that confronts the politics of technology by perceiving information technologies as social media rather than simple tools.

Chapter 3 ("Technological Cultures") identifies the emergence of a new occupational group of information technology specialists, comprised of several technological cultures within the district. This group is mapped across organizational levels, and its functions are explained. I argue that technological cultures are integrating into places of power and altering all aspects of organizational operations, transforming the school system into a post-Fordist organization — that is, with distributed operations yet centralized control. IT specialists weather the frequent storms of organizational restructuring through the maintenance of vibrant informal networks, and these could serve as a model for human-centered relations in the organization as a whole.

Chapter 4 ("Fragmented Centralization") expands on the organizational domain introduced in Chapter 3 to explain the splintering of power and responsibility within the "decentralized" Los Angeles school system. It shows how, especially with regard to information technology, decision-making power in the organization is becoming more centralized while accountability for centrally made decisions is becoming more distributed and decentralized. Through this process, school systems become post-Fordist organizations that demand flexibility of workers and students and increase their workloads, while — perhaps unwittingly — serving the interests of global capital.

Chapter 5 ("Policy Games") follows the translation of technology grants and their policies to reveal the human agency and values at work in the implementation of technological networks in schools. It argues that myths of autonomous technology or technological transparency cloud the panoply of negotiations that take place, subsequently removing decisions about technology from public participation or scrutiny. Because technical specifications for government funding are unforgivingly rigid, they aggravate existing territorial disputes among technological cultures in the district. Technology policy thereby reinforces Fordist rigidity in technological realms that are typically viewed as supporting post-Fordist flexibility. An alternative approach would allow greater leeway for the setting of specifications by those at school districts and school sites. This would better serve the specific needs of those at schools.

Chapter 6 ("Flexible Governance") investigates changes occurring in governance structures with information technology. It analyzes physical and virtual governance interfaces, regulatory apparatuses for technology use, and institutional cultures in L.A. Unified for their combined effect on public relationships with — and within — governmental bodies. The chapter argues that structural constraints are being solidified for the disciplining of publics and that the design of digital government interfaces or technology regulations should be seen instead as an opportunity for establishing mechanisms for public involvement.

Chapter 7 ("Future Imaginaries") draws on the discourses and activities of actors in L.A. Unified to map imaginations for technological change and possible future worlds. It locates dominant symbols of global technological change within articulations of the future, the development of data-mining systems, product-based conferences, and student sketches of future learning spaces. It argues that the social construction of imaginations for change reinforces student control and abjection by convincing them and others that technologies are their only hope for achieving social or economic equality and then denying them the fruits of that promise. Imaginations for flexible futures, by contrast, can flourish when dominant symbols are critically interrogated and when all experiences are placed on equal footing as legitimate material for imaginative acts.

Chapter 8 ("Neoliberal Orders") concludes by calling for the actualization of latent alternatives to states of discipline and control. Actors in school systems do possess agency to negotiate the dominant trajectories being established, and information technologies can be used to catalyze student learning and collective empowerment. Intelligent tactical resistance on the local level is required to conjure these alternate realities into existence and to leverage them against the silencing force of neoliberal orders.

1
POLITICS OF SPACE

Space is a social morphology; it is to lived experience what form itself is to the living organism, and just as intimately bound up with function and structure.

Henri Lefebvre 1991, 94

The limits of possible spaces are the limits of possible modes of corporeality: the body's infinite pliability is a measure of the infinite plasticity of the spatiotemporal universe in which it is housed and through which bodies become real, are lived, and have effects.

Elizabeth Grosz 2001, 33

Entering into the worlds of public education in Los Angeles after many years' absence, I navigated the spaces as a stranger. Often I did not know where to enter, what the protocols were for passing security desks and gaining clearance, where my informants or interviewees were located, or how others would respond to my intruding presence. This outsider vantage point made for frequent uneasiness on my part, but it rendered these sites productively strange to me, for as a body negotiating terrain for the first time, I was acutely aware of symbolic ambiguities, sonic and visual disruptions, and physical obstacles to movement. At each of the dozen schools I visited, from elementary to middle to high schools, I interviewed technology coordinators and had them walk and talk me through (or around) their many technological infrastructures in progress: server rooms, trenches, repair areas, classrooms, computer labs, phone rooms, libraries. Throughout these tours, coordinators would comment on the archaeology of networks in those particular schools, short- and long-term goals, administrative and/or teacher opposition, construction mishaps, contractor disappearance, and, without exception, the politics of the Los Angeles Unified School District. I would take pictures of rooms, watch people interact and bodies flow through spaces, and talk with students, teachers, and administrators. The recurring referent was that of flux, of new socio-spatial orders merging with older ones and of people's contributions and responses to these alterations.

The dominant architectural leitmotif of most schools in L.A. Unified, some well over a hundred years old, is that of discipline, order, containment, and standardization. These schools are concrete edifices, surrounded by fences (some with barbed wire), and divided into box-shaped classrooms, which contain neat rows of desks or tables, often bolted to the floor. This style is not surprising given the historical and political motivations behind the compulsory schooling movement that inspired the construction of such schools. By 1900, most states had passed compulsory education laws in an attempt to "Americanize" the 18.2 million immigrants who arrived between 1890 and 1920 (Sokal 1987; Brown 1992).

In conjunction with the introduction of psychological aptitude tests, school architecture injected an ideology of scientific rationality (e.g., standardization and differentiation) into education, intended to sort and tame bodies with the goal of combating the perceived risk of anomie that "uneducated" foreigners represented (Chapman 1988). The history of compulsory education can also be read as a positive, progressive effort to include and provide for all students irrespective of their differences or backgrounds. The point of discussing compulsory education here, however, is to comment on how ideologies and rationalities become embedded within built form. Thus, even if one celebrates the inclusive mission of compulsory education, the architectural manifestations remain those of standardization and compartmentalization: every student has a place, but all are also intended to remain in those places.

This older school model, which continues to serve as an architectural template for newer schools, can be linked, without too much strain, to another prominent institutional order that emerged in the early twentieth century: Fordism. Characterized by mass production, mass consumption, vertical integration, standardization, and the interchangeability of parts and workers (Amin 1994; Abu-Lughod 1999), Fordism encapsulates an ideology of rigid economic efficiency that penetrated deeply into private and public domains, such as industry and education.[1]

If one can judge the promise of the current information technology (IT) "revolution" by its surrounding rhetoric, it is, by contrast, uniquely post-Fordist. IT pundits such as Nicholas Negroponte (1997) proclaim: "Being digital has three physiological effects on the shape of our world. It decentralizes, it flattens, and it makes things bigger and smaller at the same time." This sentiment is echoed in the media and then rearticulated by those in public institutions like L.A. Unified. For instance, in an interview with a mid-level technologist in the district, he opined:

> A society that doesn't integrate technology, be it industrial or third world, will be a third world society in a matter of a few years. . . . Where in our society, education has typically been patterned on an industrial model – kid walks in door, spends time, and kid leaves door. . . . Now what we've done is that we have technology that can distribute *any kind* of education, no matter how sophisticated, to anyone, anywhere in the world, at any time. So what we've done now is we've said, (a) you don't have to have money to go to college and get educated, (b) even if you live in the highlands of Ireland and you're still driving around a donkey and a cart, you can get information to do brain surgery if you need it. So the whole concept of education, delivery of knowledge, and thus producing educated individuals, is now suddenly free for all . . . . So the whole level of how much you need to know and how fast information changes has accelerated beyond a pace that's ever been known in history.

These proclamations are post-Fordist in that they espouse a technology-driven change in production concepts and models, away from standardized mass-production and toward specialized just-in-time production, away from geographical boundaries and toward global distribution, away from temporally bounded creation processes and toward rapidly accelerated innovation, away from centralized organizations and toward decentralized collaborative entities, away from a producer paradigm and toward a consumer orientation. As with many similar articulations, these quotes by

Negroponte and the district technologist imply that if such changes are embraced, they will lead to universal prosperity, democracy, and equality.

In contrast, many scholars question the presumed benefits of post-Fordism and its globalization context, saying that it is most likely a deleterious extension of capitalism rather than a departure from it, and that it leads to increased disparities between social groups rather than establishing conditions of mutual advantage (e.g., Harvey 1990; Castells 1996; Graham & Marvin 2001). For the present purposes, I would like to put this argument on hold and instead investigate how these two production models (Fordism and post-Fordism) — whether virtual, real, or both — clash, intermingle, and integrate in spatial forms, on the ground, generating new social relations and subsequently shaping the future in unanticipated and unforeseeable ways.

The integration of Fordist and post-Fordist production models in public education is really one of ideological synthesis, where the built world functions as a stubborn palimpsest, a continuously rewritten script whose previous lines, directions, and motivations can never be completely effaced. In this chapter, I observe these clashes through two lenses. First, ideological changes are read through the practices of students and teachers in existing technology classrooms. These snapshots of people in school spaces reveal the continuous reconstitution of mostly static, already constructed spaces, where the actions (and nonactions) of new occupants and new mentalities intermingle with sedimented materialities and institutional histories. I develop the concept of *built pedagogy* to account for the politics of spaces and their capacity to teach individuals how they should act in the world. Second, ideological changes are perceived through the ongoing redesign of educational spaces by school-site personnel. The process of integrating new information technologies into older school spaces highlights problems of material resistance to technologies that are often celebrated for their flexibility and virtuality.

Recognizing that spaces of education are spaces of cultural reproduction, I next argue that the pressures of globalization, including the valuing of compliant students and workers, are quietly reinforced through material impositions on social development and exchange. In answer to this trend toward self-flexibility demanded of actors in the system, a model of structural flexibility is proposed for the design of polyvalent spaces that empower rather than discipline their occupants.

Syncretic Spaces

The Fordist-informed design of older schools and classrooms makes the integration of IT a difficult endeavor in many ways. As computers and their networks are introduced into classrooms that previously had no machines, they are typically placed along the back and side walls. This design is chosen for purposes of providing easy, safe, and inexpensive electrical and data supply but also so as not to intrude overmuch into the existing territory of classrooms. As a result of these and other social reasons (see Chapter 2), computers are not often incorporated into daily classroom instruction. In other spaces that have previously housed machines, whether computers or typewriters before them, the design layout significantly departs from this periphery model, and computers are centrally deployed on tables lined up in neat rows across the room. The first space that I describe matches this latter layout of centralized computer placement.

Space 1: Computer Classroom at a High School

Tucked away behind lockers and colorful student wall murals on the second floor of the high school, this computer classroom is completely devoid of any windows or adornment; it is spare in spite of its relatively large size of roughly 26 by 40 feet, with room for forty students (Figure 1.1). Fluorescent lights glare from above, giving all bodies a yellowish tint, and sounds are muffled as they bounce off the scuffed floor tiles and up into the pock-marked drop ceiling. A sink area in the back of the room indicates a past life for this space, possibly as an arts-and-crafts room or science lab. There are two columns of tables, divided into five rows, with a protective barrier of desks and tables at the front of the room insulating the teacher from the students. All the tables are bolted to the floor to prevent their movement, and several big gouges in the floor tiles betray the destructive results of attempts at bolt removal. Awkwardly, metal-coated power outlets rise out of the floor like symmetrically planted land mines, serving as infrastructural traces of a past technological revolution: the electric typewriter.

The African American teacher in this room laconically greets his mostly Latino students by name as they wander in, and judging from their interchanges, they seem to have a good rapport. Students chat a little in Spanish or hum as they work on their lesson of transcribing a business letter; they peck along with one or two fingers while the teacher remains

Figure 1.1 Centralized computer layout.

mostly concealed behind his barricade of furniture. Occasionally students will get up and wander over to their friends to help them with their work; in order to occupy himself, the teacher removes a large pink feather duster from inside his file cabinet and dusts off the tops of unused machines. Midway through the period, one student coaxingly asks him if it is wrong to have someone else type the drill for him, to which the teacher responds: "Don't play me like that; I can tell whether you typed it or not too." With the ice broken, students ask the teacher whom he voted for in the 2000 presidential elections held the previous day (the results being still in dispute). His response: "A person."

"Which candidate do you think is a better person?" the students press on.

"Ralph Nader, but I didn't vote for him."

"Yeah," students pick up the drift, "only white people and rich people vote for Bush."

He carefully corrects them, "Conservatives vote for Bush."

"I want another Clinton," a male student interjects.

"That's why Gore didn't win," the teacher closes the conversation.

In this exchange, the teacher's guarded enunciations transmit and mutually reinforce the signals of temperance and caution radiating out from this fortified space; just as the protective barrier of desks distances the teacher from the students, so does his control over the discussion keep personal divulgence and student connection at bay. The space provides a social script for him (and the students) to follow.

As I converse with the teacher after class, it is clear that he feels constrained by the typing-class layout, a remnant from another era. He confides that a cluster configuration would be much better for student collaboration and visibility (since they are now hidden behind monitor screens) and that he thinks other teachers would agree with him and be comfortable with a cluster design. I detect from his tone that he thinks I might have some leverage to make such changes occur, perhaps because I am frequently seen with the school's technology coordinator and seem to have his confidence. The obstacles to rearranging a room, however, are severe: there is no budget for new furniture, only for new computers; the floor would likely be destroyed in the process of unbolting the existing tables; a new floor could be requested from L.A. Unified, but it would probably take a year or more before it was actually installed; and the labor would be a strain on the school's limited technology staff of teaching assistants. Regardless of what the teacher says, he seems very comfortable with his current configuration, which grants him symbolic authority over the space.

Space 2: Computer Classroom at a High School

At a high school just outside of downtown Los Angeles, close to where several freeways merge in a maze-like, spaghetti-junction mess, I attend a meeting of technologists after school hours. During a break in the meeting, I take to wandering the halls, where I spy an older Latino teacher working alone in his computer classroom and decide to approach him. He explains to me the evolution of network installation at the high school and, indirectly, of his classroom. The district was using funds from a local bond measure to wire the school, but when contractors accidentally drilled into asbestos, the school had to be closed for 2 weeks of cleanup. Construction then stopped altogether for 9 months while contractors and the district fought over who should be held responsible for the added expenses and potential lawsuits. It took more than a year from the initial health alert for the network to be completed and its ownership to be signed over to the school.

The teacher had a fair degree of autonomy in choosing the actual layout of the room, and he elected to make the "side" of the classroom into its "front," so that it could contain three long rows and two columns, with an aisle down the center (see Figure 1.2 for a picture of a similar space, not the actual room described). The effect of this configuration is increased visibility: the students can see the teacher and television screens up front without too much strain, and the teacher can easily walk to the back of the three rows and view every student's monitor screen with one quick glance. Monitors face away from the windows at the front of the room, dissipating any glare problems from the external light. The teacher demonstrates the Apple Network Administrative Toolkit (ANAT) that he has running on the 30 networked computers in the room, showing me how he can "take control" of all the machines at once, a smaller grouping of them, or an individual workstation from his terminal at the front.

Figure 1.2 High-visibility classroom.

Moreover, if he so chooses, he can view the image of any student's monitor on his computer screen without the student's awareness and without disrupting his or her activities. The idea behind such technological control is augmented pedagogical attention, not discipline, he stresses, although ANAT can be used that way. My interlocutor confesses that such virtual monitoring is way too cumbersome, so he opts for "walking the aisles" instead.

The teacher continues to explain that this space is designed for instructional activities, lessons of leading and following, rather than those of self-exploration or collaboration. All the same, he does encourage students to engage in the kinds of collaborative projects that would be better served by a cluster arrangement of desks and machines, and he says that students have no problem getting up and walking over to others to see what they are doing and asking them how they are doing it. The range of student activities is determined by the tone of the instructor, he avers, and I agree, but the room does afford wandering and collaboration by means of its spaciousness (it is about the size of the first room described yet contains only one-quarter the number of computer stations and seats).

Space 3: Applied Math and Science Academy at a Middle School

An old wood shop at an L.A. Unified middle school has been converted into a multimedia classroom, and the room's spaciousness and high ceilings provide a sense of ease and mobility (Figure 1.3). The layout resembles a plus sign (+), creating areas for separate tasks without rigid boundaries. Modular technology stations line the perimeter, leaving the center open for students to work on projects or walk between stations. Ten square tables are set up in this center area; their shape was specifically chosen, I am told, to create a defined sense of shared territory and to discourage too much wandering. (Rectangular tables were attempted first but were too bulky; round tables were tried second but encouraged too much movement.) From this center area, I can easily observe what students are working on at each computer. Looking up, I see that overhead beams and pipes have been painted in bright, cheerful colors: orange, red, green, purple, and yellow. Skylights and windows illuminate the room with natural light, increasing its sense of internal expansiveness and external connectedness, but as

Figure 1.3 Converted woodshop.

unusual as classrooms with natural overhead light are in L.A. Unified, even more rare are the Plexiglas filters on the windows, which remove both heat and glare. A newly installed air conditioner further transforms this room into a cool oasis on this blistering spring afternoon.

Lessons in this room follow a series of prescripted modules organized around themes (space technology, aerodynamics, alternative energy, multimedia production, health management, etc.), and each of the 24 technology stations supports one of these themes. All work in this class is peer-graded, and from the first assignment students learn to evaluate both end products and participation. Throughout the year, seventh- and eighth-grade students work on collaborative projects that integrate multiple subject areas, such as building rockets, experimenting with wind tunnels, designing cars with the use of software applications, checking each other's blood pressure, producing videos with the music department, and much more. Rather than limiting student involvement, the module format provides the necessary scaffolding for students to participate fully in content creation.

When students first enter class, they stand silently and wait. This is obviously a ritual, because they are quiet for at least a full minute before the Japanese-American teacher instructs them on what to do with their projects. Today half the students work at stations while the others rehearse a video shoot that will take place later in the week. For this video production, the students have collectively decided on a topic of interest to them, written a script, and plotted an action scene. They will edit the film and screen it when they are done shooting. Every student on this production team has selected a role (director, camera operator, actor, technician), and they use real film as they run through the scene. The teacher tells them that if they are planning an outdoor shot, they should just use their imaginations today and focus on acting.

Students are autonomous in this learning environment, and they move freely yet purposefully around the room. When the room's phone rings while I am interviewing the teacher, a student nearby answers it, and following a poster outlining phone etiquette, he determines that the call is not urgent and takes a message. As with the modules, this poster presents another example of the many support structures that aid students in running the business of the classroom, which is their learning. When a student approaches us and gestures toward a pair of scissors, the teacher engages him in conversation: "Why do you want the scissors? What are you going to do with them?" When the student leaves, the teacher tells me that he takes every opportunity to help them practice communicating in English, because the (mostly Latino) students do not converse in English on their own. These interactions with the phone and scissors show how even "noninstructional" moments can teach responsibility, critical thinking, and language skills.

With the demise of vocational "shop" programs in public education, many technology teachers have claimed these large, abandoned rooms for the openness and flexibility they provide. At this middle school, a small group of individuals took advantage of a National Guard–sponsored Applied Math and Science Academy (AMSA) program to convert this wood shop into a project-based technology lab. They appropriated an existing T1 network line that was not being used and rerouted it to the lab for Internet connectivity, and the teacher and others redesigned the space by tearing out tables, painting the walls and pipes, carpeting the floor, purchasing new furniture, and adding storage and special editing rooms at the corners (which created the area's plus-sign layout). When the National Guard dropped this "soft" recruiting program and stripped its funding, other AMSA schools sought corporate sponsorship with companies like Boeing, but the teacher in this space kept the program afloat by soliciting the school itself for funding. He explains to me that they have tried to maintain the program more or less as it was set up, just in case the Guard ever wants to come back and renew funding.

Through a combination of business savvy, manipulation of informal networks, and creative individual investment, the AMSA teacher is able to navigate *external* policies to serve the *internal* needs of the class, effectively blurring the boundaries between outside/inside. Through the district, he buys special durable furniture from a company that offers a 10-year warrantee or from sources of used furniture or government sales. He claims that most people do not know about these furniture options and that the purchasing department of the district does not advertise them. He constantly promotes the AMSA program to Board of Education members and parents by keeping track of student scores in related courses (math and science) and conducting student surveys. This tracking is not obligatory, but it serves as a public relations interface and garners additional support for the program. The teacher tells me that the district usually encourages all computer use, regardless of its effectiveness, but that L.A. Unified especially likes to boast of successful and interesting examples of technology use. In a climate of non-guaranteed funding, this lab ensures its continuation by publicizing its activities widely.

The spaces described in this section signify three different locations along the spectrum from Fordist to post-Fordist production regimes in public education. In the first space — the one with a centralized layout in an old typing classroom — the professed values of the IT revolution (speed, mobility, and flexibility) conflict sharply with the constraints of extant materialities. The result of this collision is a disciplinary space that defies alteration, lending the room to rote exercises on stationary computers and reduced overall autonomy for students and teachers. The second space — the one with high visibility and a network software system — departs from the first through the warm ambience supplied by decoration and outside light, the tone established by the teacher, and the meaning ascribed to the material configuration. Because the teacher was involved in creating this space, even though obstacles were encountered and lengthy delays incurred, the result is one with an explicit pedagogical purpose. This space empowers its occupants with increased mobility and visibility but also disciplines through its central orientation and stable rows of tables. So in large part, the positive values attributed to this space and translated into student lessons (and vice versa) are mutable and could shift when the teacher retires and another takes his place. The room lies somewhere between the ideals of Fordism and post-Fordism. The third space — the one with an open layout and lab modules — exploits a historical, programmatic departure from vocational "shops" in public education to establish an open yet supported decentralized educational context. This is one case — there are several other, similar examples across L.A. Unified — where the shift away from a mass-production model actually opened up large rooms for enterprising teachers and technologists to essentially start from scratch without many impediments apart from shipping out older equipment and cleaning up. The lessons afforded by this final space are decidedly participatory, collaborative, exploratory, and empowering.

The point of describing these three spaces is not to argue that Fordist-informed spaces are educationally disabling and disempowering while post-Fordist ones are enabling and empowering (although this is likely the case), but instead to illustrate the inseparability of the two regimes, to reveal that there are no clean breaks. Whether older spaces enforce discipline or encourage autonomy, they continue to constrain and inflect any new designs or pedagogical changes; spaces and practices co-construct one another in iterative development patterns, and rooms continue to teach older lessons even when individuals, curricula, or technologies move on. Still, realizing that technological change is contingent, embodied, and politically situated can open up education to the future potentialities harbored in material forms.

Built Pedagogy

Scholars in the field of science and technology studies (STS) have advanced a number of concepts for thinking about the often elusive but always political ramifications of technological systems and spaces. Central to most STS approaches are the premises of social construction and artifactual agency. This means, first, that technologies must be understood as outgrowths of social actions and therefore always historically contingent (Bijker & Law 1992) and, second, that technologies function in the world as heterogeneous social "actants" that influentially shape all domains of human (and nonhuman) behavior, thought, and action (Latour 1987). A symmetrical relationship exists between these two theoretical strands, such that social construction illustrates how human actors affect technological artifacts and systems, and the actant approach shows how technological artifacts and systems influence human actors. A term that I call *built pedagogy* draws on these STS tenets to account for the politics embedded in and catalyzed by technological systems and their spatial forms.

Built pedagogy describes how spaces teach individuals proper comportment through affordances that privilege certain movements, activities, or states of being over others (Monahan 2002b). Built pedagogy further signifies the ideologies and values embodied in material structures, in tangent with the social practices that constitute space and saturate it with meaning (Winner 1986; Sclove 1995). Subject positions are learned in dialogue with the instructions spaces give; in public education, these are predominately positions of compartmentalization and self-discipline, where architectural norms are internalized within bodies and carried out into the world. Importantly, built pedagogy manifests itself everywhere (homes, schools, offices, streets), teaching bodies what should and should not be done in silent, subtle, and insistent ways.

The concept of built pedagogy facilitates inquiry into technological infrastructures (or "technological spaces") for the politics they embody, for the actions they catalyze and foreclose, and for the experiences they generate. As a quick illustration, a classroom wired for the use of desktop computers possesses a valence (or a "charge") for discipline because tables and other furniture must remain stationary or else the wiring will be damaged.[2] This same room has systemic dependencies upon electrical power, imperatives for cooling systems for the machines, and demands for technological staff and institutional policies to keep the machines operational. Finally, this classroom can contribute to emotional states of apathy, anger, or disappointment if occupants feel disempowered and isolated, or, conversely, states of excitement, happiness, and fulfillment if occupants feel empowered and socially involved. Together, these factors script a built pedagogy for the space that is both political and personal.[3]

If we accept the premise of built pedagogy, this increases the importance of studying design imperatives, processes, and contingencies, as they act upon existing material forms to reshape not only our environment but our internalized sense of self. The design of technological infrastructures in L.A. Unified lends itself remarkably well to such a political analysis because its schools are undergoing massive construction projects to install telecommunications networks for Internet access. Consequently, this is an especially liminal period where spaces are in dramatic flux and design processes are visible to a degree that may not be the case once these technologies are integrated, spaces transformed, and practices normalized. Yet the perdurable quality of previous built forms — walls; floors; ceilings; desks; electrical supplies; heating, ventilation, and air-conditioning (HVAC) systems; etc. — imposes governing logics and constraints that refract current agendas and values. As observed with the classrooms described in the previous section, the politics of existing spaces partially mold those of emerging spaces (which I identify as Fordist and post-Fordist, respectively), so there is never a clean break or a fresh start, no matter how much politicians, technologists, architects, or parents fantasize about one.

In order to capture the social significance of emerging technological spaces, one must eschew neat prophesies about future digital worlds and instead delve into the messy materialities that always already constitute all change and existence. If we are to move beyond perceptions of (technological) spaces as empty and apolitical containers (perceptions that hide rationalities of exclusion), we must get our hands dirty through observations of socio-spatial reconstructions on the ground. Only by acknowledging and self-reflexively contending with these multiple flows and reticulations can the design of technological spaces (or analyses of them) begin to construct (or posit) built pedagogies of empowerment, participation, and equality.

Designing the Future

Attending to spatial configurations and technology practices, the previous sections described a range of built pedagogies across one ideological spectrum, from Fordism to post-Fordism. They demonstrated some of the politics of spaces in public education, revealing that the greater the structural flexibility of previous configurations, the greater the potential for accommodating changes that support a multiplicity of social actions in the future. But spaces are in greater flux than these mostly synchronic snapshots betray; they are being redefined not only through practice-generated symbolic meanings but also through ongoing material alterations that dialectically interact with social events to construct meaning. Understanding design in action is a necessary step for evaluating (and achieving) structural flexibility in built forms. In terms of the production metaphors under scrutiny here, this narrative must now shift attention from the product to the process, from designs to designing, with the aim of carving out discursive room for different, legitimate understandings of space and its politics. Let us begin by following some of the actors engaged in technology infrastructure design.

A cadre of male college students[4] infiltrates a science classroom on the third floor of my primary field site, Concrete High. Equipped with boxes of category 5 copper cable (CAT5), duct tape, various pliers, flashlights, plastic ties, box cutters, a ladder, and long coils of bright orange polyvinyl-chloride (PVC) conduit, they set to work on a cable "pull" to connect incoming computers to a currently unusable school network. This part-time school technology staff works as a team. One worker steadies the ladder as another ascends. He exercises caution in removing dusty panels from the drop ceiling, for empty bottles, cans, and dead pigeons are frequent finds in these overhead caverns. PVC tubing is passed up to the worker on the ladder, whose head is concealed within the opaque void created by the removal of the ceiling tile. The workers joke about the unpredictable elasticity of the tubing, which can smack a person in the face or cause him to slice his own hands with razor blades while trying to cut it — both events have occurred in the recent past. The worker on the ladder strings the conduit from one ceiling tile to another (to which the CAT5 will be pulled) and uses plastic ties to secure it. This placement is complicated by the need to avoid the fluorescent light fixtures, which wreak havoc on data signals. Once the tubing is in position, the group cuts the conduit to the appropriate length and triple ties and tapes the cord that runs throughout the tubing to the tube's end. They are now prepared to "pull cable," yet after 45 minutes of work, they sense that they have fulfilled their manual labor duties for the day, so they call it quits. The always-on emergency fluorescent lights flicker and hum as the technical staff retreats silently from the classroom.

Students at Concrete High view these activities and intrusions with vague curiosity as welcome distractions from classroom monotony. The episode described above occurred after school, but similar technical work often goes on during class hours. Teachers at this school view such restructuring with guarded suspicion, for while many of them believe computer literacy to be necessary for students to succeed after high school, their own pedagogical uncertainty and territoriality compel them to resist. Nonetheless, in 2000, the state of California provided funds to establish a 4.75-to-1 student-to-computer ratio in all public high schools, leading to changes in all classroom spaces in spite of resistance. Technically, funding bills like the one referred to here (Assembly Bill 2882) do not "require" schools to apply for them and comply with their rules. However, because public schools are in constant need of funds, any missed opportunity to secure "free money" would be interpreted as negligent or incompetent; thus, there is little room for schools to opt out.

The description of workers preparing a CAT5 cable pull emphasizes the often hidden materiality of technology design, and once these projects are completed, the technical augmentations will further modulate bodies in space in unanticipated if not unpredictable ways. For example, the very presence of visual images on computer monitors draws students' attention away from all auditory stimuli such as instruction, discussion, questions, or even the class bell. Computer monitors have a profound material-virtual effect on social possibilities in these spaces; in response, several school sites have implemented network management programs of the kind related above, which freeze students' screens in order to combat this attention problem. Computer monitors on desks also introduce classroom visibility complications that hinder other visual learning experiences, such as viewing the blackboard, teacher, or other students.

The networking of computers in existing classrooms usually requires that desks touch the walls somehow, because this is where the electrical conduit and data drops are. This poses additional complications: if desks must always tie back to the wall, one cannot move furniture in the classroom. Additionally, electrical lines are often enclosed in metal conduit to protect them and students from harm, but this impermeable casing coupled with warranty restrictions prevents even technical staff from redesigning rooms. Teachers and students must adapt their activities to the inflexible structures that surround them. It should be said that while wireless technologies may solve some of these problems, they embody a host of other demands and constraints: the need for carts and/or cases for laptops, policies for replacing the fragile devices when broken, higher repair and maintenance costs, periodic battery replacements, electrical charging facilities, daily labor routines for charging them, and more.

The usual process of technology integration betrays an exclusionary politics on the material level. The built pedagogy is one of students and teachers adapting to the constraints of their technological worlds, not one of designing their worlds with technology to meet their needs. Authority may become displaced in these classrooms, but it is delegated to the technical infrastructure and not to the human participants. Ironically, unlike examples of voluntary technology delegation for purposes of human efficiency or discipline (Latour 1992), this material transference of classroom power to technology is largely the unintentional result of designing for network or administrative efficiency rather than for learning enhancement.

That said, technology coordinators at schools and the individuals laying the networks in these rooms do care about creating effective learning environments, but they operate within their own set of constraints, which limit design possibilities. Their budgets do not include much if any money for furniture; they face opposition from teachers and staff; they are under strict time pressures; and they must design around existing classroom obstacles such as tables bolted to the floor. Following from Michel de Certeau (1984), who grouped practices into "tactical" and "strategic" categories (the former being improvised and transient appropriations of spaces, and the latter being planned creations of durable and disciplinary places), the designs of technology coordinators are strategic in that they structure material contexts that affect the experiences of others (students and teachers) yet tactical in that they muddle their way through obstacles in *bricoleur* fashion.

What is known as "participatory design" (the design of spaces, technologies, or systems in meaningful collaboration with occupants or users) might offer one approach for investing individuals in design processes and outcomes (Schuler & Namioka 1993). Growing out of work and trade union practices in Scandinavia in the 1960s and '70s, participatory design has since expanded to the development of computer information systems in workplaces such as hospitals, universities, and city governments (Clement & Besselaar 1993). A key tenet of participatory design is that all users are experts in what they do, and that designers can tap this expertise to generate better and more democratic outcomes (Trigg & Clement 2000). In this case, however, the potentiality of participatory design is exacerbated by time constraints and cultural obstacles. For instance, I sought out the teacher of the science classroom described above and requested his input on the furniture layout for the computer portion of his classroom. His complete disinterest startled me, until I discovered that this teacher did not want to use the computers being installed in his classroom anyway. Without the teacher's involvement in the initial framing of the design problem (under what circumstances should computers be used in public education, how should they be used, and for what purposes or pedagogical goals), my question was meaningless.

This section has sought to convey a sense of the disruption, contingency, and obduracy presented by the process of designing techno-spatialities. Such conditions are typically hidden by a number of factors, mainly the disconnection of schools from communities and an encompassing mythos of spatial emptiness, technological purity, and technological determinism — or the view that technologies autonomously determine social changes, irrespective of human choice or agency. Unlike other forms of infrastructure design, such as road construction, the creation of telecommunications networks in schools is almost completely beyond public sight and thus outside of public awareness or criticism. Dominant spatial and technical mythologies reinforce this shielding from external scrutiny by communicating that there is no point in looking or questioning anyway because the outcome is predestined and apolitical, but this could be a treacherous form of technological myopia, as the lives of more than 700,000 students in this school district alone are shaped by these experiences of "inevitable" disruption and educational postponement.

This is not to say that students and other occupants of schools do not "learn" from these experiences. This is, in part, why the concept of built pedagogy is so important: the tacit curricula of built space can have many times more influence on identity construction than abstract(ed), subject-based lessons (Dewey 1944). But since the construction of a technology network takes years to coordinate and because all networks will likely have to be replaced within 10 years (as one high-level technology administrator admitted to me), such lessons of disruption and deferral are becoming the status quo.

Globalization Counterfoil

If the contours of techno-spatial designs are to a large extent motivated and planned, even if contingencies and interpretive flexibilities undercut overarching strategies or determined outcomes, what are the forces behind such motivations? Within what greater networks are these operations embedded? What informs the agency of the designers, or the policymakers that collaborate with them, to catalyze technological change of this magnitude? Or, more to the point of this chapter, what are the built pedagogies or ideological encodings at work here?

One does not have to pry too deeply into the social imaginary to get responses about the *needs* for technological literacy, global competitiveness, and future opportunities. L.A. Unified's "Instructional Technology Plan" illustrates this position:

> Society is completing an evolutionary shift from the Industrial Age to the Digital Age. Accordingly, educational institutions must realign their practices with Information Age standards. Those that lag behind in technology capacity, infrastructure, technology education, and establishment of support structures risk being unable to fulfill their mission of preparing students for the future.

> Technology has been a driver of change in such diverse areas as global communications, economics, the arts, politics, and environmental issues. While the world of business has readily adapted to and thrived upon technology innovation, the world of education has been relatively slow to reform . . . .

> Our changing society and workplace require citizens who can take responsibility for their own learning and well being on a life-long basis. In addition, we need the citizens to be able to work collaboratively, innovate,

and be creative. Educational reforms, which help develop our citizens, are dependent on the adequate and appropriate infusion of technology for their support. The time to think and plan strategically to further enhance instructional technology in LAUSD is here. (LAUSD 2002)

The impression one gets from this passage is that network technologies of the kinds used by "the world of business" are like tickets for a brighter future; the exact destination is unknown, but it is certain that many are being left behind, especially the poor and the marginalized. Thus, the mandate for "universal access," no matter how manufactured the needs or projected benefits are, resonates intensely with democratic ideals, cultivating a social fiat for equal access, even if it is only circuit deep.

Globalization, in its many forms, is one, perhaps too encompassing answer to the above question about motivating forces. It becomes the historical context and justification for profound changes in urban and social structures, and it compels individuals and institutions to embrace network technologies that epitomize connectivity, opportunity, innovation, and "the future," as it both rationalizes market-based approaches to education and supports IT markets with massive, state-subsidized expenditures on equipment and services. What these new technologized spaces are expected to shape, as the above quote and my many interviewees stressed, are flexible students (and future employees) who can multitask, who are self-motivated, who adapt easily to change, who thrive on instability, and who innovate under pressure.

The irony of this globalization paradigm, as the previous sections have illustrated, is that the ideals of opportunity, achieved through flexibility, do not often find reference in emerging technological spaces. I speculate that this is the case in part because the preponderant myth of technological purity and cleanliness disallows inquiry into the messy syntheses of built pedagogies. Yet when extant buildings and classrooms are modified for technology use, they carry the remainder of their disciplinary state into their new forms, often augmenting previous regimes of regimentation with IT enhancements. The results, in other words, are much more rigid and intractable than either of the ideals of Fordist or post-Fordist spaces would be in isolation. Furthermore, because technological spaces present manifold dependencies and demands for more equipment, security, energy, space, and HVAC systems, they subordinate human bodies in proportion to these nonhuman imperatives. Finally, the rhetoric of creating conditions of opportunity through technology functions as a promise whose delivery is deferred, apparently so that individuals will exchange freedom and autonomy *today* to support the needs of global capital. Flexible individuals are efficient and compliant, reducing labor costs for industry, whereas flexible spaces are expensive and unruly, possessing the potential for power disruption and redistribution.

One of the keys to unlocking the manacles placed on more equitable and lasting change is a symbolic one: what Ivan Illich might call a "counterfoil" reconceptualization of space and IT. Illich (1973, 77) explains counterfoil research as consisting of two interrelated tasks: "to provide guidelines for detecting the incipient stages of murderous logic in a tool [i.e., technologies that lead to increased, obligatory dependencies to the detriment of sociality]; and to devise tools and tool systems that optimize the balance of life, thereby maximizing liberty for all." Whereas dominant perceptions of space as an empty container or of IT as a realm of pure virtuality can lead to an artificial sterilization of technological spaces (divorced from their built pedagogies), this chapter has thus far offered (and attempted to perform) a counterfoil approach that accentuates the necessary materiality of all spaces and technologies. There are several motivations for taking this tack: first, to achieve greater empirical accuracy; second, not to reinforce simplifications that advance exploitative conditions; third, to trace the many cultural, political, and economic paths that weave into (and out of) educational transformations — a task this book as a whole seeks to accomplish; and fourth, to gain insight into the subject positions and identities that spaces co-construct with social actors.

The approach to the design of technological spaces that I am advocating for here, then, would begin with an analysis of bodies and stress relationships among them and the built world; it would challenge power differentials that often remain hidden in naturalized spatial configurations; it would critique overt and covert politics embedded in socio-spatial arrangements; it would strategize perturbations to maintain an open field for alternate subject positions and life-worlds; and it would improvise non-disciplinary, fluid designs to modulate existing materialities in community-, self-, and other-enabling ways. Because all these tactics depend on continuity and relationality, of people and places within states of flux, this counterfoil approach to emergent life-worlds is decidedly feminist and analog in its orientation.

In drawing a parallel between feminist and analog approaches to design, I am suggesting first that feminist design is about process, disruption, and challenges to the status quo; as such, its qualities cannot be pinned down once and for all in any space or artifact, because it is always an endeavor predicated on relationality and flux (Weisman 1992 ;Grosz 2001). Second, I am referring to a more technical definition of *analog* as information embodied within and constituent of physical representations (Eglash 1998), such that the representation of information alteration is also the means of transforming information (e.g., turning a volume knob on an older car stereo).

A digital approach, in contrast to this proposed intervention into techno-spatial re-creation, more often than not circumscribes planning agendas to the elision of continuity, connectivity, and fluidity. The digital is the supposedly clean trajectory, the apolitical realm, the disconnected exchange, and the pure representation, each without a remainder or a place. In terms of globalization, the digital could be read as an electronic or economic utopic no-place, an imperative and a rationalization for creating and disposing of waste, exploiting others, and deferring responsibility far into the future while erasing traces of it in the present and the past.[5] By way of response to such a reading, the next section proffers a range of analog alternatives for embodied flexible trajectories, for the creation and re-creation of spaces open to difference.

Spatial Flexibility

What is the importance of flexibility in built forms? Like a mantra, flexibility becomes more valued and less definite with each verbal repetition, yet for all the calls for mutable individuals in an unpredictable world, very little attention has been given to flexible conditions for diverse human actions. Put differently, people are compelled to adapt to their worlds, but their worlds are seldom made to adapt to them, and this is especially true for learning and working spaces undergoing technological changes.[6] The previous examples of classroom spaces and design processes began an inquiry into the politics and tenacity of built pedagogies and highlighted the unavoidable clash of production regimes and ideologies in all techno-spatial adjustments. Globalization was depicted as a motivating force that encourages a digital sort of material and political disconnect in perspective, even as the technological networks are being plugged in and turned on. This section picks up from there to direct inquiry into flexible possibilities on the spatial level, to shift the wider globalization discussion away from the needs of capital (speed, networks, loose markets, expendable labor and resources) toward the needs of people living, learning, and working in messy, imperfect, constructed places.

Spatial flexibility is one important dimension of the latent opportunities for social empowerment within globalization. If the dominant globalization ideology calls for that which is protean and innovative, then a strong case can and should be made for flexible conditions that support these *and other* desired modalities. Because flexible spaces, especially those that incorporate information technology, are capital-intensive, then perhaps only by fastening their creation to the fears and desires of institutions in the global political economy can they come into being. Once enacted, flexible spaces can move beyond the transient goals of the marketplace to establish long-term conditions for democratic participation and sociality, or a built pedagogy of collective empowerment. There are risks of dancing with global capital to craft edifices of the future, but, put bluntly, a space that allows for discipline and empowerment is better than one that simply disciplines.

I offer several properties of flexible space that could be drawn upon to evaluate existing spatial conditions or employed to engage in new design (or redesign) projects. Flexible spaces encourage flows of individuals, sight, sound, and air to reinforce a sense of interconnection and openness; they lend themselves to multiple uses, depending on need or whim, and readily accommodate new, unforeseen functions and activities; finally, flexible spaces invite manipulation and appropriation so that individuals can actively participate in determining the governing structures of their lives. The combined effect of flexible spatial properties is an environment that radiates a sense of possibility, fosters democratic exchanges, and supports the vagaries of social life.[7]

In the three classroom examples given earlier, the first example of a centralized layout for computers enforced a rigid and disciplinary space, devoid of most of these flexible attributes. The second space, which employed a network administrator program, possessed a disciplinary valence but introduced greater flexibility by allowing actors increased lines of sight and providing social proximity for individuals. The final multimedia space catalyzed the greatest flexibility through its openness and interconnectivity, tipping the techno-spatial scale in favor of social interactions over the needs of computers.

It is worth mentioning that a correspondence exists between the level of participation occupants had in redesigning these three spaces and the practice outcomes for teachers and students in those rooms. The greater the participation, the less disciplinary were the social results. Be that as it may, the obduracy of the built environment means that spaces will outlast the current generation of occupants and materialities will impose their built pedagogies on future populations. For this reason, it is imperative for those designing technological spaces to imagine a future beyond current uses of space and then to ameliorate as many constraints and rigidities as possible in the present. One way to achieve such a design ethic is by having individual designers visit technological spaces that are considered "innovative" by educators, observe interactions in these spaces, and talk with the occupants about the design of those spaces. However, because flexible spaces generally require greater financial allocations, an ethic of future potentiality needs the support of educational institutions and the general public if it is to succeed.

The discussion of spatial flexibility presented here is not intended to serve as a unifying template for "good" technology-infused classrooms but instead as an invitation to prioritize issues of embodiment and openness to futurity in all acts of spatial creation. Working with these criteria or other comparable ones implies attending to the ramifying effects of built pedagogies on social relations and tempering adverse global-technological imperatives in their perhaps necessary translation into built form. Spatial flexibility is also an invitation to enter into a dialogue about social responsibility, to move toward conditions of equality and empowerment, and to imagine what the steps toward reaching those goals might look like. Finally, this larger invitation is to reinscribe global flows through all spatial design to support many possible routes for legitimate participation and identity formation — multiple pathways for thought, action, and inaction — rather than succumb to disciplinary worlds that demand individual adaptation and autonomy depletion.

Conclusion

This chapter has argued that technological infrastructures and their attendant spatial counterparts embody politics and shape social relations by design. The prosaic assumption that space is merely a passive and neutral container, an empty vacuum patiently waiting to be filled by objects and (inter)actions, is a patriarchal product of Enlightenment models of rational thought and action. Historically, this narrative of empty and unused space has also been employed to justify imperialist projects of colonial expansion (Fabian 1983, 144). Space is not simply a medium but a situated and contingent plane, continuously reconstructed through practices and movements, through the interchange of bodies and symbols. The meanings and politics of spaces are grounded in historical materialities that mutually coexist with present conditions, introducing iterative developments riddled with constraints, latencies, and inflections. The past, in other words, haunts the present with its structural forms and symbolic formulae.

The production of space, as Henri Lefebvre (1991) reminds us, is itself a political act because of the social relations it gives rise to (or delimits) and the decision-making processes that it obscures. Both aspects are clearly legible in the urban topographies of cities like Los Angeles, instantiated in sprawling metropolises, inadequate public transportation systems, and fortified enclaves of commerce, dwelling, and education. Rather than being "natural developments" or rational adaptations to existing terrain, every spatial articulation involves decisions, yet not only are most people excluded from participation in those decisions, but many negotiations are effectively and intentionally erased from social memory and substituted with myths of the inevitable present (Fulton 1997; Klein 1997). In turn, the urban spatial forms spawned by development processes engender remarkably similar social relations of exclusion and erasure: ethnic segregation, class polarization, gender inequality, and homelessness.

Technological infrastructures, like the spaces they are nested within and linked across, betray similar orientations to social groups. Undeniably designed and planned, infrastructures interimplicate with spatial events and material presences to create orders of meaning and possibility (Bowker & Star 1999). As with the design of urban space, processes of technological planning and implementation are hidden from view, participation is restricted, and outcomes are normalized. Infrastructures are political social structures that modulate the functions and relations of bodies in space. Yet the political orientations of infrastructures are concealed by the restriction of individual involvement at the incipient stages of material production, prior to the concretization of built form, and by the sedimentation of social-spatial movement and interpretation after construction, which conceals alternative ways of being.

In his 1967 lecture "Of Other Spaces," Michel Foucault (1986) delineated a series of "other spaces" that lie outside of routine experience, functioning as counter-sites, mirroring, inverting, and challenging the logic of all other places (these counter-sites included prisons, museums, retirement homes, cemeteries, fairgrounds, and more). He called these other spaces *heterotopias*, which are beyond the everyday, yet — in contrast to utopias — are real and situated, offering insight into cultural values and social structures in their juxtaposition with usual places of work, leisure, or exchange. Foucault presented two categories of heterotopias: those of "crisis" and those of "deviation." The former accommodate individuals in transition, such as adolescents, the elderly, and menstruating or pregnant women, while the latter house social deviants such as criminals, the infirm, and the indigent.

Public schools, I assert, serve heterotopically as liminal spaces of crisis *and* deviation. They hold individuals who are in a state of crisis, but they also contain those who deviate from social norms on account of their liminal status. Schools are quotidian places that operate on the margins of everyday awareness, and, as such, they ground otherness on the inside of urban and corporeal bodies. These bodies do not simply contest or represent larger society; they also operate as sites of embodied contestation and contested representation.

The production regimes of Fordism and post-Fordism present two forces in dispute and in conflict in public education. The embedding of technological infrastructures within older materialities gives rise to new forms of discipline and new avenues of potentiality; in this way, schools clearly mirror societal tensions over globalization and networked realities. I have called the lessons that constructed spaces teach us *built pedagogy*, and I have drawn attention to the tenacity, power, and discreteness of built pedagogies as they modulate individuals and their identities. Yet spaces are continuously interpreted, constituted, and reconstituted by the interrelation of people and objects; thus, the symbolic meaning of space is underdetermined and co-constructed in the ever-present dialogue between the material and the social. This is most easily seen in the present redesign of space, in the tactical agency allotted to and appropriated by those who are inscribing new spatial modalities and foreclosing others through acts of technological incarnation.

This chapter issues an invitation for an approach to technological spaces that moves beyond demands for flexible and docile bodies. The globalization counterfoil offered here advocates for flexible, participatory, and polyvalent spaces to accommodate the disparate, variable, and unpredictable needs of individuals. This is a call to place the needs of people above the needs of space or capital; to create architectural possibilities, not prescriptions; and to begin rescripting existing territories with opportunities for other modes of being and becoming. To initiate such a venture implies engendering new ways of seeing: to perceive space not as an empty vacuum but as an embodiment of practices and relations. This visual adjustment affords a critical evaluation of all spatial politics and an opportunity to learn from mythic and real heterotopias.

2
JUST ANOTHER TOOL?

We cannot begin a reform of education unless we first understand that neither individual learning nor social equality can be enhanced by the ritual of schooling. We cannot go beyond the consumer society unless we first understand that obligatory public schools inevitably reproduce such a society, no matter what is taught in them. . . . In a schooled world the road to happiness is paved with a consumer's index.

Ivan Illich 1971, 55–58

[T]he much vaunted "flexibility" of the new forms of global economy involve not simply new forms of connection but new forms of disconnection as well.

James Ferguson 2002, 141

"Computers are tools, just like pencils." This is a statement echoed by many technologists, teachers, administrators, and policymakers in public school systems. It is a deceptively simple statement that smoothes over many of the chaotic elements of the current information technology (IT) revolution of Internet connectivity in public education: infrastructure construction projects, organizational restructuring, technology-driven curricular changes, enhanced security systems, acceptable use policies, and increased costs and dependencies. Of course, neither computers nor pencils simply appear in classrooms on their own, but what does it mean that the two are so quickly equated? If the power of the pencil lies in its simplicity, versatility, and mobility, then the comparison suggests that computers adapt somewhat synergistically to individual needs and that they are largely disconnected from systemic dependencies, politics, and social relations.[1] This chapter challenges these assumptions by arguing that the current state of technology-based instruction in public education reinscribes larger social transformations that are under way with globalization, demanding a great degree of individual flexibility and supporting the ongoing commodification and privatization of public institutions.

To begin this inquiry into the implications of IT instruction in public education, this chapter first provides an overview of John Dewey's progressive philosophy of education as a touchstone for analyzing current technology practices in school classrooms.[2] Next, it discusses technology pedagogy in relation to perceptions of inequalities of gender and race in the district, drawing attention to the risk of occluding difference under commodification regimes. It then documents those pedagogies that my interviewees and informants find valuable and evaluates these exemplars in relation to the ambitions of progressive education. The combination of these elements — technology practices of classroom instruction, perceptions of social inequality, and expressions of value — reveals that the goals of public education as an institution are becoming increasingly narrow in spite of the liberating promises of globalization and IT. As a corrective, I offer a conceptually different approach to technology pedagogy, one that perceives computers as *media* instead of *tools* and that introduces elements of structural flexibility into what are currently ideologically inflexible regimes in public education.[3]

Philosophical Backdrop

In John Dewey's originative work of educational philosophy, *Democracy and Education* (first published in 1916), he advanced a conception of learning as an eminently social practice necessarily situated in a material environment.[4] Rather than viewing learning as a unidirectional transference of knowledge, his progressive educational approach stressed action, communication, participation, and experience, the goal being the continual *process* of individual growth directed toward social aims. Education conceived of as a social practice opened up inquiry to the many networks that play upon institutionalized public education and are reproduced by it, including class differentiation, market demands, and ideas of progress. Institutionalized education was something Dewey perceived as necessary in developed and "civilized" societies whose store of symbolic knowledge far surpassed the ability of everyday rituals to inculcate it. The key threats to progressive or constructive education, John Dewey (1944, 109–110) believed, were the myriad external aims imposed on learning processes, eclipsing student-centered growth and development:

> The vice of externally imposed ends has deep roots. Teachers receive them from superior authorities; these authorities accept them from what is current in the community. The teachers impose them upon children. As a first consequence, the intelligence of the teacher is not free; it is confined to receiving the aims laid down from above. Too rarely is the individual teacher so free from the dictation of authoritative supervisor, textbook on methods, prescribed course of study, etc. that he can let his mind come to close quarters with the pupil's mind and the subject matter. This distrust of the teacher's experience is then reflected in lack of confidence in the response of pupils. . . . In education, the currency of these externally imposed aims is responsible for the emphasis put upon the notion of preparation for a remote future and for rendering the work of both teacher and pupil mechanical and slavish.

This is a remarkable passage, for it expresses quite clearly (almost a century ago) many of today's sentiments, especially as held by teachers, toward standardized tests, curricular benchmarks, and other mandated impositions such as computer use in classrooms.

In effect, the formulation of learning as a social practice rendered visible the many external pressures that Dewey then sought to mitigate in order to preserve the unencumbered growth process of individuals. What Dewey did not pursue was the *necessity* of ideological impositions by means of the larger social context within which educational institutions operate and from which they cannot be divorced. This is the lens that Ivan Illich (1971) selects for his condemnation of all institutionalized learning. For Illich, educational institutions are inimical to individual growth because they perforce function as products of capitalist society, which in turn produce consumers rather than lifelong learners. Michael Apple (2000) and others have since noted how globalization penetrates into public education through the combination of certain rationalities, both neoliberal (e.g., privatization, vouchers, flexible and docile students) and neoconservative (e.g., standards, accountability, traditional values), leading to the overall "depoliticization of life." Under globalization rubrics, Apple explains, the domestic world is considered "private" and therefore not political, and the public world is considered "economic" and therefore not political. This emerging depoliticized world, propagated through education, not only proscribes the kind of progressive education espoused by Dewey but also insidiously eliminates democracy by denying legitimate public space for discussion and critique.

Placing the functions and configurations of educational institutions within this expanded political and economic universe does not deny once and for all the constructivist aims of progressive education, but it does introduce a series of complex interrelations within which pedagogical ideals must operate in conversation, and it does invite the tracing (and perhaps erasing and redrawing) of the "external impositions" that always exist *within* schools. This holds true more than ever for the redesign of educational spaces and pedagogies through the introduction of information technologies. For IT is not only a means of global expansion; it also represents a system for linking students and public institutions intimately to globalization processes, thereby reproducing and reinforcing rationalities of global competition and interconnection. Given this encompassing political orientation, the question posed in this chapter is not so much "Do computers work?" but "What social relations do they produce?"

Classroom Pedagogy and IT

In conjunction with the politics-of-space premise of the last chapter, which drew upon science and technology studies (STS) to introduce the concept of *built pedagogy*, the field of "anthropology of practices" directs attention to social actions and interactions of individuals, spaces, and symbols. Together these frameworks facilitate identification of the manifold political (and other) meanings in what people do. From this theoretical starting point, this section describes and decodes three everyday tactical uses of technological spaces in Los Angeles public schools. The examples — which I label "disciplinary scare tactics," "isolation and social disconnect," and "panoptic flexibility" — convey only some of the many uses of computers in the Los Angeles Unified School District, but based on my research, they are representative examples. They are chosen to direct inquiry into the tacit curriculum or unanticipated learning — rather than intentional pedagogy — that takes place in IT classrooms. This tacit curriculum, at least in these examples, points to a troubling connection between neoliberalism and public education.

Practice I: Disciplinary Scare Tactics

A group of thirty students, followed by their teacher, file into the computer lab at Concrete High. In this windowless room housing thirty-eight computers, one group of tables with desktop computers forms a small island in the middle of the room while the rest of the lab's furniture and equipment hugs the walls. Blue snakes of CAT5 data cable descend from the drop ceiling, wrap themselves around trellised power conduit, and connect computers to a local area network (LAN). The walls are painted pastel shades of mauve and blue-gray and display colorful motivational posters with messages such as "Cheer up!" and "Writing is nothing more than a guided dream."

As students take their seats, their first time in this lab, the school's technology coordinator emerges from the doorway connecting his office to this room. He is a tall, imposing figure with wispy white hair, and his voice bellows out over the heads of the students as he begins his ritual scare speech, scripted more to instill fear and caution in the students when they are around the expensive computer equipment than to communicate specific rules of conduct. He makes a series of rapid-fire points:

- Because this lab's equipment is paid for by federal dollars, students will be prosecuted under federal laws, which are harsher than state ones, for any acts of vandalism or theft.
- Thirteen people have been sent to jail or detention centers in the past year.
- The minimum jail sentence for those under age 17 is 4 months; for those 17 and over, it's 6 months.
- No liquid, food, gum, or makeup is allowed in this space.
- If you play computer games or install programs on computers, even on your own laptops (which no students in this impoverished school own), you will be sent to another high school.

- The surveillance cameras in the lab (tucked away in the corners of the ceiling) will watch you at all times.

During this speech, English as a Second Language (ESL) students pay very close attention; others chuckle nervously, whispering to each other that it is not true. The technology coordinator reads their body language and assures them that he is dead serious and that he is telling them this for their own protection. I question him later about this approach, and he confesses that the point about playing games is true, but only two people have been jailed, and that was because of an inside job of stealing equipment. When I suggest a communal approach of "let us protect what we have," he asserts that such a tactic would work only for "good kids," but "bad kids" want to damage what any authority figure holds dear.

There are several lessons, other than the intended one of protecting machines, that students can learn from such disciplinary experiences. As students told me in interviews, they learn that computers are highly valued, perhaps more so than students, and that students, too, must value and respect property, even if the property is intended for their use. I speculate that they also learn that their proper mode of comportment is one of passivity, acquiescence, and self-discipline, not exploration or experimentation. Finally, it appears to me that they learn that they are not trusted to adhere to stated policies or to be presented with the real consequences of breaking rules. (Teachers and technology coordinators have very real interests in preventing theft or vandalism, but rather than explore their subject positions here, the emphasis of this section is to query what lessons students might derive from technology practices in classrooms.)

Given the many potential lessons communicated by this one example alone, which is replicated in many forms throughout the day, it is not surprising that the students who do come to class appear unenthusiastic. Many other students in this school of over four thousand choose to roam the hallways and the heat-baked asphalt grounds behind locked gates and tattered barbed wire rather than to attend classes, so that hundreds are physically present at school but otherwise "absent" during any given period. The exception to this migratory pattern occurs during testing and attendance weeks, when school performance is gauged and budgets determined, respectively; at these times, teachers and staff routinely round up wandering students and confine them to classrooms. Aside from these few days throughout the year, administrative pressure is not exerted to put students in classes, and most teachers and staff members feel that it is not their responsibility to engage in what they see as policing work. This is "just-in-time" education, but it is calibrated to institutional needs, not to student learning or growth.

Lessons of discipline, passivity, and apathy may not serve students well for individual growth, yet these lessons do prepare students, as future workers, to accept their plight as low-skill, low-wage, low-benefits, and low-job-security laborers. These lessons cultivate states of democratic illiteracy, where students maintain unfamiliarity with any concrete manifestation of democratic processes. Finally, students acquire an appreciation for the value of commercial products and a respect for private property. In these ways, the global economy is supported by the human capital of students socialized in public education.

Practice II: Isolation and Social Disconnect

On Valentine's Day in the same school's computer lab, a teacher ushers in her class to work on the practical and imaginary task of mapping out their college schedules (even if many will not be going to college). Once the students begin the assignment, she promptly leaves the room to take a break and does not return for the rest of the period. A college teaching assistant (TA) is watching the equipment from the next room, but besides us, no other adults are present, and no one is instructing or assisting the students. The TA relates that this is a common occurrence: teachers use the computer lab as a "free period" for themselves. Meanwhile, most of the male students talk, while the female students use the computers to make Valentine's Day cards for their boyfriends.

During another period, a different teacher brings her class into the same lab and insists, even though there is more than enough room, that all other students in the lab leave (i.e., those who are there during their free period). She then orders one of the student TAs — she does not even know his name — to patch her computer's image through the overhead projector. Soon, students in this class are pecking away at their keyboards with one or two fingers, busily transcribing previously handwritten papers. The hawk-like teacher homes in on one black student who is sitting at his machine and not typing anything. She says, "The printed assignment is due at the end of the period, so you'd better get to work on your bibliography." He abrasively informs her that he does not have any sources because he was absent from the previous class. She curtly responds, "Tough!" and then walks away, leaving the student to mumble, "Fuck you, bitch," under his breath.

In one final example from the same computer lab, students avidly copy images from Microsoft's encyclopedia program Encarta and paste them into Microsoft's PowerPoint presentation program. This is part of a larger "research" project on notable historical figures, and every time these students come to the lab they work on cutting and pasting all period long. One of them tells me that these PowerPoint exercises do not work because he never reads what he is copying or discusses it with anyone; his project is a series of disconnected images. It would be much better, he continues, if students had to present the material to the class or engage in collaborative group projects. After class, the teacher tells me that students work better in the lab than in regular classrooms because they are obviously engaged and busy, and if they fail to learn anything else, then at least they will know how to use computers. When I ask whether they share their reports with each other, he shakes his head despondently, saying that such presentations would be a waste of time because they are never good enough for others to learn from.

What can these examples from the high school computer lab tell us about globalization and education? In cities such as Los Angeles, one dimension of globalization is the establishment of high-tech and financial industries that then require a vast service sector of unskilled and unstable jobs — such as data entry, office temp work, janitorial and housecleaning services, and so on — to support them (Sassen 1991). These classroom examples can be read as preparing students for this demand through a tacit curriculum and built pedagogy instructing them to fend for themselves and to appear busy, regardless of the subject matter. These examples offer insight into the constraints and double-binds placed on all actors in public institutions that are struggling to fulfill service missions within a hostile climate of privatization. The teacher who vacated the room was tactically poaching off of an educational system that, as a rule, overworks teachers and undervalues their labor. In a profession where content and responsibilities are increasingly prescribed, the establishment of a computer lab granted her freedom to maneuver in self-selected ways but resulted in the neglect of students. The teacher who assumed a harsh disciplinary tone with students erected a rigid emotional barrier to preclude intimacy and defer conversations about the purpose or relevance of mindless computer activities (which are disparagingly called "drill and kill" by district technology coordinators). Such a stance alienated students but served to protect her from a possibly demoralizing self-reflexive appraisal of her own teaching or from recognition of the constricted opportunities for effective teaching and learning within the public school context. The last teacher was outwardly more self-aware than the first two but was unwilling to trust students to pursue work in conversation with their classmates. Thus, not only were students' cut-and-pasted images disconnected, but students were also artificially isolated from their peers and from a full range of individual growth within this social context.

Practice III: Panoptic Flexibility

In a computer lab at an old high school in shadeless and hot South Central Los Angeles, two teachers preside over a massive room of fifty-four students, all hunkered down in front of their own bulbous, blue Apple iMac desktops. The two male teachers are perched on a riser in the "front" of the classroom overlooking all the monitors, while students sit with their backs to the instructors. In an uncommon display of design foresight, both teachers and students face a series of large windows at the "back" of the classroom, such that a sense of outside connection is established, but the glare from the sunlight does not reflect off the computer screens (see Figure 2.1).

I enter this space while a class is already in progress and observe students working quietly and individually on the computers. One of the teachers directs me up to the riser and explains to me that the students in this room are in two separate classes (or "tracks") and are therefore working on different projects: introduction to computers in the first class and Web design, digital art, or other self-selected topics in the second. He then enumerates the many elements of control that are exercised over student instruction, from meticulously constructed Web-based lessons to teachers' superior visibility of all student activities and, not least of all, the technological dominance over students' computers through the network

Figure 2.1 Panoptic computer lab.

software. Proudly yet purposefully, he demonstrates "taking over" the machines of a group of students through his network connected computer. Students cry out "hey!" and turn around to see why they have been interrupted in mid-task. Having their attention, he explains to them a procedure for adding shadows to buttons in Web pages; he then executes the procedure on his machine, with the sequence of mouse-drags and clicks faithfully reproduced on each of these students' monitors; finally, he relinquishes control by disengaging his virtual network tentacles from their iMacs. Throughout this demonstration, the rest of the students continued unperturbed, working on their previously assigned tasks. "It's not '1984,' even though it looks like it!" the teacher concludes. (I was the last person to leave this classroom after the bell rang, and, with permission, I stayed a few minutes longer to take several pictures. As I left, the door shut behind me, making a latching noise, but I thought I should verify that the room was secure. As I reached for the knob, my hand grasped air: the teachers had somehow taken the knob with them as an added precaution to protect the room's valuable contents!)

Unlike the other practices described above, the activities in this classroom did not abandon students or directly alienate them; they created instead a strong sense of structured discipline, with active classroom control ensured through technological prostheses. The design of this space obviously lent itself to such interactions, but the addition of teachers who seemed as compassionate as they were firm, and the apparently "cutting edge" lessons that students were encouraged to pursue (e.g., making Web pages), created a productive amalgam for individual-based learning.

The unintentional lessons are a bit harder to decipher. Both the layout of the classroom and the use of network monitoring are reminiscent of Jeremy Bentham's design for a "panopticon" (or "all-seeing") prison. As Bentham envisioned it, a circular prison with illuminated cells and a watchtower in the center would ensure superior monitoring of inmates, whereby they would internalize a state of constant self-discipline because they would never be able to determine whether or not guards were observing them (Kaschadt 2002). The intention of this utilitarian design was one of social rehabilitation of prisoners, but as Michel Foucault (1977) has famously theorized, variants of this architectural model have been replicated throughout modern society (in schools, hospitals, prisons, mental institutions), compelling all individuals to internalize discipline and become passive (and apolitical) "docile bodies" in the face of such normalized institutional power.

The panoptic technologies at work in this computer lab may require educational individualization, because the eye-in-the-sky that can swoop down to monitor, control, or direct you is most effective when there is only one "you" to monitor, control, or direct. Thus, students may be grouped for management purposes but not for collective activities based on social interaction. The disciplinary learning-scaffolding here may afford self-motivated, individual activities, but it simultaneously deters unsanctioned actions within the classroom. This socio-technical space teaches students that they, too, can gain technological (and by extension economic) power provided that they work diligently alone and refrain from the temptations of social distraction.

This built pedagogy of surveillance and panopticism reinforces an ethic of self-discipline and undistracted labor while simultaneously developing subject positions that embrace external monitoring and control. These external forces, unannounced and therefore always anticipated, mobilize fear and promises of material gain to elicit acceptable behaviors of individual work and collective silence. As David Lyon (2001) suggests for other contexts, subject positions that are adopted in response to conditions of ubiquitous surveillance perfectly suit the labor needs and political indifference of the global economy.

Together, the three types of classroom interactions described in this section paint a range of disciplinary activities within globally insinuated technological spaces, where in each case technology modulates power differentials between individuals in varied social positions (e.g., students and teachers). These technological "tools," in other words, reconfigure social relations, potentially removing control from teachers, who then respond by transferring disciplinary functions to the technology (security cameras, network administration programs, and mindless rote exercises) or by reasserting (or abandoning) social control through alienation tactics (scare speeches, abrasive attitudes, or absenteeism). Importantly, it is the value attributed to technologies and their configuration within spaces that lends them this disruptive potential; as technologies become important *actants* in these social worlds, they do not so much shift power to students or to teachers as they leach (or are delegated) power within these contexts. The net effect, however, is one of discipline, individualization, and social disconnect. Learning as a social activity of individual growth is subordinated to (but not necessarily supplanted by) the globalizing rationalities that network technologies embody and reproduce.

I have sought to show how the lessons that students receive in technology classrooms are shaped by the combination of social practices, technical valences, and spatial designs. But the ideologies crafted in schools are surely inflected by those circulating beyond the schoolyard. The claim here is that even though it is largely unintentional, what may be poor pedagogy for individual and social growth is ideally suited for the production of workers who can meet the needs of global capital without challenging the political status quo.

Interpretations of Inequality

Public education may familiarize students with new workplace training and labor routines in the post-Fordist era, but globalization researchers (e.g., Ong 1991; Keil 1998; Valle & Torres 2000) have also documented new relations of race, class, and gender that deserve exploration in the domain of public education. This section analyzes perceptions of race, class, and gender inequality in L.A. Unified, specifically in regard to IT, to see what insights public schools can offer to the picture of shifting relations within globalization.

If IT in public school systems is supposed to help students overcome structural disadvantages such as poverty, unequal opportunity, or institutional racism (which is in fact the discourse of "digital divides" and "universal access" that, to a certain extent, propels technological policies and laws), one would expect individuals in L.A. Unified to have developed nuanced and critical understandings of race, class, and gender in technological contexts. For the most part, judging from all my interviews and conversations, this is not the case. As a general summary of responses, interviewees were quite comfortable talking about class issues and the promises of technology for correcting class inequity; they were slightly less comfortable but still vocal in discussing differing levels of technological acumen and proficiency between men and women; but, with rare exceptions, articulations of race or ethnicity were completely absent, and through their guarded responses, interviewees subtly let me know that issues of race were off-topic, inappropriate, and likely irrelevant. Because this was the most interesting "finding" within these three categories, let me begin by offering an illustration and an interpretation of it.

The following passage from an interview with an African American business teacher typifies this penchant to redirect race-oriented questions back to issues of class:

Do different ethnic groups use technologies in different ways?

I think they would use it in different ways depending upon their exposure, depending upon their educational levels, because a lot of times it's not used because they don't know how, you know? So it's going to depend upon how well you prepare them and they know what they're doing, and then they can see the uses of technology — how valuable it is to use it. Otherwise, they would make no difference. It just depends upon the exposure of the person. Maybe a person in a higher economic situation would have computer exposure much quicker than a person in a lower economic area. They wouldn't have it available to them, so they wouldn't know how to use it as well as a person up here [holds her hand up high]. So, I don't think it's ethnic or not; I think it's exposure. It's exposure and use of it — "know how."

Okay. So if there is an ethnic difference in use of technologies, you would attribute that more to socioeconomic status —

Yes, not the other way around.

This teacher recognizes the link between race and class, but she attributes any lack of access or any differences in patterns of use to degrees of technological "exposure," not to ethnic identities or racial biases. Put otherwise, as a social category, race is subordinated to class. This, at least, is the surface story that I am told, and the perception of technology as economically enabling helps sustain this version.

It is not surprising that questions concerning technology and ethnicity gravitate back toward class when technologies are perceived almost entirely as economic enablers. One possible explanation for interviewees' reluctance to discuss race issues is the ultra-ethnically diverse context of Los Angeles, with its frequent racial clashes (mostly undocumented altercations) and its constant threat of conflict eruption. This environment sustains a palpable racial tension, like a harmonic overtone that all can hear if they choose to listen. In places of heterogeneity and disenfranchisement, such as public schools, it is impossible not to register this note, to heed its warning and attempt to channel it into productive, if fleeting, resolution. Questions like mine about how students from different ethnic backgrounds utilize or relate to technologies aggravated this implied balance and expected silence, and they violated some unspoken rule about keeping demons at bay by not naming them. Thus, my interlocutors avoided giving me vocal feedback by shifting the conversation to the safer issue of class.

On another level, the shifting of race-based analyses to issues of class evokes entrenched ideologies of universalism in U.S. public education. Public schools serve as official sites for the cultural drama of equality of opportunity, regardless of the particularisms of race and ethnicity, and actors perceive class differences in education as legitimate outcomes of a meritocractic competition that rewards talent and work over biological difference. Class is easy to speak about because of its association with such "legitimate" universalism: the production of achieved difference is contingent on blindness to ascribed difference. Thus, diverting discussions of race to issues of class is an important part of the educational ritual of universalizing the particular. Recognizing race means coming to terms with what my interviewees perceive to be the illegitimate intrusion of particularism into the universalizing agenda of public education.

There were a few exceptions to this pattern of deflecting volatile race issues, but these anomalous statements were very general in nature and doubly and triply qualified to avoid any misunderstanding on my part or any wrongful attribution of "racism" to their assertions. In one instance, a Caucasian teacher explained to me what he called "the cultural winds" at play in student academic (including technological) achievement: Latino families push their children toward trade training with the aim of them getting jobs, while Latino peers are neutral to the issue and so present no competing crosscurrents for this goal. African American families, he explained, motivate their children less forcefully toward vocational training, and these students' peers are determinedly anti-intellectual (e.g., harassing those who carry backpacks or books), presenting a strong counterforce to individual advancement. This theory of cultural crosscurrents offers insight into some of the reasons behind behavioral differences, but it simultaneously eschews any discussion of ethnic or racial identity in relation to differences in technology use.

Discussions of gender and technology, by contrast, yielded much more colorful and passionate opinions and convictions. Given the widespread associations between high technology and sexiness, it is not surprising to observe how technology use in schools is both gendered and gendering. To this end, this next passage, taken from an interview with a woman who is chair of the business department at a high school, is analyzed for its gender stereotypes and sexual undertones. I began by asking her whether computer use at the school reproduced stereotypes of men using technologies more than women. She responded:

> I kind of think that's going to be a "has-been." I think that it will get better. But basically, because men are more, initially more manipulative —

Just manipulative, period?

[both laugh]

Yeah, period — with their hands. And that's one of the things that men have always been famous for, to fix things. And I think they're "fix-its." Men are "fix-its." Women are usually more compassionate; they're the ones that keep things together, and all that. But men, they usually take things apart and put 'em back together.

Tinkerers?

Yeah, they're tinkerers. But I don't think that will stay that way. I think that women will enter into the market and I think that they will do an acceptable job, because women have something that men don't have: "stick-to-it-ness." They will stay there until it's done. Men will kind of tinker and go on. And I think that quality will help us [women] in that area . . . I think [men] will have some competition.

Because women will start to become more technically proficient also?

Right. And I think men will have competition in that area, and I'm sure they're already getting it, from the women, but they're going to have more, because women seem to stay with it longer. They'll stay with any-thing longer, than men. And men want to get it [claps her hands up and down], get it and get gone. But women, because of their perseverance, they're going to give men a really good turn, for those competitive jobs . . . I think that when these jobs level off, there will be higher jobs, and I think because women have entered into the market, they're going to be in com-petition for those higher jobs also, and they're going to be right there giving men a headache! [she laughs]

It is difficult *not* to read this passage as a play of stereotypes about gender and sexual behavior: men "manipulate" while women tolerate patiently; men want to "get it and get gone" while women want to see things through. However, as the interviewee augurs, difference and ine-quality are in the past, because in the near future, men will have "competi-tion" from women. Again, particularism is subordinated to a more universalistic interpretation of IT and education, where ITs are figured as passive, neutral, and gender-neutral tools with potential for leveraging more equitable relations at some time in the future. Of course, the past and the present remain times in which women's subordinate role in society is recognized. Thus, this description signals a tension between IT pedagogy as a mechanism of gender neutralization and equalization and as a continuation of long-standing patriarchal structures that link technological progress to masculinity.

To conclude this section, articulations of class differences were the most prevalent responses to questions about inequality and technology. Almost all of them matched the sentiment expressed in the first quote on ethnicity above (maintaining that socioeconomic status determines access or exposure), or they adopted a tone conveying dire if amorphous imperatives for equipping students for a global workforce. Technology is interpreted as helping to level the playing field by establishing equal starting points. As one teacher described her self-appointed mission: "Make these kids computer literate, so that they can cope and they can compete with other people in the work market." However, the problem with perceiving technologies as *only* catalysts for competitive individualism is that this symbolically purifies technologies, shielding them from critical reflective discourse on how inequality might be reproduced through their use.

As an indicator of shifting power relations within the global economy, the findings from L.A. Unified indicate a disturbing trend, one of masking possible issues of race and gender differences behind class determinants. This was done perhaps out of fear of aggravating existing tensions or upsetting dominant mythologies about color-blind technologies and equal opportunities for technological empowerment. I do not take the reduction of race and gender to the category of class to mean that these are unimportant distinctions for my interviewees, because especially with race, interviewees were too consistently insistent on changing the subject. The denotation of their remarks was "this isn't important," but the connotation was "this is too volatile." The issue was explosive not only because Los Angeles is a city that knows race riots but also because American schools are stages for the performance of the American Dream.

The redirection of conversations about race and gender to class issues makes it difficult to spot discrimination or injustice within existing conditions and to make recommendations for alteration. A current, if general, "take" on social relations under the IT revolution is that there are dramatically fewer women occupying technical positions — 20 percent of the IT workforce (AAUW 2000) — and these positions remain predominately on the low-skill and low-wage levels (Eubanks 2004). Moreover, in education, poor minority students are more likely to be given repetitive, "drill and kill" exercises on computers than their white, more affluent counterparts, who are given more contextualized assignments (ETS 1999). Such observations are then manifested in the actual technology practices of students in L.A. Unified, where, as noted above, students are more often than not placed into instructional situations that teach discipline, individualization, and alienation. Where there are opportunities for students to engage in technical occupations in schools, such as repairing computers or serving as computer lab TAs, they are often economically exploited for this work, and women are systematically excluded from such positions. Thus, as currently configured, IT in schools may aggravate existing inequalities while reinforcing lessons about the inevitability of inequality, in spite of proclamations about equal opportunity.

Expressions of Value: School Academies and Enterprises

Thus far, this chapter has advanced a conceptualization of learning as a social practice, has described several trends in IT pedagogy, and has drawn on field interviews to offer interpretations of inequality with technology. If what Dewey called the "external" pressures placed on education are necessarily internalized and then reproduced in locally specific ways, as I have argued, then we should try to identify these pressures at their sites of intersection with education in order to demystify or denaturalize their effects and implications.

Because determinations of value are often contingent upon systems of exchange that transcend immediate settings, one way to get at these places of intersection is to pay attention to what pedagogical situations become exemplars of economic value and innovation. This section traces two developments that my informants held up as examples of pedagogical success — "academies" and "enterprises" — in order to identify where globalization ideologies overlap with situated educational aims, and to what effect.

In L.A. Unified, technologists and teachers admire what are known as "schools within schools," such as "media academies" and "enterprises" located on the grounds of existing high schools and serving as extensions of them. Interested students must apply for these rare public programs and are not guaranteed acceptance. With media academies, once students are accepted, they are given preferential treatment: they take all their "electives" within the academy, usually learning special skills like video editing or computer animation; they generally have smaller class sizes and more exposure to cutting-edge technologies; they comprise a small cohort of students (about two hundred) within a larger school of three to four thousand; their core classes are "integrated," such that they learn history, English, and social studies, for instance, while creating their own media productions; they are appointed professional, outside mentors to instruct them in their fields of interest; and, when such are available, they are given internships during their senior year. Students of high school academies have a 90 percent graduation rate, program directors told me, compared with a 60 percent graduation rate for all other students in these schools. The programs are, therefore, truly elite within the public school system.

School enterprises share a similar positional orientation within schools, but they are usually profit-making ventures that are run almost entirely by students (under some supervision). For example, in one enterprise, students manage the building and selling of computers to outside companies, including the installation and maintenance of networks. In another example, students grow food in the school's gardens, make salad dressings, and then sell those products to local supermarkets under the brand "Food from the 'Hood!" (http://www.foodfromthe hood.com). In a conversation about the creation of a technology-based school enterprise with a previous director, this woman asserted that the idea was to involve students in a "real world" venture through the establishment of a separate corporation that operated within a school but outside of the school district's control. Through legal incorporation, students were promoted to the status of "executives" and "stockholders," and the district was legally unable to take its usual 7 percent share of all school donations. Unlike the academies, which are still framed in educational metaphors, the enterprises unabashedly conflate business and educational goals.

These two expressions of "value" within L.A. Unified (school academies and enterprises) each operate at the intersections of internal educational missions and external pressures (the false internal/external distinction is used here simply as a heuristic for investigating learning environments within larger social contexts). The underlying theme that runs through each of these expressions is one of an economic marketplace, defined by a state of competition for scarce resources. School academies and enterprises exist mainly for the sake of preparing students for the marketplace; other kinds of learning undoubtedly take place, but the primary lessons are acquiring technical and/or business skills for individual gain. One grave risk of such an emphasis on preparing students for the workplace, as noted by Michael Apple (2000) and Joel Spring (1998), is the globalization and commodification of education, whereby room for political critique or even for the discussion of democratic goals is slowly eliminated. Put otherwise, the prioritization of vocational goals, and the assessment of educational progress in relation to industry, privileges an economic perspective to the detriment of any less economically infused learning activities. This is a subtle process that can be seen more readily in the valuing of school academies, enterprises, and high-tech classrooms than in its corollary — the cutting of arts and humanities curricula.

When these economic measures of performance operate as cultural dominants in L.A. Unified and other institutions, they support what Hank Bromley (1998) has called the "rationalization of public life," as is seen with technology pedagogies that result in experiences of atomization and social disconnect. In the computer classrooms, students' social disconnect as they engage in individual projects and as they exercise panoptic self-discipline shares structural similarity to the disconnect reached by valorizing vocational training programs for their economic accomplishments alone and the disconnect that teachers enact regarding racism and sexism. It is in these and other ways that *disconnection becomes the experience* for students and teachers; it is what is learned and what is taught, and, not coincidentally, it produces subjectivities valued by global capitalism: socially and politically alienated labor forces that are also active consumers.

Conclusion: From Tools to Media

This chapter began with a common expression of computers being tools just like pencils. Given the many ways that pedagogy with IT alters social relations in classrooms and further enmeshes both the organization of L.A. Unified and its members in the global political economy, this pencil/computer comparison could be a dangerous oversimplification that obscures the profound changes taking place. In light of the evident social transformations documented here, it makes eminent sense to perceive technologies as political, as components of complex systems that bring about conditions largely beyond our control or comprehension. As Langdon Winner (1977, 29) writes:

> Is technology a neutral tool to human ends? No longer can an affirmative answer be given without severe qualifications. The most spectacular of our implements often frustrate our ends and intentions for them. . . . Far from being merely neutral, our technologies provide a positive content to the arena of life in which they are applied, enhancing certain ends, denying or even destroying others.

Following from the previous sections' critique of the social disconnect resulting from market-based evaluations of educational performance, conceptions of computers as simple tools reinforce this disconnect by deflecting questions of implications beyond the classroom and then individualizing learning within the classroom by parsing it into discrete technological performances. Just as valuing education *foremost* for its workplace training is dangerously limiting, so does the equation of pencils and computers falsely constrict learning possibilities and evaluations of them.

In response to the call for progressive education made by Dewey, a more structurally flexible approach to understanding the role of computers in constructing social relations, identities, and (dis)connections would be to conceive of them less as *tools* and more as *media* that are components of larger socio-technical systems. Media, as Malcolm McCullough (1996) gracefully presents them, are substances or contexts that mediate human action and may be altered with tools; by mediating, they serve as acts of communication and invitations to interpretation. McCullough says:

> When the tools are complex, when artifacts produced are abstract, or when tools provide the only means of access to the medium (all common conditions in high technology), it can be difficult to say where a tool ends and a medium begins. But we can say that under skilled practice even these tools become transparent, and that a sense of a medium eventually emerges. (1996, 193–194)

Media imply an invitation to alteration, but they simultaneously tend toward transparency, which, as I see it, is both their power and their limitation. Transparent contexts seemingly enable unhindered action or creation, but that is because the limits and rules of action have become internalized, accepted, and taken for granted. As with jazz music, internalizing the strict rules of structural and tonal form can invite one to push on those rules and to innovate; however, one must constantly both accept that invitation and keep it at bay to avoid the unmusical poles of sterility or cacophony. Through action or play, one must constantly strive to reinvent old rules or create new ones, and the same should hold true for educational computing. Contexts for learning with technology should afford a multiplicity of learning styles and activities, and they should also motivate the reevaluation and rescripting of the rules for learning.

In analyzing classroom practices with IT for their learning potential, I find it useful to graph them onto what Donna Haraway (1992) calls a "semiotic square" along the axes of tool-medium and material-virtual (see Figure 2.2). The use of pencils or similar implements would fall into the quadrant of *material-tool*; classroom spaces, sounds, stages, canvases, or even the human body are *material-medium*; the kinds of cut-and-paste, document transcription, or rote use of computers described above fit into the *virtual-tool* quadrant; and uses of computer programs as media for creation, perhaps for art creation with animation software or composition with word processing programs would map onto the *virtual-medium* quadrant. Such categorization definitely depends on a subjective assessment of situated activities, but it should not be interpreted as a solidification of boundaries between categories — lines exist, but they should be thought of as permeable and transparent, like the media they are intended to describe and ultimately engender.

When computers are thought of as tools, they tend to yield mechanical tasks and situations of social disconnect. But as a rule, the "media" approach to computers, which perceives them as part of complex systems of interdependencies and as contexts for creative expression and knowledge production, catalyzes empowering learning activities because constraints and interconnections become the explicit terrain for practices (Monahan 2004b). A good example of a technological medium is the multimedia lab in a former wood shop space described in Chapter 1. In that open space for learning, technology is used to create a context for collective discovery rather than being used only as a tool for discrete

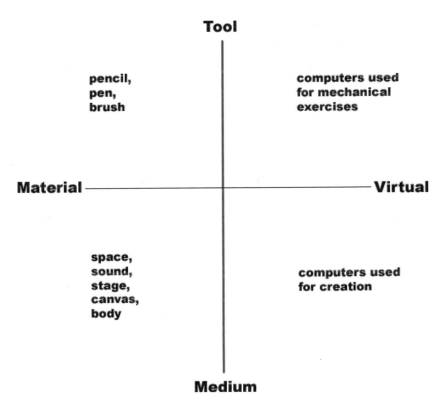

Figure 2.2 Semiotic square of educational technologies.

actions or marketplace training. While this space is also part of an "academy" and the lessons are intended to be of a "real world" nature, the tone is decidedly one of creativity and collaboration rather than of individual gain in a global marketplace. Thus, since academies and multimedia curricula do possess potential to bring about learning experiences of deep social connection, one cannot simply dismiss all academies as elitist or isolating. It could be that because this positive example exists in a middle school and the other ones exist in high schools, the instructors do not feel the same pressure to prepare students for workplace training and economic competition.

By implying contexts of constraint, media also draw attention to their embeddedness within larger social milieu, to the field of relations that make certain actions possible or impossible, valuable or worthless. That said, any evaluation of learning should fall back on the question of what kinds of social relations are being produced. As an illustration, the "1984" classroom described above could easily be seen as a virtual medium, yet it clearly produced a climate of isolation and self-discipline — it is a virtual medium with results that empower in the economic dimension, but probably not in terms of sociality.

Importantly, arguing for computers as productive media does not deny their tool-like properties (any more than student learning denies test-score representations of that learning), but it does shift the focus to lines of connection and constraint, such that possibilities remain visible for changing the social fabric that media co-constitute, along with human actions and interactions. The concept of media is more flexible in this way, but, not surprisingly, it is typically avoided by those working with educational technology: not only do media create space for social learning and individual growth, an invitation that can be accepted or declined, but they compel us to face the implications of larger connections and to take responsibility for our roles within those networks. As I see it, it is this daunting ethical challenge that must be accepted if learning is to be taken seriously and if vibrant and enriching social life-worlds are to be preserved under economic globalization.

3
TECHNOLOGICAL CULTURES

Technology is not politics pursued by other means; it is politics
constructed by technological means.

Bryan Pfaffenberger 1992, 1

In *The Visible Hand: The Managerial Revolution in American Business*,
Alfred Chandler (1977) identifies a unique moment in the development of
modern industrial capitalism. From the late nineteenth to the early twentieth centuries, a many-tiered, hierarchically ordered managerial "class" arose
to govern complex, multiunit businesses through "scientific" control of all
the stages of production and distribution. This class dramatically altered
both the nature of businesses and the markets in which they operate, ushering in a period of Fordism predicated on systems of mass production,
mass consumption, and scientific management. Building on this work,
I assert that the post-Fordist era of flexible accumulation is being accom-
panied by an analogous rise of a managerial group of information technology (IT) specialists.[1] While my data are drawn from a service-oriented
organization in the public sector, I expect that similar developments are
occurring in nongovernmental organizations and service, manufacturing,
and other industries in the private sector as well.

The history of public school systems is marked by persistent conflict
between administrators and teachers; traditionally, this has been a gendered struggle, with men occupying the administrative roles and women
the teaching roles. The many phases of educational technology to hit the

schools throughout the twentieth century — film, radio, television, personal computers — were impelled by these male administrators, who wanted to revolutionize learning through various forms of mechanization that would *coincidentally* diminish the autonomy of female teachers in classrooms (Cuban 1986; Apple & Jungck 1998). While administrative colonizations of classroom activities are stronger than ever, in the form of standards, benchmarks, and compulsory testing, the latest wave of educational technology to hit the schools has grown out of *teachers'* efforts within schools. The early catalysts for Internet access in public schools were teachers with a technological bent, a good many of whom were women.

Whereas all the mechanical advances of the past failed to stick, let alone revolutionize education, the Internet and multimedia production appear to have taken hold. The reasons for this probably have more to do with the wider media-generated myth that computer access provides social and economic empowerment than with school politics and practices; however, the grassroots origins of technological networks in schools certainly resonate with teachers and lend the movement legitimacy. Perhaps more important for the continued utilization of new technologies are the accompanying infrastructural investments and spatial reconfigurations: when the U.S. E-Rate program alone has allocated $8.1 billion since 1998 for technological infrastructures (Dillon 2004), material and financial investments stoke the fires of the technological imperative. Furthermore, these material conditions of commitment seemingly mandate the creation of official IT positions within school districts to manage the technologies. It is these positions, I argue, that split the classic dichotomy between administrators and teachers, leading to profound destabilizations of authority and responsibility and to many contentious turf wars.

The larger group of technology specialists is comprised of various "technological cultures" within the school district, and these cultures are often more unified by organizational position (e.g., school-site technology coordinator) than by geographic location. Following from other anthropological investigations into science and technology (Pfaffenberger 1990; Hess 1995; Downey & Dumit 1997; Fortun 2001), I maintain that it is crucial to study subgroups of technologists as cultural entities, because they tend to share worldviews, values, specialized languages, and political orientations that shape their practices. Most importantly, technological cultures function as agents of change throughout the modern world, and public education is no exception. By better understanding the operations of these cultures, we can cease fetishizing technology and attend to the actual production of technological worlds as expressions of globalization.

Emergence of IT Specialists

It is difficult to provide a uniform representation of IT specialists in the Los Angeles Unified School District because this group is constituted by multiple technological cultures. What binds these specialists together as a group is their relative technical expertise vis-à-vis other employees and their commitment to the use of IT in schools. IT specialists are increasingly influential in making decisions about the district as a whole, including not only technology policies that govern equipment purchases and infrastructure design but also technology policies that shape curricula, information reporting, and space allocations. This is not to say that IT specialists always agree or that their decisions always trump those of administrators or teachers, only that their influence is strong and their presence growing. The goal in this chapter is to map this group that has emerged during the past decade in order to learn about what kinds of power they do have and how they are contributing to organizational restructuring that supports neoliberal agendas in public education.[2]

There are many strata of IT specialists and the organizational terrain is in flux, so, in the spirit of California's predictably unpredictable — yet assuredly present — seismic activity, consider the following outline of IT positions as a contingent topographical sketch (see Table 3.1). At the geographical plate of school sites reside *technology coordinators, network administrators*, and *support staff*. Technology coordinators oversee the operations at individual schools, including implementing ad hoc networks; negotiating with contractors and facility managers; creating mission statements for long-term technology development; purchasing computers, furniture, peripherals, and network devices; supporting and fixing school equipment; and so on. Over the past ten to fifteen years, technology coordinators have applied for grant money and used it to meet what they perceived to be the specific needs of their schools, and they now increasingly decide space allocations (classrooms, storage closets, and offices) and supervise network

Table 3.1

Strata of emerging IT occupational groups in L.A. Unified.

Stratum	Group
School Site	Technology Coordinators
	Network Administrators
	Support Staff
Local District	Instructional Technology Applications Facilitators (ITAFs)
	Complex Project Managers
	Business Managers
Central District	Program Administrators
	Information Managers
	Technology Administrators
	Policymakers
External Providers	Contractors
	Vendors

administrators and support staff. Currently, most high schools have some form of technology coordinator position, even if the responsibilities are shared among multiple teachers without additional salary benefits. Dedicated coordinator positions are rare below the high school level.

Network administrators ensure, at a root level, that systems are functioning properly, from server efficiency, to printing capability, to user logins, to data backups, to security protections, and more. Yet in most cases that I saw, network administrators collaborated closely with technology coordinators to manage the social as well as the technical components of system operations. They supervised support staff, assisted teachers with hardware problems, and advised technology coordinators on equipment purchasing and implementation plans. Granted, at the moment, many high schools and most middle and elementary schools cannot fund and therefore do not have network administrator positions.

At the high school level, support staff positions have the label of "teaching assistant" (TA) and are occupied by college students or current students at the school. The division of labor I observed was one where college TAs primarily fixed nonoperational equipment and installed networks, while student TAs assisted teachers and supervised activities in computer labs. At the site where I did most of my fieldwork, there was some fluidity with these responsibilities: the technology coordinator or network administrator sometimes told college TAs to perform nonmaintenance tasks, and college TAs selectively permitted student TAs to enter their space. Students in both TA positions frequently reminded me that they were severely underpaid for the technical work they were doing, which was a belief shared by the technology coordinator. College TAs received $9 an hour, while student TAs received the federal Title I "student aid" wage of $5.15 an hour (the state minimum wage was $6.75 at this time). On the other hand, TAs' conviction of being underpaid provided them with a rich rationalization for engaging in what Michel de Certeau (1984) calls *la perruque*, or the diverting of work time and resources for personal projects. In their case, especially when their boss, the technology coordinator, was not around, they would often play games, watch movies, do homework, or search out and compare specifications for computer hardware they were personally interested in rather than perform work-related tasks.

At the geographical plate of the local district, the primary IT position is that of *instructional technology applications facilitator*, a cumbersome title that compels everyone to refer to these individuals as "ITAFs." The functions that ITAFs actually facilitate are communication, translation, and negotiation between school site technology coordinators and central-level district administrators. For example, when contractors fail to perform their tasks and leave schools with gaping trenches or nonfunctional networks for months on end, technology coordinators contact ITAFs, who then find out what is going on and lodge complaints with central administrators to get things moving again. To a lesser degree, at least during this initial infrastructure-building phase, ITAFs organize teacher development sessions and facilitate the placement of technology teachers and coordinators throughout the district.

There are other important technology roles, if not positions, at the local district level that involve providing contractors with blueprints of schools and sometimes walking them through these facilities, inspecting completed networks and requesting changes, and "signing off" once networks are completed to specification. Traditionally, these tasks fall under the responsibility of *complex project managers*, but many of these people do not have the necessary expertise to plan for or evaluate data networks, and in at least one case that I observed, these tasks fell under the purview of *business managers* in local district offices. I expect that a position or positions will solidify around this facilities role in the near future, but at the time of my research, ITAFs and technology coordinators were in the dark about whom they should contact to perform these essential duties.

At the geographical plate of the central district, technology personnel include *program administrators, information managers, technology administrators,* and *policymakers*. There is an Information Technology Division (ITD) and an Instructional Technology Branch (ITB) in the school district, each with its own internal structure, but because crucial technology tasks are also distributed to individuals who are not formally associated with ITD or ITB, I have elected to adopt the more inclusive categories listed above. Furthermore, it is important to note that many central and local district IT people originated from school sites and climbed into these positions over time. This does not indicate, however, that IT groups maintain an up-to-date awareness of and sensitivity for the constraints and responsibilities of their interorganizational counterparts.

All program administrators, or district-level ITAFs, are located in downtown Los Angeles, but they are spread out in separate building locations: some in the main L.A. Unified facilities at 450 North Grand Avenue, some in imposing skyscrapers further down on Grand, and others in the labyrinthian 3rd Street Annex. Program administrators oversee large-scale construction projects, such as the networking of all 459 schools that qualified for E-Rate funds — a monumental task with an imposing deadline that was divided between four contractors: IBM, PacBell, Vector, and Wareforce. Other program administrators manage the specifications and distribution of computers that are purchased through state grants, such as California Assembly Bill 2882, which allocated funds to reduce the student-to-computer ratio to 4.75 to 1 in all public high schools. Finally, some program administrators serve more of a recognizable ITAF function of organizing staff development sessions.

Information managers deal with the technical side of technology use in the central district. Network services personnel, statisticians, and auditors all fall under this category, and some sample tasks include monitoring the student information system (SIS), centrally maintaining Internet access for schools and staff, updating Web content on LAUSD.NET, producing reports for policymakers, conducting software audits, and performing a host of related activities.

The presence of technology administrators represents a major development in the value placed on information technology and on information derived through the use of technology.[3] These positions carry titles like "assistant superintendent," "chief information officer," and "chief technology officer," and their organizational and physical proximity to Board of Education members and the superintendent is a sign of their increasing importance and influence. The primary tasks of technology administrators are supervising programs and serving as liaisons between policymakers and program administrators. In this second capacity, the position is isomorphic to ITAFs, who mediate between local and central levels: technology administrators provide information to policymakers, gently negotiate policies with them, communicate those policies to program administrators, collect information and suggestions from these staff members, and translate that information back to policymakers in the form of policy recommendations.

Finally, policymakers are gradually becoming much more interested in crafting technology policies and evaluating the cost-efficiency and, to a lesser extent, the educational efficacy of technology programs. There is a Business, Finance, Audit, and Technology (BFAT) standing committee of the Board of Education, comprised of four board members and three outside members, that generates its own policy agendas, orders reports and takes policy recommendations from technology staff, and then proposes policy to the Board of Education as a whole. One example of this process is the creation of acceptable use policies that comply with the Children's Internet Protection Act (CIPA) of 2000 — a law that requires schools and libraries to filter "objectionable" Internet content. (This act was deemed unconstitutional by the U.S. District Court for the Eastern District of Pennsylvania on May 31, 2002 [Clark & Wasson 2002], but the U.S. Supreme Court declared that it was constitutional on June 23, 2003.) Other examples of technology policy include establishing a district-wide information technology plan and implementing the "Waterford Early Reading Program," which is a computer-based, automated reading program approved in 2001 for 244 elementary schools at the cost of $44 million (LAUSD 2001). Additionally, the fact that several Board of Education members have worked for private technology companies further attests to the convergence of technology and policy interests.

The last geographical plate holds a group of IT service and product providers associated with L.A. Unified but outside of the organization proper. I choose the terms *contractors* and *vendors* to differentiate, respectively, between the services and products they provide, but in conversations these categories are often conflated. Contractors and their host of subcontractors are responsible for district-supported, as opposed to ad hoc, technological infrastructure construction or alteration. This group is worthy of being included in any analysis of IT specialists within the organization because not only do they reconfigure space and, by extension, pedagogical practices, but they also actively negotiate with program administrators and others over specifications. Moreover, even when digging up schools, tearing through walls, and drilling through ceilings, contractors must interpret *how* to perform their tasks to the agreed upon specifications in materially messy contexts; for instance, they must make on-the-fly decisions about where to put data drops or what to do when they encounter plumbing not sketched on blueprints.

A similar case can be made for vendors, such as software or hardware providers. These people often cultivate relationships with technology coordinators over many years. Trusted vendors can recommend products that are then used to modify educational environments and experiences. At the district level, some vendors develop exclusive, if perhaps illegal, relationships with program administrators or employees in the purchasing department, and they inflect the technological configuration of schools through these alliances.

Across these four imbricated strata (school site, local district, central district, and external providers), I have plotted positions that, taken as a whole, constitute a powerful present and emergent IT occupational group consisting of multiple technological cultures. This IT group, while clearly not homogeneous or unified, is gradually gaining authority over the domains previously controlled by other groups. At the school site, for example, technology coordinators are in some cases able to charge onto the hallowed ground of teachers and administrators — classrooms and offices — and requisition these spaces for technological purposes, such as computer labs. At the other end of the spectrum, technologists at the main district offices have all but taken over one of the largest buildings (the "G" building), they wield an enormous budget (over $400 million per year), and they drive curriculum changes (e.g., the currently mandated, software-based Waterford reading program referred to above).

If this occupational group of IT specialists could be seen as ushering in a particular rationality, in a parallel manner to the Fordist one of the managerial "class" that Chandler depicts, I would describe it as post-Fordist. Similar to managerialism, IT occupations embody a technological and scientific imperative, manifested as a fervent belief in technological progress and in many cases quantifiable measures (e.g., of test scores or student-to-computer ratios). At the same time, IT specialists are wrapped up in a process of decentralization that places more responsibility on individuals for self-management and flexible adaptation to organizational changes.

The stress on individuals flexibly adapting rather than on organizations being multiply enabling is epitomized by a "CAN-DO WINNING ATTITUDES" motivational plaque hanging in the main ITD conference room in L.A. Unified. The text on this plaque is divided into two sections, between old-school rigid thinking and new-school flexible thinking; sample quotes are "It's not my job; I'll be glad to take the responsibility," "It's contrary to policy; anything's possible," "Let somebody else deal with it; I'm ready to learn something new." As with corporate training practices in the private sector, flexibility is something demanded of bodies in the post-Fordist economy (Martin 1994).

Finally, a litigious culture of contract and license compliance and associated audits, what Marilyn Strathern (2000) has coined "audit culture," imposes self-discipline on IT and other employees and restricts policy possibilities. What is interesting about this current transition period is that value systems are not uniform across IT groups and design processes are clearly contingent and socially constructed, so conflict is as visible as cultural agency in this liminal terrain.

Engineering a Power Vacuum

Thus far this chapter has offered a rough map of an emerging IT occupational group, made up of various technological cultures within L.A. Unified. As Michel de Certeau (1984, 129) reminds us, however, "What the map cuts up, the story cuts across," so the next sections begin to fill in some of that missing story by analyzing the motivations and agency of technologists across organizational domains. Not only is information technology an important catalyst of organizational change, but the specialists charged with managing IT infrastructures and projects act directly as agents of that change.

One Board of Education member I interviewed claimed that technology, through the information access it enables, is breaking up existing territories and creating a positive "power vacuum" in the district. She further explained: "You don't have power based on information as much anymore, because so much is available on the Web. And the more we can get onto the Web, the less people can hoard information and use it for power chips." In the context of our conversation, I understood her to mean that IT creates a state of transparency with policymaking and subsequently equalizes bureaucratic control. Judging by the elaborate, stratified group of IT positions documented in the previous section, one might counter that any existing organizational vacuum is quickly being filled by technologists.

I would like to proffer, however, a more nuanced reading of the situation. I would place agency into the hands of IT specialists and assert that *technologists are restructuring the relational networks that constitute the organization.* By drawing on cultural myths of technological imperatives, which present technologies as correctives for social and economic inequalities, IT specialists are able to insinuate themselves into influential organizational positions and then deploy an infrastructure that necessitates continual upkeep and upgrades by individuals in these occupational groups. IT positions, in other words, are validated by the materialities and dependencies they facilitate.

In some cases, this strategy of constructing relations of dependency is conscious and intentional. Take as an illustration the following passage from an interview with two information managers (I will call them M1 and M2) in L.A. Unified's Information Technology Division (ITD):

> M1: If technology truly becomes an integral part of our everyday [lives], you can't live without it. Like the book, like the chalk — no one would debate that there should be a classroom without a whiteboard, chalkboard, whatever. Nobody would debate that any teacher should have books or be able to provide a place for that child to sit.

M2: What if every teacher did their attendance on computer, period. No more role books; no more turning in paper stuff. It's all done on the computer. You think that network wouldn't be up 99.99% of the time? This is our income! [Meaning that the school district relies on attendance reporting for its income.] That network would work! And it would be supported at the school level, and at every level. So—

M1: So if it truly becomes an integral part of our daily administrative and instructional, whatever, basis, then there will be no choice but to find a way to make sure that it's supported . . . . Why? Because *even* the board member who doesn't have e-mail for an hour will be freaking out, and when they're up there voting, they're saying: "But I remember what it was like when I wasn't getting my e-mail or when I tried to watch, to do that PowerPoint presentation," because it becomes an integral part of my daily life. When the superintendent is doing e-mail — and they're all doing it now, they're starting, and they're becoming very dependent upon it — or going to a Web site to get information or to find out what the district is doing, or any of that stuff. Or the sharing of knowledge and all that stuff. If it stays on the fringe, it's easy to take off. That's why I always used to go out to schools and say, "I don't believe in instructional technology plans; I don't believe in instructional technology plans. What I believe in are instructional plans that have technology woven into them. So, if you give me an instructional technology plan and the *instructional technology plan* is here and your *instructional plan* is here, you know what? That's useless to me; it's useless to the school, because as soon as you can't do something because you don't have the money, or the resources, or the people, or the time, or whatever, ah you know what? 'Oh we'll start this one in six months, but this one is required.' Don't do that; do an instructional plan with technology woven into it. End of story. It's not an afterthought; it is a part of your everyday lives."

What you're describing sounds like a litmus test, that if it becomes integral to instruction too, not just—

M1: Absolutely, to every element, to every element.

—record keeping, then it will be maintained and

M1: Absolutely.

—*and someone will support it. And if people, whether it's the larger culture or it's just not integrated, if they decide this isn't really important to learning, then it's going to—*

M1: They won't.

—*be cut.*

M1: I don't think anyone will ever say, "This is not important to learning." It'll be, "You know, we're faced with the sheer nature of we have to cut something. Which finger would you have me cut off?"

[*Laughs*]

M1: Right, okay? I wouldn't want to choose any of them! But you know what? "I need to do this; I need to do this; I need to do this; I need to do this" [He counts on his fingers]. Which one do I need to do more, and which one can I live without? And if it's not an integral part, then I can live without it.

One of the primary motivating reasons for integrating technology seamlessly into the educational environment is a concern that IT jobs will be modified or redistributed in the near future (keeping in mind that few people are fired when the school system is formally restructured). Albeit no technologists expressed instrumental personal reasons for desiring technology integration (most do believe in the efficacy of technology for teaching and learning), many articulated concerns about what would happen when the current inflow of federal, state, and local grant money dried up. In an interview, a program administrator vocalized this well:

> If what happens is what I'm reading is going to happen, we're going to see a dip in financing and everything in terms of schools getting funds. We're probably also going to see some of the things that we've got going take a hit. One of those will be support personnel: ITAFs [and] if we happen by some miracle [to] get the network support people [at school sites], we'll see them go by the wayside first. And that may, if it's at the wrong time, we'll end up with a lot of metal on our hands, a lot of metal and plastic, and nothing to really show for it.

That must be a major concern.

It is, and one of the things I'd like to make sure we keep in the forefront is that the least amount of impact we have in installing these things, and the more it seems to be part of the environment as we go through it and keeping everybody up to speed, the more entrenched it'll become and the less easy it will be to rip this stuff out.

Interestingly, the potential threat to IT positions was not perceived as occurring across the board. Most interviewees saw technology coordinators as protected by their school "fiefdoms" — insulated realms that would find a way to keep crucial technical positions intact, whether by allowing teaching leave, or through Title I[4] funding, or through some other arrangement. The IT people at the central district level saw their positions as assured likewise by means of the vast technical and social infrastructure they oversaw. It was the ITAF positions at the local district level that were seen to be at greatest risk, perhaps because they are nomadic in nature: ITAFs wander from school site to school site, organize professional development meetings, and otherwise mediate between local and central levels. Without a social *and* material infrastructure to justify their positions, and without a secure sense of place (schools and downtown offices are entrenched fortresses compared to the recently created local district offices), ITAFs may have little leverage to defend their stations, but they can tactically migrate to new positions when their jobs are jeopardized (probably by emphasizing the instructional and training parts of their job descriptions instead of their technical management skills). This tactic of achieving a degree of job security through enhanced mobility can be read as a uniquely post-Fordist arrangement, with parallels to contract migratory workers in the global political economy (Diamond 2002).

So, where the board member's comment about a "power vacuum" implies that technology is an equalizing force that neutralizes power asymmetries in the organization, this interpretation elides the agency of IT specialists to nurture dependencies that happen to grant them more job stability and resource control in L.A. Unified. In some cases, technology may enable equal access to information and thereby correct power imbalances caused by information hoarding. That said, giving all the volition to technology sets up a false sense of *fait accompli*, deflecting attention away from the many individual choices made and actions taken in the ongoing construction of technological systems in public education.

The Power of Informal Networks

The technological cultures in L.A. Unified are continuously tested and reconstituted. Bound together like rafts on a turbulent sea of constant policy changes and structural adjustments, informal networks of technologists (and other groups) keep the district afloat and operational, with its cultures intact, despite the many waves of organizational restructuring. Technological cultures are especially adept at adapting to organizational change, because in keeping with their grassroots origins, they have long fostered an informal community of knowledge and labor exchange. One of the networks for such exchange is a group called the Instructional Technology Commission (ITC), which usually holds monthly meetings at schools throughout the regular school year and runs an electronic discussion "listserv" out of Bell High School. The members of ITC accomplish many things: they gather and disseminate information about new grants, laws, policies, technologies, software, and training; they share best-case instructional and technological practices; they help each other troubleshoot technical problems; they assist in placing technology personnel in jobs throughout the district; and they express criticism of or support for district policies, which are activities that often result in the modification of central district policies and/or processes. Most of all, ITC provides members with a sense of being involved in a collective endeavor; it is a "place" for individual technologists who would otherwise be as isolated as they are scattered across Los Angeles.

ITC is not really a commission in any official sense. The founders of this group told me they chose the name in order for their acronym to appear before the acronym of the district's Information Technology Division (ITD) on meeting agendas and minutes. One can speculate that the district formed the Instructional Technology Branch (ITB) to "one-up" ITC in this ongoing symbolic competition. Because ITC has no official organizational status, it easily weathers the frequent storms of reorganization in the district and provides coherence for what would otherwise seem a very murky environment. While central IT people seldom come to the physical ITC meetings, in spite of their assertions to the contrary, these administrators do read and contribute to the listserv discussions and debates and, in interviews, administrators refer to these interactions as "participatory" processes. There are certainly symbolic power struggles on this listserv, and many people do not contribute for fear of being reprimanded by central administrators, but it does offer an arena for productive contestation, mostly instigated by technologists at schools: protesting technical specifications set by central administrators; prodding administrators to determine the correct process for getting a school network legally "signed off"; and questioning the legality of the ways in which grant monies are being allocated. These conflicts galvanize responses and inspire movement to get things accomplished (a technology coordinator put it well in saying that such "conflicts are healthy because the district isn't"). These disputes, however, serve an additional social purpose of testing and reinscribing territorial boundaries in this volatile district.

ITC is but a visible representation of informal networks that exist throughout L.A. Unified and ensure functionality within states of seemingly constant bureaucratic flux and indeterminacy. The following story, recounted by an ITAF, captures the tone of this more general networked condition. The context for this narrative is a school site trying to figure out who should officially "sign off" on an installed telecommunications network at a Central Los Angeles school so that it could be used and another infrastructure project with a strict deadline for completion could be started:

> A lot of people just don't know what their job is, and things come up that nobody has thought about, like how to sign off a network. And it's easy for someone to look at something like signing off a network and say, "Well that doesn't fit into my job classification." End of chapter. And what happens is everybody is saying, "Well that doesn't fit into my job classification," and there's no one to do it.
>
> *And this is what happened [at this school] because it was the business manager here [at the local district] who had responsibility for signing off?*
>
> Well, he was not aware that he had that responsibility until the [school] situation came up, because no one ever told him that that was his responsibility, because it never occurred to anyone that that would be something that would have to be done. The real breakdown was that the inspection

unit did the inspection and didn't inform the school that they had completed the inspection, nor give the school any documentation that the inspection had been completed. They not only didn't do that, but they didn't notify us in our local district that it was done, so none of us knew what the inspection unit had done. The ball was dropped because the inspection unit didn't communicate with us. And the inspection unit is used to being autonomous, so they didn't fully understand why it's so important that they do this communication.

This is an inspection unit within the district?

Within the district, yes. It's within the district.

And they're centrally located, these people?

Yes . . . but it's my understanding that they're to be regionalized, too. But they're probably in the process of being split up, and they're in transition, too. So they're moving from the central to the regional, so there would be confusion there, too . . .

About the network, was it signed off?

Yes.

Was it signed off a long time ago, or—?

When I succeeded in talking to a substitute complex project manager—

[Both Laugh]

because the complex project manager was on vacation. He happened to have worked in the inspection unit before he became a complex project manager. So he called a friend of his in the inspection unit, and my impression is that the network had been signed off for about a month. I think the most positive spin I can put on the whole debacle, and using the word "debacle" has its own spin, is that it was a growing pain. Certainly there were lessons learned by the confusion that will make it easier for other schools, but it was an embarrassing organizational foul-up.

I was struck by what you were saying about the informal networks: that the substitute complex project manager, used to be in inspections, had a friend there—

Right, right.

I hear this a lot, where even though you do have rigid hierarchies, or decentralized structures with hierarchies within them, you do have proper modes of getting business done in L.A. Unified. And yet, whenever anything really gets done, like in this instance, or maybe if there's a special problem, it's not the proper channels, but it's the informal networks of people knowing people who know people across this spidery district that get things accomplished.

I think that's an extremely astute observation. It is where things get done. And that is where someone like me, who's coming into the district later in my career, is at a disadvantage. Because people that have been in the district 20 and 30 years have rubbed shoulders with lots of different people, and their contact web is much bigger. And you're right, that's the way a lot of business is done. . . . And especially when we're in a period of transition like this where we don't yet have a very functional organizational structure. When the published organizational structure is not real functional, people have to resort to their informal webs to get things done, so there's a lot of that happening right now.

Sticking with the cultures of technologists in L.A. Unified, another practice mobilized by informal networks is the creative bending of rules in order to further the educational mission of technology use. On the equipment side of this equation, examples are numerous, including things like technology coordinators providing teachers with replacement laptops when they have broken the ones they were first issued, and ITAFs replacing broken network switches at schools with other "found" or self-purchased ones rather than wading through the paperwork morass of contractual replacement equipment. Similarly, when an elementary school had equipment stolen and the insurance company stalled in replacing it, ITAFs and technology coordinators borrowed equipment from other schools in order to get the school network online. And for another example, when the district sends out "software inspection teams" to audit schools for compliance with software licenses, instead of performing random spot checks, schools are often given a 2-week notice by these inner-district auditors to get things in order and then given several weeks to correct any problems the auditors found. In each of these instances, individuals improvise across their networks in order to establish or maintain functional technological infrastructures for students and teachers to use; these are tactics employed on the margins of school policies, but without them, many district projects would come to a screeching halt.

A final tactical practice facilitated by informal networks is that of identifying and exploiting *latent possibilities* in social and material infrastructures. Most schools that have technology coordinators, for example, support these positions through innovative combinations of existing financial resources: with Title I funds (designated for schools with impoverished student populations), with short-term technology grants (such as California's "Digital High School"), or through a part-time teaching leave (granted by school administrators, but the time must be covered by other teachers). A number of middle and high schools I visited had appropriated existing T1 Internet lines from some past (usually administrative) network effort and rerouted these lines for instructional use. Similarly, some of the best computer lab spaces I saw were ones that had previously been abandoned, unwanted "shop" rooms that were cleaned out and converted by motivated teachers and technology coordinators (see Chapter 1 for details on one example). In each of these cases, it is only by harnessing an intimate knowledge of funding possibilities, facility histories, and school politics across informal networks that change occurs.

This section has demonstrated the power of informal networks to maintain organizational operations but also to advance technological agendas in schools. The Instructional Technology Commission (ITC) group forms a coherent community of technology practitioners and establishes a context for collaboration and participation across the district. While a wider culture of territoriality persists, the flow of individuals across territories over time leaves a string of contacts that can be called on when needs arise. Policies establish norms of acceptable and legal behavior, but when they hinder educational projects or the design of functional classrooms, actors creatively bend the rules or walk on the margins of officially sanctioned conduct in order to get things done. Finally, the cultivation of knowledge networks within individual schools allows for the realization of latent possibilities hidden within social and material infrastructures.

Conclusion

This chapter introduced some of the many technological cultures in L.A. Unified, their political strategies for cultivating dependencies, and their constitution through informal networks. The insertion of technology specialists into all organizational levels of public education represents a destabilization of traditional power relations between administrators and teachers. Contrary to mainstream notions about the natural evolution of technology, however, these technologists demonstrate clear agency in the integration of information technology into vital organizational functions, thereby assuring themselves of job security well into the future. In response to the confusion generated by frequent organizational restructuring (and especially by the most recent form of post-Fordist decentralization, which is covered in detail in the next chapter), the technological community has developed vibrant informal networks to support the systems that they have charged themselves with governing. Informal networks could serve as a model for human-centered flexible relations within the organization, because while they may bend the rigid rules of the school district, they also spur innovation, tap latent possibilities, and provide local responsiveness to students and teachers. That said, informal networks would not be so necessary if the institution of public education and its organizational manifestations adapted better to the needs of people rather than forcing people to adapt to them.

4
FRAGMENTED
CENTRALIZATION

[F]lexibility has little or nothing to do with decentralizing either political or economic power and everything to do with maintaining highly centralized control through decentralizing tactics.

David Harvey 1991, 73

In this neoliberal era of increased public suspicion of government bureaucracies, the restructuring of public institutions is about relinquishing territory to the private sector and reestablishing control, or at least the appearance of control, over inefficiencies. In public education, restructuring has been a frequently employed strategy for responding to a host of pressures that haunt policymakers and bureaucrats: fiscal responsibility, test-score improvement, safe and timely school facility construction, curricular innovation, grant compliance, student security, and, most recently, functional technological infrastructures.

Organizational restructuring is not a new phenomenon in public education, but there is a discernible historical trajectory in restructuring movements that cannot be explained as back-and-forth pendulum swings along a centralization/decentralization spectrum. Throughout most of the twentieth century, educational restructuring has led to greater centralization, larger schools, more subjects taught, more middle management, and less teacher autonomy. A call for local control and experimental pedagogy in the 1960s led to a partial decentralization of school districts, typified by

New York City's borough system, but the experiment did not much alter the larger development pattern. Whereas in 1931 there were nearly 130,000 school districts in the United States, by 1987 there were fewer than 16,000 (Tyack 1990, 184). The current wave of restructuring should be seen, therefore, as a new mutation in the larger historical pattern of centralization.

In the context of neoliberal pressures and this history of centralization, this chapter questions the development of organizational "decentralization" in school districts.[1] Decentralization is a phenomenon worth studying because it highlights links between public institutions and the global political economy. Along with labor outsourcing, just-in-time production, computerized automation, and other flexible accumulation strategies, decentralization has been theorized as a post-Fordist organizational reaction to globalization (Harvey 1990; Amin 1994). Los Angeles has been identified as epitomizing these flexible production traits (Scott & Soja 1996; Monahan 2002a), but thus far little research has been done on post-Fordist manifestations in large public institutions such as school systems. Notwithstanding this lacuna, most public institutions are undergoing radical neoliberal restructuring — from welfare systems (Eubanks 2004) to military operations (Hartung 2004) to medical research (Fisher 2005). The main argument advanced here is that in spite of the strong rhetoric of decentralization and the ostensible decentralizing valences of information technologies, a form of centralized control persists — yet is masked — within public education.

Public school systems are morphing through a process of *fragmented centralization,* such that decision-making authority is becoming more centralized while accountability for centrally made decisions is becoming more distributed down the hierarchy chain. This splintering of authority and responsibility gives organizations the appearance of responsible management but simultaneously decreases worker autonomy while intensifying workloads. I adopt the term "fragmented centralization" from David Tyack (1990), who uses it to describe New York's borough school system, but I develop it to analyze issues of power within educational structures, incorporating what Jill Blackmore (2000) calls "centralized-decentralization" — the simultaneous existence of Fordist and post-Fordist attributes in educational organizations.

Organizational Restructuring and Technology Projects

To an outsider and probably to many insiders, the organizational makeup of the Los Angeles Unified School District appears inscrutable. Employees, claiming to have seen multiple organizational iterations in their time, rattle off names for groupings of schools — families, clusters, regions, local districts, mini-districts. The current incarnation is called "decentralized" and consists of administrators and policymakers at central district offices located in downtown L.A. who set policies, establish programs, initiate construction projects, and otherwise oversee the operations of the district. L.A. Unified is then divided into 11 "local districts," each with its own superintendent and administrative personnel who preside over an average of 73 schools and 68,000 students. Each of these local districts is then further divided into "families" of schools, usually consisting of one high school and all the elementary and middle schools that feed students into that local area high school. L.A. Unified's vast size makes it the third largest employer in the region (City of L.A. 2003), with an annual budget of $13.35 billion (LAUSD 2004) and therefore vital to include in any study of economic and industrial trends in this global city. Yet in all the research on industrial and regional transformation in Los Angeles, the school system has been given only peripheral attention, if any.

The latest restructuring happened in the summer of 2000 and was instigated as a response to the Belmont Learning Complex debacle, where an L.A. Unified high school was built on a 35-acre former oil field with toxic levels of hydrogen sulfide and potentially explosive methane (Smith 2000). As work continues on Belmont, it is reported to be "the most expensive high school project in America" (Moore 2002), with total costs projected at $270 million (Madigan 2004). Still, public demands for accountability and outcome assessment are part of a growing neoliberal cultural orientation that is vital to globalization and that transcends isolated construction disasters.

Organizational statistics and mappings render a surface description of L.A. Unified but fail to convey a sense of what this entity is. What is an organization, after all, and how can one move beyond surface significations to a deeper understanding of its operations? I approach organizations as *assemblages of categorical relations*. In other words, organizations are socially embedded entities whose structures shape individual and collective cognition and behavior (Douglas 1986). As socially situated collectives, organizations are constantly co-constructed by informal and emergent practices, historical biographies, and contemporary contingencies (Scott 1995). Thus, building locations, chains of command, and budgetary controls can shift with only nominal effects on the quotidian functions or identity of the organization as a whole. One can approach the complexity of collective behavior and perhaps achieve an understanding of significant change by studying the manifold relationships and power differentials, whether perceived or actual, among groups.

As the last chapter indicated, periodic restructuring has reinforced, especially in areas of technology projects, the need for local self-sufficiency and informal networks. The building of technological infrastructures requires not only financial resources but also a sustained vision and the cultivation of an expert community. Technology planners at individual schools have learned to insulate themselves from the vicissitudes of the district as an administrative body by strategically promulgating local autonomy and securing, whenever possible, financial support from outside the district; for instance, schools have a history of applying for their own technology grants. Informal networks across L.A. Unified have been the mechanisms that have allowed schools to achieve degrees of autonomy from official district projects and protocols. Individuals at school sites also draw on the larger public sentiment of bureaucratic mistrust to gain rhetorical advantage over the central administration. Because the mission of the organization is "improved student achievement," those in everyday contact with students possess symbolic leverage over administrators who seldom see any students.

The development of technological infrastructures in L.A. Unified started as a grassroots endeavor at individual school sites and has only recently been centralized and standardized. As an example, individuals at one flagship high school I visited, which serves an extreme low-income and minority student population of 4,700 students, started building an infrastructure in the mid-1980s and boast that they had a fully functional network long before the district achieved one in the mid-1990s. These interviewees claim that they encountered nothing but resistance from "downtown" administrators, who did not see any value in technology and were (and still are) mainly concerned with the production of statistics, not with meeting student needs.

Individuals at this school applied for a small technology grant over fifteen years ago and were soon thereafter mysteriously contacted by the U.S. Defense Advanced Research Projects Agency (DARPA), which asked the grant writers whether they wanted assistance from the Department of Defense for a pilot program. One of the women at this school said she gave DARPA representatives a 5-minute presentation of her vision, which was a fully networked high school providing community access and leadership and resources for elementary and middle schools. She told me that DARPA responded by saying "great" and then awarded the school close to $1 million and an on-site training person for 6 months. Individuals at this school have continued to maintain autonomy from the larger organization by applying for other grants individually, because "the district was taking too long." For instance, in the late-1990s, they secured $1.2 million from California's Digital High School (DHS) program and $4.2 million from E-Rate, the federal government's technology discount program for schools and libraries.

This school's success has set a model for schools in the rest of the district to follow, but its financial (and spatial) autonomy has also given it continued positional advantage over district officials and their technology mandates. The network administrator at this school related to me a story that affirms this point about territorial control. He first professed to be quite open to anyone visiting and viewing the school's equipment — a point that was supported by his gracious acceptance of my intrusion. Nonetheless, he continued, when two district subcontractors came in to check out the school's network and ignorantly started tugging on the fragile fiberoptic wires, he forcibly removed them from the school site. A few days later the technology staff at this school received the district's "technology plan" for proposition BB, which is a local school bond measure, and they were aghast to see specifications for inferior hubs when the school was already using far more efficient switches. In response, the personnel at this school organized a meeting of technology coordinators from several schools and invited the downtown administrator charged with setting specifications to attend. At the meeting, they informed the administrator that if they were given hubs, they would throw them in the trash, and other school coordinators seconded the threat. When I questioned the sincerity of this threat, the technology coordinator told me that they would have stuck the hubs in a closet somewhere to collect dust, but this does not undermine the effectiveness of the ultimatum: if the media were alerted to the fact that L.A. Unified was wasting taxpayer dollars on obsolete equipment that did not serve the needs of students, district administrators would feel the heat. A few days later, central administrators capitulated and distributed a new set of specifications that included an option for the more efficient switches.

This example of confrontation with central administrators illustrates how spatial territorial rights (control over what happens at school sites), degrees of financial autonomy (lack of complete dependency on the school system), individual insulation (protection from retaliation by those outside of the school), informal networks (mobilizing a community of practitioners), and symbolic leverage (tacit threats of whistle-blowing to the media) act together to create conditions for appropriate technology design. In this setting, technology staff act as agents who can draw on their histories of success to modify policies even when they occupy institutional positions lower than those of central administrators. The power balance described here is quickly changing, however, and local control achieved through grassroots mobilization is being lost.

Fragmented Centralization as an Organizational Structure

The unfolding of information technology (IT) projects and programs in L.A. Unified establishes an identifiable pattern of fragmented centralization, meaning the simultaneous centralization of decision-making authority and decentralization of accountability (across multiple peripheries) for the measured "success" of those decisions. This trend in relationships among technologists serves as a barometer of a sea change in the organization as a whole (e.g., policies on curricula, standards, and testing each reveal similar qualities).[2] One high-level technology administrator put it succinctly by telling me that the underlying goal for all technology decisions was "standardization without centralization." If this is the case, then the question of where standards are set and by whom determines where power is shifting, on the one hand, and where autonomy is lost, on the other.

The term *fragmented centralization* describes the latest development in the organizational restructuring of public education while specifically accounting for power shifts that occur during this process. Fragmented centralization is a theoretically helpful concept because, by attending to multiple sites across the organization, it avoids forcing data into simple core-periphery categories, which has been a problem with other theories of global development, such as world systems theory (Nash 1981; Wallerstein 1990). Consequently, networks of power (whether of class, gender, race, or professional status) can be mapped for their multiple hierarchies and power differentials across and within organizational registers. The concept is appropriate for Los Angeles institutions, because the city itself has long been recognized as a "fragmented metropolis" of uneven development and economic inequality (Fogelson 1967), and the school system molds itself to these urban and social conditions.

The impetus for the contemporary process of fragmented centralization in Los Angeles has its roots in globalizing pressures that are felt in many sectors, both public and private. Over L.A. Unified looms the shadow of privatization, which could be the bane of public institutions in this era of neoliberalism. Fear of privatization, dissolution, or state takeover compels the city government to provide a semblance of local accountability and responsiveness. Furthermore, what has been called the postmodern urban form — characterized by suburbanization, edge cities, and gated communities (Dear 2000) — establishes a political topography that may motivate fragmented centralization, especially within public institutions. As Michael Dear (2002, 16) explains, "it is no longer the center that organizes the urban hinterlands [in Los Angeles], but the hinterlands that determine what remains of the center." The center — in this case the central offices of the school district — must give the appearance of being responsive and accountable to demands from the periphery suburbs or risk losing almost all control over policies and resources. This risk is made palpable by a growing movement for the wealthier San Fernando Valley to secede from the City of Los Angeles, thus stripping the city of vital economic resources needed for public programs. The San Fernando Valley secession movement recently gained ground by getting a ballot measure approved for the November 2002 elections, and although the measure did not pass, policymakers are certainly aware of and responding to this ever-present possibility.

In L.A. Unified, the Board of Education and the superintendent mandated decentralization of the school system into 11 "local districts" in 2000, which accomplished a type of local responsiveness, but by giving each of these local districts moderate budgetary control, this form also abdicated central authorities of responsibility for future problems. A sense of arbitrary restructuring for the sake of inoculation against an externally enforced breakup of the district is prevalent. One program administrator expressed it as follows:

> I don't think that the restructuring of the district has had much effect one way or the other, other than appeasing those people that were looking for a breakup of the district. I think it's held that at bay a little longer. I don't think it's produced any kind of positive effect yet in terms of student achievement — it may. I do think that it's brought localized control, which can contribute to student achievement, but again, there's your 5-year rule [meaning the district is restructured on an average of every 5 years]: we won't know. The problem is we may have people making decisions again in 2 years. We were joking this morning at lunch: "What's it going to be next? Are we going to be eight districts, nine districts, are there going to be letters, numbers?" And each of us is talking about all the things we've gone through in our careers at L.A. Unified.

> *How many restructurings?*

> Well, we've had zones, districts, little districts, clusters, regions, areas, you name it — going back 20, 25 years. It's kind of funny the way we do these things.

Yet, in spite of surface efforts at decentralization, it is my contention that a high degree of central control is maintained: most policies are still set by members of the Board of Education, purchasing is centrally coordinated, average daily attendance and payroll time reporting are still centralized, legal counsel and auditors still operate centrally, and IT decisions are almost all now made by central administrators.[3] Financial allocations over personnel in each school and in each local district are determined by a formula, set centrally, that allots personnel budgets according to the number of students served in that school or local district, respectively.

In the IT realm, the process of fragmented centralization is marked by a series of colonizations of previously protected territories, and these colonizations occur under the rhetorical cover of power vacuums, neutral technologies, and technological imperatives. In addition to what I described in previous chapters as space and budgetary controls absorbed by IT specialists, examples of territorial invasions and centralizing trends are manifold:

- Librarians who guarded computer passwords in attempts to regulate Internet use by students are foiled by the establishment of a central system of school-level student IDs and passwords, thereby diminishing librarians' gatekeeping ability.
- Teachers who have a history of teaching computer classes are suddenly told that only math, computer science, business, and vocational teachers are equipped to teach such classes — unless, of course, such experienced teachers wanted to bypass this arbitrary ruling by undergoing training for an "add-on credential."
- Centrally located administrators now set specifications for computer equipment purchased for schools, whereas previous specifications for equipment purchased with grant money were set by individual schools. The onus is then placed on resource-strapped IT staff at schools to support multiple platforms without any extra assistance.
- Central administrators determine and coordinate construction timetables and hardware specifications for the federal government's E-Rate program, whereas schools handled such arrangements themselves in the past. Oftentimes the burden falls on individuals at school sites, who must pursue individual contractors or pressure local district ITAFs to figure out why construction has stalled and how to get it started again.
- Policymakers and central administrators have now set rules to preclude any new technology grants submitted by individual schools; grants now must be orchestrated by the central district. Moreover, all grants must now accord with the newly written District Technology Plan.
- The Instructional Technology Commission's (ITC) online discussion group, which has grassroots origins and has been a

place for the open exchange of ideas, is now seen by participants as being "policed" by central administrators, who publicly reprimand anyone who questions their authority or decisions. This results in many participants self-policing their own contributions for fear of making enemies.

• Central administrators chastise school-site technology coordinators who want to participate in specification writing, telling them that the job of technology coordinators is to demonstrate, through standardized tests, that computers augment student learning. Here, the inclusion of local knowledge in decisions is restricted, but determinations of the efficacy of computer use in education, which should have been made at the policy level, are delegated to school-site personnel.

The point of enumerating these many examples is not to say that all central control has negative effects but rather to illustrate a general organizational trend: participation and autonomy are diminished at the local level as decisions are centralized, yet labor and accountability are simultaneously intensified for those on the periphery.

Decentralized distribution of responsibility for centrally made decisions, on the other hand, can be seen in almost every aspect of public education, but especially in policies concerning information technology:

• Local districts and individual schools must directly contend with centrally managed but incomplete telecommunications networks in schools. This includes both the instructional burden of teaching mandatory "technology standards" to students when the equipment is nonfunctional and the material burden of navigating around partially completed construction projects that leave classrooms closed and trenches exposed across school sites, sometimes for well over a year.

• Policies on instructional curricula, standards, and testing are set by centrally located administrators (sometimes at the state or federal level) and reinforced through prescribed instructional software, but individual schools, teachers, parents, and ultimately students are held accountable for successfully executing those policies. This phenomenon is brought into stark relief with such punitive measures as putting entire schools or districts "on probation" when students or districts fail to improve their test scores, which is a central component of President Bush's No Child Left Behind Act of 2001.

- L.A. Unified requires that acceptable use policies (AUPs) and release forms be signed by every student and by parents or guardians of minors; otherwise, students are unable to use the Internet in any classes or in school libraries. These documents remove all legal burden, whether from lawsuits or for crimes, from the district, placing it squarely on the shoulders of students and their parents or guardians. Until students turn in these documents and pass an Internet etiquette test, they are unable to use computers, in spite of the fact that networked computers are now being placed in every classroom and "technology standards" are pushing all teachers to use the machines. AUPs and Internet tests represent another facet of fragmented centralization: computers may be reputed as valuable and necessary by those deciding technology policy, but any foreseeable or unforeseeable risks resulting from that "necessary" use must be taken by those who are most vulnerable.

Rationales for fragmented centralization are clearly embedded in and constrained by larger political and cultural contexts. First, the design of large technology grants that are tied to student poverty levels (like the federal E-Rate program) or to low student performance on tests (like local bond measure BB) or to number of students in a school (like California's Assembly Bill 2882) all lend themselves to central administration in order to ensure equitable resource distribution and grant compliance. Instead of dealing with each school or local district on an individual basis, those awarding grants would prefer to simplify the process by outsourcing the assessment of needs and the routing of resources to main district offices. As one L.A. Unified program administrator said to me: "It's a matter of efficiency. If I can get one guy in L.A. to give me all the data I need — you're looking at the one guy — it's a lot easier than if I have to hear it from 126 different schools." This point was later affirmed in an interview with a policymaker in the governor's office for the secretary of education.

Second, the management of grants quickly becomes work of creative financing, which lies beyond the resources of most schools or local districts. Here is a quick introduction to this accounting complexity: The federal E-Rate program is really a "discount" technology grant that requires a financial outlay from other sources, such as school districts. Digital High School (DHS) is a state-sponsored grant that requires matching funds from another source. L.A. Unified does not match the funds out of its general budget but instead draws matching funds for DHS from E-Rate, and vice versa. Things get a step more complicated when grants used to equip schools, such as Proposition BB and E-Rate, have different technical specifications for network equipment — CAT5 cable and hubs, and fiberoptic cable and switches, respectively. Then, to ratchet everything up one more notch, E-Rate has a rigid time limit for completion; otherwise, the funds are forfeited. And because all construction contracts must be based on competitive bidding and there is a dearth of able contractors in the area, E-Rate schools are prioritized. This, in turn, requires a holistic view of district construction projects, but it is not clear, even to those in top management positions, whether such prioritization (of some student populations over others) is legal.

Third, the appearance of professional computer networks in schools is important to policymakers, parents, and other visitors, but professional appearances cost more money and cannot easily be achieved by school-site employees. Technology administrators and policymakers stressed this point by saying that the district needed to move from "hobbyist" to "enterprise" approaches to technology design, and that the "home brew" history of network projects in L.A. schools — which often look sloppy, with cables dangled from drop ceilings and strapped to the outside of electrical conduit — had to give way to clean- and neat-looking designs by professionals.

Finally, the material components of technological networks, something often neglected in analyses of technology, may themselves act as *gravity wells* that compel central control in spite of the many unbound web metaphors used to describe them. In L.A. Unified, all the mainframe servers for data collection, storage, and Internet routing are centrally located in the "G" building of the main district offices in downtown Los Angeles. These servers are visible at the entrance to the Information

Technology Division offices, impressively shielded behind a glass enclosure and forbiddingly inaccessible without an authorized key card. It is here, and not in the boardroom or classroom, that the primary business functions of the district are managed: payroll time reporting, average daily attendance, student information system, decision support system, purchasing data, budgets, and Internet routing. So despite the model of 11 semi-independent districts, the hardwired information networks continue to be sited downtown because efficient and secure technological design dictates it. As with the military command-and-control systems that inspired today's telecommunications networks, the politics generated by these technological systems are those of centralized control, regardless of the decentralized operations of virtual networks (Edwards 1996).

Each of these rationales for central control of IT and its design are embedded in ideologies and interdependencies that link L.A. Unified to globalization processes. The allocation of public grant monies for needy student populations has its impetus in rhetorics of digital divides and national competitiveness (Monahan 2001), where discursive themes stress either the need for computer-literate students entering a global workforce or the economic necessity of supporting the technology industry in the United States. The management of multiple grants becomes a two-sided coin of securing outside funding and ensuring legality every step of the way. These two sides are linked by the fact that mistakes in design processes — such as the Belmont Learning Complex — imperil students and waste public funds, thereby diminishing public support for the organization as a whole and jeopardizing future bonds or grants. Unfortunately, the combination of needing to secure outside funding, complying with the legal stipulations on that funding, and engaging in competitive bidding processes places public education in the procedural confines of "free market" inflexibility. My informants stress that this "private sector" approach to the management of grants is markedly different from past district responsibilities with state or federal funding, because the district must now demonstrate compliance on a greater level than before and risks losing entire pots of money if procedures are not strictly adhered to or deadlines not met.

The appearance of professional computer networks matters most for convincing visitors to classrooms — diplomats, superintendents, principals, parents, or researchers — that state-of-the-art education is occurring in those spaces; such appearances generate a symbolic if specious bridge for students to cross over from classroom spaces to the business environments that such classrooms emulate. Finally, the centralizing tendencies of technological infrastructures now manifest themselves in what Saskia Sassen (1991, 2000) flags as the "concentrated sited materialities" or "global cities" of service support structures for global capitalism. The insertion of technological networks into schools plugs education (and the production of computer-literate students) into this wider grid of global flows and dependencies.

Fragmented centralization is not simply the reproduction of centralized management control of the past. Instead, fragmented centralization is a unique form of centralization that allows for the decentralization of certain responsibilities as part of its structural logic. Centralization is now a stealth endeavor hidden in the seemingly apolitical setting of specifications and standards while risk and responsibility are fragmented and copiously distributed to those on multiple peripheries throughout the organization.

A Post-Fordist Organization?

It may not seem obvious to analyze post-Fordist structures within public institutions, because post-Fordism has been used predominately to describe the organization of private companies. Unlike corporations, public institutions have competing social *and* economic missions and radically different governance structures, but these differences make the organizational changes under way all the more important to study. After all, the public sector — from education to welfare to security — is being privatized rapidly, yet the implications for organizational missions or public experiences are very poorly understood at this stage. Therefore, while it may be analytically useful to maintain the differences between public and private institutions, it is not necessarily empirically accurate or theoretically generative to view them as separate and distinct.

Of the main strands of post-Fordist theory, the *flexible specialization* approach of Michael Piore and Charles Sabel (1984) outlines the ideal type of an individually empowering and efficient organizational structure and provides a comparative perspective for evaluating the constitution of public education. According to this model, as summarized by Ash Amin (1994, 21), the ideal flexible organization will demonstrate these arrangements:

> division of tasks within the production cycle . . . reintegration of research and design, management, white-collar and blue-collar work . . . reversal of the Fordist and Taylorist tendency towards deskilling and worker isolation, through greater reliance on skills, polyvalence, worker participation and collaboration . . . decentralization of decision-making authority . . . deployment of multi-purpose technologies (rather than task-specific ones) . . . [and] the sedimentation of a culture of cooperation, trust and negotiability between firms.

Many critiques can be and have been leveled at flexible specialization as a model of what post-Fordism is or should be, namely that it is market-deterministic and it uncritically romanticizes skilled, craft production. My purpose in invoking it here is to provide a heuristic for speaking about the possibility of flexible and empowering structures in public education.

At first blush, the restructuring of L.A. Unified into eleven local districts seems to have met several of the flexible specialization criteria admirably: division of tasks, reskilling, and cooperation. In fact, one thing that restructuring accomplished well was to create an environment that requires teamwork; previously, entire divisions of personnel were centrally located, but they are now more distributed, with one or several individuals present in each local district office. This is the "knowledge worker" model of management (Drucker 1999), where all individuals must be experts in their fields because they must work with others who do not, and should not have to, know the details of their specialties. Such positions may be empowering for those who want to be actively involved in and responsible for knowledge production, communication, and management, but some individuals do not thrive under such conditions, as the following story told by a local district ITAF makes clear:

> [The facilities division] had over time kind of evolved a system of how to manage plants centrally. But that was with them all working together in one office and having their very bureaucratic, ritualistic ways of doing things. But now that office has been split up and it's in eleven different areas, and most of the people have been moved to other positions, so

people that were doing this in the old bureaucratic system now have other jobs or have retired because they just couldn't deal with another reorganization. . . . [The facilities person assigned to our local district] was not asked to leave by the local district but chose to resign because he was having a difficult time regionalizing. He wanted to maintain his ties and his supervisory structure with the general district. And the local superintendent was saying, "I'm going to be your boss," and he said, "I resign."

While not all individuals can be expected to thrive under the pressure and responsibility of being knowledge workers, most technologists I spoke with took great pleasure in describing the esoterica of their jobs, had no qualms about confessing ignorance in other areas, and appreciated opportunities for participation that genuinely affects outcomes.

Decentralized and participatory organizations that rely heavily on information technology to facilitate knowledge production and sharing do hold a promise for increased efficiency, productivity, and worker investment (Osborne & Gaebler 1992; Hakken 1999; Reich 2000). This belief has led some scholars to proclaim that such revolutionary "informating" processes mean "dismantling the very same managerial hierarchy that once brought greatness" (Zuboff, cited in Thompson 2003). It should be evident that these optimistic projections are not realized in the current organizational form of L.A. Unified because of centralizing tendencies that persist in practice. Thus, the key flexible specialization criterion of decentralized decision-making authority is not met; as a result, a culture of cooperation and trust is not sedimented. Instead, territorial conflicts pass for respectful negotiations.

There are some logical reasons why L.A. Unified continues along a fragmented centralization path in spite of its efforts to reinvigorate its culture under a knowledge-worker paradigm. The first reason has to do with the school district's institutional history. Just like material infrastructures, organizations like L.A. Unified are large, tenacious entities that defy rapid change, in part because most individuals within them have grown comfortable with a culture of bounded territories and status quo operations. An ongoing history of conflict and struggle for existing territorial demarcations — classroom autonomy, curriculum development, employee salaries and duties, managerial oversight, and so on — entrenches a commitment to policing hard-won territory and a grudging respect for the status quo.[4] These dispositions are inculcated, internalized, and reinforced with every quotidian interaction in spite of the district's structure du jour.

The demands of globalization on state and industry further support fragmented centralization. As the example of IT demonstrates, grant programs with outside agencies insist on the centralization of management, both because external funders, such as the state of California, seek to outsource the labor of distributing funds and because of the legal and procedural complexity (including liability issues) of coordinating multiple grants. Grant givers, then, are engaged in a similar process of fragmented centralization: distributing responsibility for management and audits to other institutional bodies while maintaining authority to set the parameters of the grants awarded. The "professional" appearance of school projects, whether construction, curricula, or technological infrastructure, is a standard set by industry and, perhaps not coincidentally, can be met only by industry; this demand does not necessarily centralize, but it does remove local self-sufficiency and autonomy. Lastly, the valence of technological networks is toward central control, and the concentrated sited materiality of mainframes and their security apparatuses has been planted at central L.A. Unified offices. The district has become a node on the larger global network — a service provider of IT workers and consumers for the sustenance of global information flows and capital accumulation.

Is L.A. Unified a post-Fordist organization? My answer is yes, but not in the idealized, flexible form proffered by Piore and Sabel. It is an organization that mutates in response to changing perceptions of the role of education in society; it accepts the responsibilities given to it by funding agencies, industry, and the public; it then distributes accountability down the organizational chain while drawing control up it; it performs elaborate rituals of disclosure and restructuring in answer to privatization threats; it develops many cooperative relationships with outside firms and contractors; it feeds the global economy with generous industry contracts and pliable workers and consumers. In other words, L.A. Unified flexibly adapts to the global political economy but does not provide a flexible environment for its workers or students.[5] This current form is the paradigm for a post-Fordist organization, but it is also one that prioritizes market logics over educational goals, intensifies workloads, and decreases worker participation and satisfaction.

Conclusion: Structural Flexibility in Organizations

It may seem counterintuitive for those who express a desire for strict compliance and accountability in public institutions, but I argue that public education would benefit from policies that encourage informal networks and improvisation. Such networks and practices not only maintain functionality in this continuously restructuring school district but also spur innovation. Although informal networks occur in most — if not all — large organizations, the frequent restructuring of L.A. Unified has probably magnified their importance, and perhaps their size and scope, in the school system. While one might argue that such networks and territories are abused for egotistical and ideological reasons, without them L.A. Unified would be dismally chaotic and hopelessly dysfunctional. The policy problem is in how to foster such informal practices while discouraging abusive and possibly harmful situations.

R. Anderson and W. Sharrock (1993) offer a partial solution with their concept of "organizational affordance," a property of the workplace environment that allows employees to simply "pick up" or acquire knowledge or skills without any specialized training. In the L.A. school system context, there are several ways that the extant affordance for informal networks can be augmented to encourage greater exchange of knowledge about individuals, practices, spaces, and policies. On the structural level, an obvious answer would be to create a more flexible organization that authentically decentralizes both responsibility *and* decision-making authority over standards and policies. Some degree of centralization, such as that over tax revenues, should be maintained to ensure equitable distribution of financial resources across the district, but many of the current functions of the organization can be moved to the local district level.

With individuals and groups, opportunities for exchange of ideas and exposure to others should be encouraged, thereby enhancing the already present networks that keep the district operational. The ITC discussion group serves as a model for exchange of individual perspectives on design processes, and similar discussion groups could be established throughout the organization. Participants in ITC discussions may feel occasional frustration that those in other organizational positions do not see the world the way they do, but the overall outcome is positive in spite of power differentials, because once an idea or a protest is documented and an entire community has written evidence of it, it makes it almost impossible for decision makers to ignore the input altogether.

Exposure to others and the subsequent expansion of individual networks could be facilitated through staged and hosted migrations of individuals to other institutional positions for a week or so. These planned visits would require employees to observe, participate in, and hopefully develop a sophisticated appreciation for the daily activities of others and the constraints placed upon them. At best, such exposure could allow the interactions of parties to flow more smoothly: individuals could provide the exact kind of useful information to the other group during future projects, or they could maneuver to pass policies or otherwise make jobs easier for their organizational counterparts. Again, such outcomes are already being achieved in moderation, but they could be greatly enhanced by planned and compensated visits across L.A. Unified.

Finally, forums could be established for the recounting of institutional stories. Be they best-case practices; origin stories of projects, programs, or groups; histories of school sites; or reflections on political changes over time — whatever the content, narratives could fill in many gaps that otherwise impede productive exchanges in L.A. Unified. Narrative exchanges could disseminate ideas for how to get things accomplished and create a shared sense of what is worth striving for. Stories could also reveal a range of latent possibilities both in social and material infrastructures, whether at school sites or in downtown offices. Conflicts may arise over competing interpretations of past or present activities, but this would at least create a space and an opportunity for discussing differing viewpoints and how they shape current projects. In other words, conflicts already manifest themselves in reactions to group policies or behaviors; having an open expression of where such conflicts originated from could bring opposing parties closer to some resolution while beneficially reinscribing institutional memory.

It is my conviction that truly decentralizing decision-making power in L.A. Unified — which would really be closer to a model of community-based schools — would provide structural flexibility and lead to greater individual investment, collaboration, and innovation. The implementation of plans of the kind outlined above (for enhancing already present exchanges of ideas and exposure to others) would enforce ad hoc yet efficient organizational oversight, making debacles on the scale of Belmont unimaginable in the future. How would such oversight work? With increased participation in projects and many eyes scrutinizing plans, collective expertise would surpass any individual's or group's. And provided that decision-making power was decentralized and distributed, such internal experts would undoubtedly have greater commitment to ensuring sound developments than outside auditors and contractors would. In its idealized form, the result of this proposal could be a flexible organization with affordances for collective knowledge production and exchange.

One major drawback of such a proposal is time investment. Requiring busy employees to participate in policy or design processes might seem unreasonable. Additionally, getting employees to involve themselves in discussion groups, to visit or host others, and to share narratives demands time that is not easily come by in this overworked environment. That said, would such allowances for these efforts really be greater than the time spent in overcoming the lengthy learning curves imposed by restructuring every few years? Would such allowances cost more than the many poorly implemented technological infrastructures or curricular programs? It does not seem likely, especially not if existing professional development hours were dedicated to the purposes I have outlined above.

Other obstacles to these proposals include inflexible funding deadlines and sedimented cultural dispositions. The next chapter advocates for increased structural flexibility in deadlines and specifications concerning technology grants, but let me mention briefly that projects that are rushed and specifications that are incompatible with existing school technology networks decrease operational efficiency and detract from the potential of learning environments. Faster is not always better. As another obstacle, extreme territoriality in school culture will certainly work against increased exchange and exposure.[6] However, because long-standing opposition between administrators and teachers is currently being disrupted by an emerging occupational group of IT specialists, an opportunity for demarcating shared, collaborative spaces within public education exists. This opportunity, if acted on promptly, could result in lasting cultural change.

5
POLICY GAMES

Irrespective of whether we choose to play the game or not, we are part of it simply because we *are played*.

Günther Anders 1987, 2

Amid organizational restructuring in public institutions, policymaking processes are becoming increasingly codified, restricted, and obscured. Especially regarding technology policy, the coils of which stretch across all domains of public education, individuals who fashion themselves as technical experts are absorbing control over many of the decisions about infrastructure design and — by extension — the attendant social relations that infrastructures govern. This chapter shows that centralized streamlining of technology specifications places undue constraints on design possibilities and that these constraints are proportional to the restriction of participation in policy processes. Policy design, in other words, embeds the values of its process into its outcomes, delimiting the range of future policies at the same time. Furthermore, nondemocratic processes tend to yield not only constricted policy outcomes but also material outcomes of limited utility and structural flexibility.

Previous chapters have traced the design of technological infrastructures in public education to points of intersection with neoliberal ideologies and globalization forces. The emphasis has been on the political valence of technological spaces, the social relations of technology practices, and the implications of organizational mutations. This chapter takes as its focus the construction of a policy arena for technology within the Los Angeles Unified School District, including the territorial conflicts, which galvanize and/or foreclose modes of participation, and the material outcomes, which embed policy worldviews into durable forms. The stress here is on the politics and contingent processes behind technology designs in this globally situated organization. The crafting of empowering policies rather than degenerative ones, I assert, hinges on their openness to interpretation and reevaluation, and this is achieved best when the policy arena itself is permeable and participatory, when it supports exceptions rather than enforces standards, when it is, in short, flexible.

This chapter follows several interpretations of technology grants and their policies to demonstrate that the design of technological systems is entirely contingent and situated and not some neutral evolutionary progression toward an unavoidable outcome. First, I provide a general overview of the interrelated technology programs for wiring schools for telecommunications access. Second, I describe the development of the federal government's E-Rate program (about which more follows in the next section) in L.A. Unified and how the translation of rigid E-Rate policies generated uncertainty, stress, and poor design outcomes. Third and last, I relate contestations across the organization's social worlds over who should set specifications for a state technology grant, and I trace some of the tactics and results of those conflicts. Whether discussing policy design, policy translation, or policy negotiation, I contend that flexible and participatory structures catalyze more productive outcomes.[1]

Policies for Infrastructure Design: The Rules of the Game

Think of the implementation of technology networks in public education as a game with continually shifting rules and resources, combative participants, and tenaciously rigid yet life-changing outcomes. In this game, technologists in the district have a finite amount of time to fit the many jagged pieces of the funding puzzle together such that a passably coherent image of functional school telecommunications networks emerges. There are several hands ticking on the game clock, what my informants call short- and long-term "drop deadlines," compelling the players to make quick decisions or to simplify the process by removing others from the game — meaning cutting some district technologists out of the policy-setting process. As an additional stressor, capital is perceptibly dry-ing up for all technology projects; grants are short-term, nonrenewable resources; support and training are the last pieces to arrive and the first to be taken away. For example, in June 2002, ongoing and promised funding for technical support and training under California's Digital High School program was "deferred," perhaps indefinitely, verifying concerns over the long-term sustainability of IT in public education, particularly in the wake of severe budget shortfalls in the state (California Department of Education 2002).

There is a complicated set of rules to this game, and participants must figure them out as they go along. First, all the funding sources carry instructions pertaining only to them, such as what the funds can and can-not be spent on, how they must be distributed, when they must be used up, and what constitutes completion. Second, grants are taken as contracts that require semi-strict compliance with their specific rules, lest a host of perils descend on the recipient: audits, lawsuits, loss of funds, or loss of future funding. Third, grants can be played off one another as "matching funds," but while this may be necessary for cash-strapped institutions, the practice increases the risk of loss should any single grant contract be bro-ken, such as with an unmet time deadline. Fourth, in the case of public education, all equipment and construction services must undergo a some-what time-consuming process of competitive bidding. In a "normal" situ-ation, this process starts with the setting of specifications in accordance with the grant's stipulations; next, vendors and contractors evaluate those specifications and submit official bids for the work; the district then awards contracts to the lowest "reasonable" bidder. Fifth and finally, the execution of grants is negotiated in a very political local context, the result of which determines who sets specifications, which contractors service which schools, and which schools get wired first.

All the rules of this funding game, however, are subject to interpreta-tion, and even arrangements of questionable legality with vendors can be achieved provided that the process gives the appearance of propriety.[2] Similarly, creative shuffling of funds between schools often occurs without too much protest because it is outside the primary interest of auditors, who are more worried about compliance with spending and specifications than with destinations. And because the technology administrators making these decisions are not elected officials, they are insulated from public scrutiny.

I suggest that the game of digitizing and automating the operations of public institutions is part of a global trend toward increased organizational interdependency and instability. Because the long-term effects of building technological infrastructures in schools cannot be forecast by the institutions charged with overseeing the plan, this game is risky on multiple levels: first, there is a possibility of losing, but the real losers will be the students with no say in the process; second, the results of partial or complete successes are indeterminate — the effects on student learning and development are unknown and unknowable; third, dependency on computer networks is rapidly becoming ensured (in the form of mandatory technology learning standards and networked administrative tasks such as grade and attendance reporting), but resources to sustain those dependencies are not guaranteed.

The first section of this chapter concerns itself with interpretations, modifications, and negotiations of specifications. As players vie for control over specifications or standards setting (i.e., what equipment will be purchased), they reveal a rich design process that flourishes beneath most people's awareness yet nonetheless structures the daily conditions of students' and others' lives. Science and technology studies (STS) scholars refer to this as the "social construction of technology" (Bijker, Hughes, & Pinch 1987; Bijker & Law 1992), meaning the dynamic, mutually shaping relationship among technologies and social practices. In this case, the emphasis is on the ways that social values, institutional constraints, and politics are embedded in technological artifacts and systems through a contingent and somewhat arbitrary design process. This means that results are not preordained, even though they give the appearance of being so after the fact. Design outcomes could always very easily have been different, and it is in order to understand and evaluate the possibilities for difference that we study the process.

Of the many puzzle pieces of technology funding that are shaped, shuffled, and forced into place, I concentrate here on the interplay of three that occupied the perennial attention of L.A. Unified technologists for the period of my fieldwork, from 2000 to 2001. First, the federal government's E-Rate (meaning "education rate") discount technology program,

which was established by the Telecommunications Act of 1996, funds up
to $2.25 billion annually for wiring public schools and libraries (NYSL
2003).[3] Second, California's Assembly Bill 2882 (AB 2882), which was
passed in 2000, allocates $175 million for the purchase of computers for
state public schools — the official goal of this program being to establish
a 4.75 to 1 student-to-computer ratio in public schools. Third, Los
Angeles' local bond measure Proposition BB, which was passed in 1997,
dedicates $900 million to new school construction and $1.5 billion for
renovating existing school facilities (Deloitte & Touche LLP 2002),
including construction and renovation for wiring schools with telecommunications networks. In reviewing the negotiation and interrelation of
these funding puzzle pieces, I hope to present the contingent and political
nature of design processes and to direct inquiry into the flexible potential
of technology policies.

Notes from the Field: The Unfolding of E-Rate Policies

My primary field site, "Concrete High," was contending with the coordination of all three of the above technology grants (E-Rate, AB 2882, and
Proposition BB) and was one of only a handful of schools in the district
whose technology projects were simultaneously funded by all three.
Schools and libraries that qualify for E-Rate technology discounts are
funded based on the application year, so that "funding year one" (FY1)
designates those that were awarded grants in 1998, FY2 designates those
awarded in 1999, and so on. Concrete High, like most schools in
L.A. Unified, was a "year three" E-Rate school and was given a deadline
of June 30, 2001, for the completion of *all* E-Rate construction. The construction of telecommunications networks in schools means the literal
trenching of campuses by contractors for the laying of data cable, drilling
through walls and ceilings to string cable, adding metal conduit along or
within walls for electrical and data access, setting up server rooms linked
to outside Internet service providers, and testing the entire system so that
classroom computers can connect reliably to the Internet.

Because the construction of networks in many schools was tied to this
June 30 deadline and because, if it were not met, the total of $228.6 mil-
lion E-Rate discounts (FY3) awarded to the district (Alther 2001) would
likely be forfeited, the technology community in L.A. Unified was under

extreme pressure for the entire duration of my fieldwork. Their stress was generated in large part by *uncertainty* about the status of construction projects at local schools, about what the specifications were for E-Rate contractors and whether or not they would be compatible with existing school networks (called "legacy networks"), and about the reliability of contractors assigned to individual schools.

This general state of uncertainty was compounded by several important factors. First, the organizational restructuring of the district in the summer of 2000 shuffled previous chains of command, leaving most people unaware of who was responsible for what or whom to contact to obtain that information. Second, coincident to that restructuring was (and is) a shift in authority for managing technology projects in the district: the shift moved control away from individuals at schools and toward centrally located administrators. Thus, amid ambiguity about what was happening and when, technology personnel in L.A. Unified were undergoing struggles over who should be in charge of making decisions that tangibly affect schools but that also legally implicate the district as a whole (e.g., for issues of grant compliance).

While tensions about the E-Rate deadline were palpable in almost all my interactions with district technologists, this general state of anxiety was seldom named directly except at monthly meetings held by the Instructional Technology Commission (ITC) or meetings held by local district instructional technology applications facilitators (ITAFs). The attendees of these meetings — mostly technology coordinators from schools — would share their disparate experiences from local school sites and collectively concatenate this partial information into a workable model of the current state of technology construction in the district. Because there was no clear narrative of what was happening with E-Rate construction and because, just like my informants, I had to piece together a story based on incomplete and always already biased perspectives, this section is written with intentional gaps — pulling data from these monthly technology meetings, Board of Education meetings, and other sources — in order to convey the experience of uncertainty and the process of knowledge construction on the ground. What follows are excerpts from my field notes relating to the iterative development of district policies for E-Rate construction.

October 26, 2000. At a "[Proposition] BB and Facilities Oversight Committee Meeting" in downtown Los Angeles, board member David Tokofsky expresses concern that the E-Rate "Army Corps" are notorious sticklers for time lines, and that he is worried about losing all E-Rate monies if the district is late with construction completion. It is appropriate for him to discuss the progress of E-Rate construction at a meeting about Proposition BB because these two funding sources for technology are intertwined in the district: in some cases Proposition BB is used to match the funds provided by E-Rate, and at some schools, such as Concrete High, construction projects from both these sources are being coordinated. Tokofsky's reference to the Army Corps of Engineers is significant because they were hired by L.A. Unified, after extreme mismanagement, to coordinate E-Rate projects among contractors. In his remarks, however, he incorrectly conflates the Army Corps with the federal government's School and Libraries Division (SLD), which oversees E-Rate, and his mistake betrays that Board of Education members are just as much in the process of figuring out what is transpiring with technology projects and policies as everyone else is.

January 25, 2001. At a "technology consortium" meeting of a local district, an ITAF reminds technology coordinators that every E-Rate school must have an Internet connection (a "fiber drop") in every classroom by July 1 or lose out on matching funds. Those present, who work at schools rather than in administrative offices, wonder aloud where the electrical power supplies to run these networks will come from, because E-Rate does not supply them and BB funds are already committed elsewhere. Pragmatic concerns about the functionality of computer networks and the risk or disruption for students and teachers occupy the minds of those on the ground at school sites.

February 15, 2001. After attending a "technology consortium" meeting of a local district, held at a middle school in Los Angeles, I run into several E-Rate construction workers digging trenches and laying cable in the dark of night. Their presence reminds me of the labor and material alteration that are needed to establish telecommunications networks: computer technologies, which are often troped as clean and seamless by the media, are messy and materially embodied through and through. This fact is easily overlooked when most people are removed from sites of infrastructure construction and most media sources — whether advertisements or editorials — equate the presence of computers with empowerment. I talk with these men for a while, and they are good-natured about their nocturnal activities.

March 11, 2001. A participant of the Instructional Technology Commission (ITC) electronic discussion group gives advanced warning that the district is planning to remove the Army Corps of Engineers from their position of overseeing E-Rate construction:

> The latest change of course concerns the role of the Army Corps of Engineers. . . . [T]he construction manager for the fiber pulling project at my school is being terminated within the month. He told me that the district is replacing all the Army Corps hired consultants, who are serving as construction managers, with the district's own people, but only about one third as many. So the number of jobs per manager will be tripled. [The construction manager] told me that he does not think the district is displeased with the Army Corps, they're just trying to save money. This kind of mid-stream change is, of course, disruptive.

The response from another member:

> OH NO!!!! Save money at what expense?!?! It seems that each time we begin a major project at our school it gets halted midstream. Then we establish a good working relationship with one person, then he's gone and someone else shows up. I realize that in any major project, adjustments must be made as we go along, but I surely pray this personnel change is a well thought out and not just a cost saving factor.

This online exchange between two technology coordinators reveals a growing level of anxiety over the unknown material effects of policy or management decisions made elsewhere. Not only do these interlocutors worry about meeting the E-Rate deadline, they are concerned foremost with reducing disruption at schools.

March 22, 2001. The Los Angeles' *Daily News* runs a front-page headline declaring: "LAUSD's online bungle: 1 of 375 schools wired by deadline, $40 million in jeopardy." The article continues:

> Los Angeles Unified School District officials promised to wire 375 schools for Internet access by March 1 when it got nearly $200 million in

federal funding but bungled the project so badly only one school has been completed. . . . With a June 30 deadline looming for spending the "E-Rate" funds to wire most schools, the LAUSD risks losing more than $40 million unless the Federal Communications Commission grants an extension, officials said Wednesday. In a frenzy now to finish as much of the work as possible before the cutoff, the LAUSD last week dumped the U.S. Army Corps of Engineers, which was brought in with much fanfare to oversee the program to prevent the kind of managerial breakdowns that have plagued many LAUSD building projects. (Barrett 2001)

This piece noticeably turns up the heat on district technologists and policymakers as the public gets wind of the fears of insiders. By alluding to the Belmont Learning Complex debacle, where an L.A. Unified school was built on a 35-acre former oil field, the article situates E-Rate construction projects within a larger history of institutional mismanagement. And because this story follows so shortly on the heels of L.A. Unified's reorganization, which was — in part — a response to calls for the breakup of the district after Belmont, another perceived waste of taxpayer dollars could have calamitous effects on the organization, creating even more disruption for students and employees.

April 18, 2001. At an Instructional Technology Commission (ITC) meeting at a South Central high school, an ITAF laments that vendors will not be paid if all the networks are not up by June 30. Of the hundreds of schools to be wired, only two networks are now operational; maybe seventy will be completed by the deadline. "This is a drop-dead date," he cautions, "something that the district has never faced before." But information is not flowing freely to contractors, he continues, mostly because plans to incorporate legacy (i.e., preexisting) networks were not included in initial contracts. Moreover, schools that have to balance year-round schedules with adult night classes are not giving contractors "reasonable" work hours, so contractors may have a just case for suing the district if they perceive that school schedules are impeding their ability to meet the contract deadline. In any event, the ITAF prophesies that technology coordinators should expect last-minute, 24-hour construction work as the deadline approaches.

April 19, 2001. At a meeting of the Board of Education's Business, Finance, Audit and Technology (BFAT) committee, staff members inform the committee that twenty schools are now wired with E-Rate funds and assure them that 70 percent of schools will be completed by the deadline. Board members nod their heads, completely unaware that this report directly contradicts what technologists are saying at school sites. It now becomes apparent to me that if construction work is not completed by the deadline, the school district will have to pay contractors out of its general fund.

May 22, 2001. At a Board of Education meeting, Dr. Paul Holmes, Director of Modernization and Existing Facilities, gives an E-Rate update: the Federal Communications Commission (FCC), which is the main governing body in charge of overseeing E-Rate, has granted the district a 3-month extension, making the new deadline September 30, 2001. Three of the four contractors currently working on more than 375 schools will finish on time. Thirty-four schools have passed "ping tests" (meaning that data is flowing across the network with few errors), and seventy-three other schools are being tested now. Ironically, this report of an FCC extension does not assuage tension over E-Rate but instead increases uncertainty for technologists in the district about which schools qualify for the extension, what will happen if this second deadline of September 30 is not met, and whether schools where E-Rate construction never started — such as Concrete High — will be cycled to the following year's deadline instead. With this extension, anxiety grew even as the deadline mutated into a less dire imperative.

May 25, 2001. In an interview with a program administrator involved with E-Rate, I am told of the many inflexibilities that continue to obstruct E-Rate projects: (1) electrical insufficiencies pose problems, because networks cannot operate without sufficient power, yet vendors are not responsible for providing adequate power; (2) health and safety issues over lead paint and asbestos slow processes down; (3) contractors had semantic differences with administrators and did not think that their contract for "network integration" meant connecting existing networks; (4) the Army Corps of Engineers told contractors to build "illegal" parallel networks in some schools; (5) there is a shortage of equipment (such as fiber-to-copper converters) and "manpower" because there are only so many qualified contractors in the area; (6) year-round and night school schedules force contractors to work on weekends, but contracts did not include the overtime pay required for weekend work; (7) the School and Libraries

Division (SLD) of the federal government does not allow any flexibility with E-Rate: every change in specifications must be applied for, and the district must wait months for approval; and (8) contracts are "locked in," so that if the price of equipment goes down, which it invariably does over the course of a project, the higher price must be paid. These comments about policy and circumstantial rigidities partially explain the uncertainties and disruptions at school sites. For instance, if administrators are waiting to hear from SLD concerning a specification adjustment or if they are searching for scarce hardware, it would be impossible for them to give technologists at school sites a clear answer about the process.

November 29, 2001. I am now out of the field and checking back with my informants to see how the extended September 30 deadline played out. A monthly "E-Rate Program Progress Report" was presented at a Board of Education committee meeting today, specifying that many "year three" schools have been given new, apparently arbitrary deadlines for E-Rate completion, such as February 28, 2002, for Concrete High. Meanwhile, E-Rate contractors will not begin construction at Concrete High until existing network construction paid for by Proposition BB is "signed-off"; otherwise, E-Rate contractors could be held liable if the BB network fails in any way. However, since a completely unrelated problem of a faulty BB fire alarm system continues to jolt students and others at this school with daily ear-piercing false alarms, the BB network cannot be signed off until this problem is corrected, because all the construction is included in the same contract. Thus, no one knows when E-Rate construction will really start at this school, and students who have tolerated incredible campus disruption continue — for better or worse — to live without the Internet in their classrooms.

In the cases described above, conditions of uncertainty coupled with an apparently strict deadline for E-Rate projects led to increased stress, discord, and disruption at schools. With such a large-scale, complex technological project, it is little wonder that so many obstacles and contingencies could not be foreseen or planned for in advance. Strict deadlines, rigid contracts, and intractable technical specifications are clearly intended to prevent graft and mismanagement while ensuring technological equity for all students, but the results fall short of these lofty goals. Paradoxically, as this section has demonstrated, inflexible policies about E-Rate spending yielded *greater* uncertainty rather than less. And if uncertainty is a key element to employee stress and material disruption, as I have observed, then more flexible policies for spending and a more open deadline for completion would have helped the district implement networks with less employee antagonism and fewer disruptions.

Negotiations over Assembly Bill 2882

Whereas the last section illustrated how the interpretation and translation of E-Rate technology policies into built form is an iterative process where employees constantly strive to overcome uncertainties and inflexibilities, this section describes polemical negotiations over the setting of equipment specifications for California's technology grant Assembly Bill 2882 (hereafter "AB 2882"). To show the different dimensions of policy negotiation in L.A. Unified, I divide this section into three parts: "Social Worlds," "Symbols as Design Agents," and "Constructing an Outcome."

Social Worlds

The design of telecommunications infrastructures in L.A. Unified presents extreme coordination challenges to the multiple networks of individuals involved in the process. Given the size of the district (806 schools), its geographical dispersion (704 square miles), and the variety of complicated tasks entailed (evaluating needs, allocating funds, setting specifications, hiring contractors, wiring schools, inspecting work, and so on), no single group can achieve a complete understanding of this vast design process. To understand how groups work together to establish infrastructures, I build on "social worlds theory" (Shibutani 1955) as deployed in the field of science and technology studies (STS).

Social worlds are groups connected through discourse and shared worldviews, not necessarily by geographical proximity or professional association (Fujimura 1987; Star & Griesemer 1989; Clarke 1990). Where most STS social worlds theory is used to analyze the construction of scientific facts, my use conveys the construction of vast technological networks and is therefore more akin to the material focus of Howard Becker's research on "art worlds" and Louis Bucciarelli's on "object worlds." Becker (1982) employs the term *art worlds* to describe the indispensable contexts for art creation: the collective coordination of conventional knowledge, its embodiment in artifacts and practices, and its dependency on extended social networks (audiences, equipment providers, curators, performers, and so on). For Bucciarelli (1994), the term *object world* describes the assemblage of social, technical, and symbolic components that make design possible within specific engineering domains (such as the construction of X-ray inspection systems or photovoltaic modules).

While the above two approaches begin with discreet artifacts and seek to explain the conditions that bring those artifacts into existence and sustain them, my use of the concept of social worlds focuses on groups that must collaborate to build nondiscreet infrastructures that always extend beyond the purview of individual designers — the product itself (infrastructure) bridges the different social networks. Leigh Star and James Griesemer (1989) have employed the term *boundary objects* to describe such bridges between social worlds, but what Joan Fujimura (1992) coins "standardized packages" probably more closely captures the structuring role of technological networks that I am specifying:

> "[S]tandardized packages" is a concept which handles both collective work across divergent social worlds and fact stabilization. A package differs from a boundary object in that it is used by researchers [policy designers in my case] to define a conceptual and technical work space which is less abstract, less ill-structured, less ambiguous, and less amorphous. (Fujimura 1992, 169)

This distinction between an object that circulates and a materiality (or package) that literally extends into social worlds is important, because how each group defines goals or problems depends on its disposition and perceived responsibility toward other designers and the larger infrastructure project.

A shortcoming of social worlds theory is that, through its emphasis on cooperation and social cohesion, it tends to neglect issues of conflict within fields of power and to neglect macrostructural restraints on social action. Yet social worlds theory has the potential to explain conflicts among groups in relation to social structures, such as organizations

(Clarke 1990). This is the approach attempted here: to draw on social worlds theory to explain technological cultures within communities of practice but also to analyze conflicts and systemic power relations among such groups. What follows is an investigation of two competing social worlds — central and local — within the organization of L.A. Unified and negotiations between them over technical specifications for California's AB 2882.

In 2000, the California State Legislature unanimously passed AB 2882 and Governor Gray Davis approved the bill with the objective of reducing student-to-computer ratios to 4.75 to 1 in all classrooms and in all public school districts across the state. Because computer access is extremely varied in schools, in part because of the varied specifications of funding sources, this legislation was intended to correct technological inequities existing among schools. Some schools have partial networks from E-Rate or Proposition BB, for instance, but, at the time, few schools had *complete* networks, that is, network drops in every classroom, connecting computers to the Internet. However, when the legislature appropriated only $175 million of the requested $800 million for AB 2882, the grand objective of total technological parity quickly changed to supplying computers for high school students alone.

My interviewee in the governor's office of the secretary for education claimed that the decision to prioritize computers for high school students over other grade levels was made with the interests of business in mind. He explained that businesses have immediate needs for a technologically literate workforce so that they, and the state of California, can compete globally. The framing of this decision in terms of business needs illustrates how discourse establishes its own symbolic infrastructure that reinscribes students' needs as those of business while eliding other educational goals.

District technology administrators, located centrally in downtown Los Angeles, are the first social world with a stake in infrastructure planning. Technology administrators in L.A. Unified are associated with the Information Technology Division (ITD) of the school district as a whole, and they oversee a range of technology projects: the district's Web pages, student information system, instructional technology training, network infrastructure coordination, and more. Technology administrators frame problems in terms of the district as a whole, whereas school site technology coordinators prioritize projects at their particular schools.[4]

Local technology coordinators and their staff represent the second social world at play in this story. In L.A. Unified, previous technology funding sources were managed by technologists at individual schools. This meant that technology coordinators at school sites assessed the technological needs of the school; applied for money to meet those needs; arranged the purchasing of equipment, software, and services; and oversaw the establishment of school networks. When technology staff exist at individual schools, which is not always the case (especially for lower grade levels), they often consist of teachers, network administrators, and student teaching assistants (TAs) both from the local school site and from outlying colleges. Some schools have skilled teams of technologists, usually drawn from teacher ranks, and have orchestrated these tasks well. Most schools, however, do not even have a full-time technology coordinator, yet alone a network administrator or a technology staff, so these other schools have not fared as well. Although there are certainly many other groups involved, my analysis will stick to actors within the central and local groups because they were the most active parties in this policy negotiation.

With AB 2882, the governor's office of the secretary for education decided to award technology funds to districts as a whole and not to individual schools. They did this so that they would not have to deal with the inconvenience of coordinating multiple grants and presumably so that districts could help all schools apply. This centralizing maneuver left L.A. Unified scrambling to figure out who should be responsible for spending the money. Because the money allotted to each school was determined by the ratio between student populations and existing computers, this was not specifically a disagreement over money. Still, school-site technology coordinators alleged that because individual schools qualified L.A. Unified for the funds through their poor student-to-computer ratios, individuals at these schools had a right to make purchasing decisions. Downtown administrators disagreed, saying that they could make decisions with a holistic view of the district's needs in mind.

A summary of the arguments between these central and local social worlds will set the stage for analysis of this policy's negotiation. District administrators claimed that central control would (1) ensure equity,

(2) achieve purchasing leverage through greater "economies of scale," (3) reduce school-site labor and class interruptions because vendors would set up all the equipment and remove all the boxes, and (4) safeguard the district from lawsuits and fraud through stern management of school and vendor compliance. Technology coordinators responded that (1) meeting students' needs requires local autonomy, (2) schools could get the same deals from vendors without central control, (3) central control would introduce unnecessary labor for schools that have to correct technology incompatibilities, and (4) central control violates fair process by excluding school participation in determining specifications. It is important to note that while these two social worlds happen to reside at opposite ends of the organizational spectrum of L.A. Unified, their disagreements stem from different approaches to problems of infrastructure planning, building, and maintenance. Before telling how this controversy over the setting of specifications for AB 2882 was resolved, we need some background on how each of these social worlds differentially perceives the task of infrastructure building.

Symbols as Design Agents

If social worlds are tied together through discourse, as was stated earlier, then one can learn about what unifies and motivates them through the language they use. This section identifies dominant symbols mobilized by members of central and local social worlds in the district and then evaluates the force of these symbols for regulating participation in technology policy.

When I interviewed central IT administrators about central/local conflicts over network infrastructure design, such as AB 2882, they frequently employed *plumbing metaphors* to explain their perspectives. In these exchanges, plumbing metaphors were used to simplify the infrastructure problem by sketching out its technical aspects while ignoring its social ones. This way of framing the problem is especially important because it demonstrates how symbols become design agents that shape desirable processes and outcomes for this social world. Take the following quote from an administrator as an example:

> Don't get me wrong, I think school-site people need to understand the
> technology, to understand the issues to make better decisions, but the

IT people should be there to implement it. I think the tech coordinator and the ITAF should understand why I need a switch versus a hub, but they should not have to worry about installing it and configuring it. That should be an IT technical person. If I'm at a school site and I'm an administrator, I need to understand that: why I want hot and cold running water. But I don't need to understand [the reasons behind it] or why I want a water heater and what's a good place to put it.

The plumbing metaphor reduces the problem to technical choices that can be best made in standardized ways that serve all schools — running water and data should be made available for everyone and in equal amounts. However, plumbing also becomes a fetish that both mystifies and dominates its creators (Edelman 1988) such that it fabricates fixed boundaries, restricts participation, and diminishes possible outcomes. The above quote betrays this conflation of the symbol (a simple technical system that can be managed externally) with what it represents (a complex social and technical infrastructure that exceeds any given social world and requires continuous maintenance), and this conflation justified the eventual exclusion of technology coordinators from participation in setting specifications for AB 2882. The metaphor, in this instance, performs a boundary-drawing function that allows only one type of professional expertise (the "IT technical person") and discounts the technical expertise of those at school sites, implying that they are superfluous and probably disruptive to the system being engineered.

The physical and social world distance between downtown IT administrators and school-site technology coordinators is great, however, and the metaphoric infrastructure of plumbing loses persuasive force along the way. In spite of the fact that allusions to plumbing came up repeatedly in interviews with administrators, none of the technology coordinators I asked had even heard of that comparison before, and they were surprised to hear it from me. Instead, the local social world of technology coordinators relies on other metaphors to help them conceptualize the larger project while lending legitimacy and meaning to their individual practices. One example I heard departs from human-made, artificial approaches to infrastructure altogether and instead compares infrastructure building to the creation of organic exoskeletons, like those of beetles, that can be abandoned and reoccupied by other creatures at a later date.

The power of the *exoskeleton metaphor* for infrastructure rests in its humble orientation toward the future, for when no one can accurately predict future needs, it becomes imperative to create flexible contexts that can be adapted for many purposes. Furthermore, exoskeletons are built from the inside out, and this resonates with how technology coordinators envision their own work: based on continuous proximal assessment of school-site needs, they build platforms for student and teacher actions. One can interpret this approach, then, as an inversion of the plumbing metaphor's insistence on materialities determining social relations; with exoskeletons, the social secretes the material. Nonetheless, this exoskeleton metaphor is limited because it neglects to articulate relationships of dependency across multiple registers or social worlds. It reflects and reproduces an attitude of complete self-reliance that belies existing conditions of extended social networks: ties to other schools, communities, the district, the state, and so forth. Finally, as with plumbing, in its strong oversimplification, the exoskeleton metaphor detracts attention from the ongoing maintenance that network infrastructures require to remain functional.

Both the plumbing and exoskeleton symbols serve as agents for the central and local L.A. Unified social worlds, respectively. They are necessary cultural lenses that these groups use to render their tasks more understandable and manageable, but these lenses reinforce singular approaches to infrastructure building, and this sometimes leads to poor outcomes. The naturalization of singular metaphors allows them to perform as agents that restrictively define the problems that individuals should solve and the processes that individuals should follow. I postulate that an appreciation for multiple metaphorical viewpoints would flexibly expand the productive potential of symbolic design agents.

Constructing an Outcome

The previous sections have described the central and local social worlds involved in building technology infrastructures in L.A. Unified and the symbols that each group uses to make sense of the complexity of this project. This section relates the resolution of the controversy over who should set the technical specifications for AB 2882 — central or local technologists — and some material outcomes of that resolution.

When centrally located technology administrators revealed their plan for standardizing AB 2882 specifications so that all computer purchases would be made by them and then shipped off to the schools, the primary forum for others to question this plan was the school-run e-mail discussion group by the Instructional Technology Commission (ITC). The organizational conflicts among IT groups in the district are refracted by this online list and are shown in the structure of textual exchanges. The usual discursive pattern in this forum consists of technology coordinators challenging centrally made decisions or articulations, technology administrators rebuking these claims by calling them "misinformed" and/or "intemperate," and then other technology coordinators admonishing administrators for policing the list and discouraging open communication. Such exchanges betray a kind of ritual where symbolic capital (Bourdieu 1977) is mobilized and each group tests the vigilance of the other over territory, rights, and expertise.

The following quote from a school-site technology coordinator, posted to the ITC list, represents the challenges raised by the social world of local technologists to the centralization of AB 2882's policymaking process:

> I still do find it difficult to swallow that, after so many difficult struggles to decentralize decision making, to bring these decisions to the site level where local site-based leaders can design and build programs that make the most sense to those of us who will have to execute the programs, that we're now back to having the District make these purchasing decisions for us.
>
> I still believe that (a) prior consultation with the end-users (the schools) was sorely lacking in this process and (b) that it would have been prudent on your part to have engaged us in the schools in a conversation about how this grant might be handled: if your "one-big-buy" idea is indeed a good one, you could have and should have convinced us of it in advance and, in the process, allowed us to positively critique your approach and measure it against our own needs.
>
> [I]f the local plans are well defended and seem reasonable, then the District should provide support and resources, not dictates, in these matters. I think that it is too bad that individual schools' hard fought and highly individualized plans were not taken into account in this process. . . .

I think District appropriation of the process, however well intended, is not the best approach to providing the equity the state is plainly seeking.

These interpretations of the policymaking process by someone in the local social world are remarkably different from the plumbing metaphors deployed by technology administrators. In contrast to the Fordist, centralizing maneuvers of downtown administrators, local technologists articulate a need for structural flexibility; together, these conflicting positions reveal one situated act in the ongoing play of global capital and local resistance.

In the above passage, the local technologist advocates for democratic process and queries its potential for translating into equitable learning environments. This democratic approach to design resonates with the organizational experiences of technology coordinators, because for them (in)equity is not an abstract concept but rather something they contend with every day in their workplaces: dilapidated inner-city schools serving low-income, minority students. Institutional parity is also a concern for school-site personnel who do not have the status or income of downtown administrators. It is telling that none of the technology administrators I interviewed recognized power distribution as an important issue, whereas this was a common source of aggravation for technology coordinators.

Challenges by local technology coordinators, like the ones quoted above, destabilized the centralized and standardized position of IT administrators, and administrators suddenly found themselves defending their decisions by claiming that there was an "open process." This move backfired when list members noted that they were never invited to participate in what administrators called an open process (a state-organized meeting to discuss specifications). In the end, administrators claimed on the discussion list that "they really listen" and made a small concession of expanding their previously set specifications to include four platforms instead of two [adding Mac iBooks (laptops) and IBM laptops to the previous choice of Mac or IBM desktops], but this alteration neither shifted decision-making power to schools nor addressed the more fundamental issue of democratic process.

After this exchange, members of the local social world ceased to push the issue further, and members of the central social world remained silent, not encouraging any more discussion or debate. The "resolution," then, was one of further entrenched central control over technology policy and several minor changes in computer hardware specifications for schools. Needless to say, both groups were dissatisfied with the process. Central administrators told me that they felt wrongly abused and needlessly distracted from their technical jobs by social problems. Coordinators, on the other hand, said that they felt frustrated that their social complaint about design process was treated as a technical complaint about specifications. Mutual dissatisfaction is easily explained: *the conflict between these groups was really a conflict between social worlds.* Both parties were speaking past one another, perhaps intentionally, because of their different interpretations of what "good design" should be. For administrators, good design manages the distribution of standardized resources and protects the district from lawsuits. For coordinators, good design catalyzes democratic participation to achieve flexible technical options for individual schools. The tensions between these groups were only compounded by territorial claims to decision-making power.

While technology coordinators verbally recognized the validity of administrators' management practices (especially for delivering computer packages to understaffed schools), it is not certain that technology administrators grew to appreciate any of their opposition's views. When I asked one key administrator what he had learned from the process, he focused on a technical rather than a social issue, saying that he would not dismiss a laptop option right away next time. He then proceeded to enumerate the many reasons why he is more convinced than ever that laptops are a bad choice for schools (e.g., they have a quicker obsolescence rate, are too individual-centered, are too fragile, etc.), so this was hardly a convincing response about how he would alter future processes.

The plumbing metaphor used by technology administrators symbolized the kind of control at a distance that they sought and achieved, but it weakened the design process for setting the specifications for California's AB 2882. The ways that administrators responded to opposition, with accusations of misinformation or with technical compromises, left the technology community in L.A. Unified (including themselves) dissatisfied and jaded. The outcome also resulted in poor infrastructure design for many schools. For example, Concrete High was given 467 computers with Microsoft Windows ME operating systems through AB 2882 in spite of the fact that their entire network runs Windows 2000. Because the school cannot afford the software licenses to upgrade these new computers, they are stuck maintaining disparate platforms. This is a large task for an understaffed school, and many other schools were placed in similar predicaments of having to shoulder the labor burden of rigid specifications set by district administrators.

In this case, design outcomes were poor because the boundaries between social worlds were not permeable or flexible enough. If administrators had solicited and embraced the flood of suggestions from other technologists in the district, they could have taken full advantage of local expertise in making decisions. If coordinators had better appreciated the legal and managerial challenges faced by administrators, they could have proposed several standardized packages for school sites to choose from. If each group had periodically spent time in each other's social worlds, they could have maintained a sympathetic understanding of the other's responsibilities and constraints. Each of these recommendations for flexible participation and information flows would improve communication and design processes in the future.

Instead of adopting malleable political stances, both social worlds adopted all-or-nothing postures: central versus local control. The oppositional framing of the issue generated pressure that led to certain productive exchanges (information dissemination and small compromises), but it simultaneously fostered antagonism and blocked greater collaboration between these groups. The few concessions made in this hostile climate were trivial compared with other obvious options, such as allowing schools to maintain responsibility for and control over their own technological infrastructures if they wanted it, and letting the district negotiate a standard package for all other schools.

The increasing centralized control of decision-making power over technology — as shown in this social worlds conflict — presents further evidence of the fragmented centralization of public institutions under globalization. Technology serves as a vehicle for transforming organizations such as L.A. Unified into post-Fordist entities, solidifying structural inflexibilities that, in turn, demand further individual flexibility to keep the systems operational — as shown, in this particular case, with the labor intensification required to maintain multiple computer operating systems. Administrators mobilized symbolic power to gain further control because emergent macro-structural conditions (of audit cultures, digital divides, privatization, organizational restructuring, and so on) encouraged them to do so.

Conclusion: Technology Policy as a Stealth Agent of Global Change

As Günther Anders (1987, 2) shrewdly observed about capitalist and technological systems: "Irrespective of whether we choose to play the game or not, we are part of it simply because we *are played*." In this chapter's context, technology policy is the game of which we are all a part because it establishes the rules and sets the board that we, as the public, are played on. Some of the constricting rules and power plays of the policy game of wiring public schools for Internet access have been explained here. First, I traced the development of the federal government's E-Rate program in L.A. Unified, illustrating how the translation of rigid E-Rate policies generated uncertainty and stress. Second, I related contestations across two of the organization's social worlds (central and local technologists) over which group should set technical specifications for the state's technology grant AB 2882. Regarding both E-Rate and AB 2882, policy design, translation, and negotiation were certainly not static, but they were unnecessarily rigid, leading to antagonism between groups, poor design outcomes, and restricted frameworks for future participation in policymaking. I claim that with each of these technology grants, more flexible policies and inclusive policymaking processes would have catalyzed better outcomes, both in terms of technological infrastructures and social relations within the district.

In this ongoing technology policy game, the design process is constituted by technologists negotiating specifications and managing the details of funding stipulations, contracts, and local materialities. Rather than being predetermined, rational, and neutral, the design of technological systems — as shown by the interchanges between technologists — is entirely political and socially constructed. Because educational environments are being radically transfigured by the building of these technological infrastructures, one would expect an in-depth public conversation or debate over the implementation and intended outcomes of these policies, yet this is not the case. Technology policy is hidden behind a cultural veil of arcane technical details on the one hand and political neutrality and necessity on the other.

Previous chapters made the case that the design of technological infrastructures in public education embeds globalization ideologies and logics into institutional and material forms such that individuals are forced to adapt to inflexible structures. This chapter extends that argument to show how attendant inflexibilities in technology policy and policymaking complicate design processes and occlude mechanisms for democratic involvement in technology decisions. Technology policy is a stealth agent of global change because it provides a vehicle for advancing fragmented centralization and industry dependencies in public institutions, yet it operates outside of public scrutiny or participation (because technical experts make the decisions, not elected representatives or some other democratic body).

Efforts at achieving structural flexibility in policy domains must contend with global forces that motivate fragmented centralization, but it helps to have some direction in navigating those flows. Edward J. Woodhouse and Dean Nieusma (2001, 89) offer four goals for making technology policy processes more flexible: "minimize up-front capital investment, keep lead time short, keep unit size small, minimize infrastructure dedicated to the new endeavor." Given the conditions I have described so far, it is not too surprising that the building of information technology infrastructures in public education misses these goals. One viable explanation is that "so little sustained effort has gone into building-in flexibility that our imaginations are imprisoned by the relative inflexible, large-scale approach [to technological systems] pursued in the twentieth century: scale it up rapidly and hope for the best" (Woodhouse & Nieusma 2001, 89).

Fortunately, there are structurally flexible alternatives for technology policy and policymaking. For starters, technologists putting the funding puzzle together in order to wire schools could benefit from less rigid constraints. Technology grants could allow recipients some leeway to determine their needs and apply the monies accordingly. For instance, a commonly voiced frustration was the incredible influx of financial support for equipment but only a meager trickle for network support or staff training. Districts should be able to redirect grants to the areas of greatest need as they perceive them. Furthermore, grants could be more flexible in their deadlines and other restrictions. If meeting a deadline means rushing a job and limiting input from schools, then the deadline works against the long-term goals of the grant; similarly, if it is extremely difficult or impossible to change equipment specifications in midstream, this allows no room for error correction. In these cases, grants that gave more control to the recipients for determining needs and establishing deadlines and specifications would contribute to conditions for functional, sustainable, and appropriate designs.

A similar argument could be made for relations among IT specialists in L.A. Unified. Many times the social worlds of central and local technologists clash, erupting into territorial disputes that deter collaboration and lead to poor designs. If the barriers between these groups were more permeable, allowing for flows of ideas and individuals across organizational domains and geographical regions, then prescribed roles of conflict and antagonism would likely dissipate, leading to better outcomes. Moreover, in order to achieve structural flexibility in technology policies, the local knowledges of those at school sites should always take precedent over the predilections of centrally located administrators. The reason for this, as articulated in this book's introduction, is to motivate power equalization among actors in the system, so that the fullest range of participation can be guaranteed into the future; leaning toward local control accomplishes this so long as there are more localities than centralities. This does not necessarily mean that specifications cannot be finalized at a central level, but school-site coordinators should be the ones writing them. This would require a reconceptualization of central administrators' responsibilities toward facilitation and synthesis instead of fiats, but if grants were simultaneously made more interpretable, the social world ethos of administrators could shift to support these modified roles.

Taking a cue from the story about technology coordinators who threatened to refuse the inferior network hubs selected by central administrators (see Chapter 4), consumerist strategies of boycotting could be mobilized by local technologists to leverage structural flexibility in policymaking. Relatedly, because a culture of strong teachers' unions already exists in the district, a more classic labor strategy of collective bargaining or organized strikes could be employed to achieve similar ends. These are some of the latent possibilities within the school system that could be considered should the gears of structural flexibility require greasing.

6
FLEXIBLE GOVERNANCE

Might the desire for some degree of collective self-legislation, the desire to participate in shaping the conditions and terms of life, remain a vital element — if also an evidently ambivalent and anxious one — of much agitation under the sign of progressive politics?

Wendy Brown 1995, 4

Government's use of digital media to engage with the public holds many promises for enhancing democracy. Yet, there are also many risks introduced by "e-government" systems, which incorporate new media technologies into existing government functions or create new functions altogether. Because such systems will likely rescript relationships between the public and public institutions, special attention must be given to keeping government as malleable, inclusive, and open as possible.

This chapter analyzes three different combinations of technology and governance in public education to highlight the subtle yet pervasive mechanisms of control that are being implemented throughout public life. The first section investigates governance interfaces in the Los Angeles Unified School District, in both physical and virtual space, and evaluates their potential for inducing public participation. The second section connects what I see to be trends toward veiled public exclusion with recent developments in information technology and intellectual property law. The third section addresses the types of institutional cultures of governance that are growing out of these technological and legal conditions. The combined picture portrays a state of individual self-governance and public exclusion that is consistent with the literature on new forms of citizenship in the global political economy (Hardt & Negri 2000; Brown 1995), but it is nonetheless disturbingly nondemocratic. I argue that the politics of technological mediation, their accompanying legal frameworks, and their associated institutional cultures must be rendered visible and openly debated if we are to achieve public institutions that foster democracy in this era of globalization.

Technology and Governance Interfaces

Board of Education meetings are the primary arena for policymaking in L.A. Unified, and because the seven board members are elected representatives of the people of Los Angeles, these meetings — which are open to the public — are the most obvious symbol of governance in this institution. Let me begin this analysis of governance interfaces, therefore, with a critical description of the experience of attending these events.

Board meetings are difficult to attend, in many respects. Checking the Board's Web page on LAUSD.NET reveals a poorly designed, almost unnavigatable textual collage of links to "Understanding Board Meetings," "Board Rules," and "Board Agendas," but finding out *where* and *when* is completely oblique. Having stumbled upon the information once before, I know that the meetings are supposedly scheduled every other Tuesday at 1 P.M. Yet more often than not, they are rescheduled, start later, or are in "closed sessions"; on rare occasions, they are held in secondary locations such as local high schools. I therefore call the board offices to verify the meeting before undertaking the taxing freeway journey into downtown L.A.

Upon arrival at L.A. Unified's "district headquarters" on Grand Avenue, almost directly on top of the 101 freeway, I pull my dilapidated car up to the security checkpoint, where a guard intones:

"What are you here for?"

"To attend the board meeting," I reply.

"Attending the meeting for whom?"

"For myself," I answer, starting to feel uneasy. "It's a *public* meeting, right?"

"Uh, yeah."

He hesitates before handing me a sticker affixed to a parking pass and saying, "Place this on your windshield."

After circling the lot for 10 minutes, both above- and underground, I realize that there are no available spaces, so I head back to the security outpost to ascertain my options.

"Go to the overflow lot on Cesar Chavez, across the street from Burger King," I'm told as the guard hands me yet another slip of paper validating my parking for this second lot.

Once parked, I cautiously cross Grand, now on foot, and discover that the main offices are imposingly inaccessible to pedestrians (see Figure 6.1). There are no clear entrances or even ground-level windows, just a solid wall of beige concrete at least three stories high and pushed right up to the sidewalk. After walking the length of the building, I determine that I must traverse the same inward route that my car took to the security booth, but there is no sidewalk here, so I apprehensively walk the tight-rope of the curb — one foot directly in front of the other — and defensively lean into the railing whenever a car edges by. Once on the grounds,

Figure 6.1 L.A. Unified's district headquarters.

I find that this massive, multibuilding complex has a distinctive institutional, "school" feel, yet it also hints at mission-style architecture and offers a green garden courtyard, which is a pleasant respite from the acres of asphalt directly outside.

The boardroom itself is a sloping auditorium: brown seats and carpets, wood-paneled walls, and two concentric semicircles of tables up front for board members and their staff. A 3-foot-high wooden barrier, which doubles as a table for the dissemination of handouts, separates the stage from the approximately one hundred and fifty seats for the audience; a speaker's podium grows out of the center of this wooden space modulator. Two armed LAUSD police officers alternate in regulating traffic through a panel opening between the stage and audience. Drab brown curtains hang from the back wall, three large sconces of gaudy unlit torch lamps mount the walls on either side of the stage, and framed color photographs of Governor Davis and President Clinton adorn the same walls (Clinton's photo was replaced by a black-and-white photo of President George W. Bush after he took office in 2001).

Most apparent of all, however, is the prevalence of media technologies in this room: two cameras, mounted near the ceiling, face the stage at 45-degree angles from both side walls; another camera shoots out from the right of the front wall, directed to catch the faces of speakers at the podium; two televisions are located on stage, mounted high up on the walls and positioned for board members to see what is being broadcast; another television screen points out at the audience from the front right; many microphones sit on the tables on the stage and at the podium; and a dedicated audiovisual booth — the control center for all media operations within this space — is planted in the back left of the room.

By 10 minutes after 1 P.M., there are about twenty people in the audience — mostly white — and two board members milling about on stage. At 1:30, six of the seven board members, the superintendent, and the "board secretariat" (who assists in running the meetings) sit in high-backed leather chairs in the inner circle while fifteen staff members sit in the decidedly less posh chairs on the outer perimeter. Well past the scheduled 1 P.M. start time, the meeting officially commences with an officer's command to "all rise" and a pledge of allegiance to the flag. The business of the day begins with "students' concerns," and several students have found their way here to bring after-school busing problems to the board's attention. Off camera, two board members talk to the secretariat throughout this presentation, but the students persevere to the end before they are thanked and dismissed.

An older speaker from the audience, a member of the public, next addresses the board in the 3 minutes allotted to him: he questions the board on the ruling to reduce "public participation" time at these meetings, but board members totally ignore him, not even making eye contact or vouchsafing a response. Another speaker from the audience addresses the superintendent directly, claiming that decentralization was supposed to change the culture of L.A. Unified, but it has not, because the board is still not accountable for its spending decisions. During this 3-minute complaint, the superintendent turns his back on the gentleman and talks to staff members; he elects not to respond in any way once the "participation" period is finished.

Having dispensed with the obligatory interchanges with the audience, the board moves on to its agenda of discussing after-school programs, the fat content in school lunches, the pros and cons of charter schools, and so on. At meetings, board members will frequently arrive late, answer cell phones, leave the room, or chat among themselves. On the unusual days when there is an audience that outnumbers the board and its staff, such as a community's protest of a school construction site (on February 13, 2001) or the vote on the teachers' union agreement for an 11 percent pay increase (on February 27, 2001), audience members whisper back and forth to each other phrases like "he's with us" or "he's not one of ours," betraying that they are, first and foremost, district bureaucrats who are as factionalized as the board itself.[1] On the usual slow days of meetings, when the seven board members and their staff outnumber the audience, they sometimes make passing reference to me as a "member of the press," apparently because members of the general public are not expected at these meetings.

The purpose of describing the experience of attending public meetings of the L.A. Board of Education is to flag the many economic, material, and cultural obstacles to participating in these (and other) governmental activities. To begin with, the time and location of these meetings pose severe impediments to most members of the public. Who has the luxury of taking off hours in the middle of the day to commute to and attend such meetings? Navigating the guards, the volatile schedule of meeting times and places, and the pedestrian-unfriendly architecture present an added range of deterrents. One must be exceedingly determined and sure of oneself to arrive at the meetings without giving up. Finally, the boardroom and its arcane rituals establish a disciplinary space of hindered mobility and communication; it is designed to make audience members passive and to deter the public from speaking (or being heard), let alone having open conversations or debates. What is more, the behavior of board members and the superintendent delegitimizes the little public participation that does occur.

Still, according to board members and administrators whom I interviewed, technology promises to render government transparent and participation facile. Board meetings are televised and rebroadcast on cable television later in the evening and on the weekend; audio versions of these meetings can be listened to from the LAUSD.NET Web site; one can download meeting minutes, agendas, and reports from the Web; and one can call or e-mail one's board member with questions or comments. However, rather than opening public governmental events up to community involvement, I claim that technologies serve to distance the public further from policymaking processes.

The act of watching television broadcasts or listening to them on the Web is a hyper-individualized and mostly noncommunicative experience. Similarly, downloading meeting minutes, agendas, or reports establishes a one-way, passive engagement with government. Such virtual re-creations of public events fail to capture what is essential about democracy — open debate, discussion, and consensus building. In this sense, technological media aggravate rather than amend the hostile indifference to public opinion visible at the actual meetings. Except for one crucial difference: the nondemocratic practices at the meetings are almost completely occluded in their media representations, because the cameras and minutes do not capture the interactions and noninteractions of individuals present. Because electronic representations are perforce abstracted models of real experiences (Agre 1997), any "truth" of transparency is a doctored reality that leaves both policymakers and the public with a specious semblance of openness that is an ersatz substitute for real participation. This would still be the case even if community members who have access to computers were to contact policymakers by e-mail. Such asynchronous exchanges would similarly conjure an illusion of involvement but would remain isolated and decontextualized, not "public" in any deep sense of the word.

Once the illusion of transparent government is projected out into the world, it is easy to lose sight of how images sanitize the events they represent. The noninteractive and nonpublic nature of image consumption is naturalized because the media themselves set up passive conditions — this is especially true of television but also of the Internet. Moreover, sanitization manifests itself in the form of blind discrimination against non-English-speaking audiences. As one public speaker brought to the attention of the board in a February 2001 meeting, 69 percent of the LAUSD community is Spanish-speaking, yet there are no translations of board meetings into Spanish either on television or on the Internet. In a private and enclosed consumption context, such as one's living room, this fact is easily hidden from those whom it does not affect. At the actual board meetings, by contrast, translation headsets are available for those who need them — provided that they have the perseverance to find out that they exist and where to obtain them.

Access alone, then, does not amount to enlightened rational actors or the creation of a politically enabling public sphere of the kind advocated for by Jürgen Habermas (1989), and even if such an open public forum were possible, marginalization and exclusion would persist, as critics of public sphere discourse illustrate (Fraser 1989; Lyotard 1979). This does not mean, however, that the project of democracy should be abandoned, but instead that efforts should be made to achieve structural flexibility in governance and due vigilance exercised to minimize material, cultural, and other obstacles to meaningful participation along the way, especially in the uncharted realms of e-government.

Public Space, Public Domain, and Globalization

The general technology-facilitated trend outlined above — of attenuated democracy and illusions of transparency — should be seen as part of globalization processes that have resonances in the urban fabric of Los Angeles itself, specifically in class polarization and the evacuation of public space. Roger Keil (1998), Allen Scott (1996), Janet Abu-Lughod (1999), and others have linked such trends to the internationalization of L.A. (in the form of foreign investment incentives, an accommodating transportation infrastructure for imports, a high-tech industry, a vast service sector, and so on). Where public spaces persist, a plethora of disciplinary designs enforce social order and segregation (Davis 1990; Flusty 1994). Such designs include social deterrents (benches that cannot be slept on, sprinkler systems that keep people away from buildings or parks, public toilets that are inaccessible or nonexistent, etc.), semiotic exclusions (defensible spaces such as "panopticon malls," office buildings, cultural centers, etc.), and physical inaccessibility (gated communities, lack of public transit, etc.). Teresa Caldeira (2000) posits that the erection of "fortified enclaves," such as gated communities and shopping malls, is a reaction against the unsettling of social boundaries — whether through the development of political democracy in Brazil or through demographic shifts in California. In both cases, the privatization of public space allows "new urban morphologies of fear" to acquire durable, material forms that threaten to perpetuate inequality, vitiate democracy, and delegitimate public institutions well into the future.

Where the city and the school district come together is in the dependency of public governance on public spaces. This section picks up the theme of the effects of globalization-spawned barriers in urban settings (walls, gates, freeways, malls) and extends it to the emerging world of technology policy and e-government. The case has already been made above that the technological mediation of policymaking impedes participation under the guise of increased transparency. The next step is to draw a comparison between the loss of public space in the urban world and the erasure of the public domain in and by the virtual world.

On the federal and state levels, laws and policies concerning information technology have been steadily chipping away at the public domain, slowly privatizing and policing media access and expression. For a quick review, the Telecommunications Act of 1996 included provisions for universal access, such as E-Rate for public schools and libraries, but it also deregulated the telecommunications industry and led to the consolidation of local media firms into national conglomerates. The Digital Millennium Copyright Act (DMCA) of 1998 eroded the public domain by (1) prohibiting the decryption of previously encrypted media, such as DVDs or computer programs, even for educational purposes; (2) individualizing accountability for intellectual property (IP) violations, thus protecting service providers over users; and (3) initiating the elimination of Web broadcasting by individuals or college radio stations that could not afford to track listeners or pay royalties. On the level of the Internet's governance structure, the 1998 congressional white paper entitled "Management of Internet Names and Addresses" delegated domain name control and policy setting to the Internet Corporation for Assigned Names and Numbers (ICANN). Here policymaking authority over an international public good was placed outside of governmental authority and public accountability.[2]

In addition to these developments, there are several other cases that offer persuasive evidence that the trend in IP law is toward the diminishment of the public domain. In 2000, in the case *Los Angeles Times v. Free Republic*, the U.S. District Court of the Central District of California decided that Internet users could not paste newspaper stories into political discussion groups for any purposes, even public comment and critique. The 1999 Uniform Computer Information Transactions Act, a draft state contract law passed in two states thus far, validates "click-wrap licenses" for computer software, disallowing reverse engineering and eliminating "first sale" and "fair use" rights — meaning that because licenses are more restrictive than copyrights, purchasers do not gain the right to resell their purchases and libraries lose the right to lend the items. Finally, the USA PATRIOT Act of 2001 and the Homeland Security Act of 2002 have authorized the removal of "sensitive" material from the public domain, such as the location of aqueducts or chemical plants that one may live near. These acts have given the FBI increased authority to intercept e-mail messages, monitor Web surfing, and track computer keystrokes with Carnivore and other surveillance programs; additionally, the FBI has ordered libraries to keep records on patrons' borrowing and browsing habits.

Many other examples could be given, but what should be observed is the trajectory toward the overprotection of IP and the policing of users at the expense of the public domain. As legal scholars caution, our current interpretive lens for looking at IP is a market-based one of property rights and incentives for creation, when what we should be most concerned about is the preservation of free speech and fair use in the realm of IT (Boyle 1997; Lessig 1999; Postigo 2003). The trade-off between these two goods — private property and the public good — is currently out of balance. As with the semblance of transparency in government or the loss of public spaces in cities, the privatization and policing of network technologies is pernicious because it occurs outside the scope of everyday awareness even as it redefines the very terrain for investigation or inquiry.

On the ground, this growing juridical regime infiltrates public institutions such as education and subtly disciplines quotidian practices. Consider the Children's Internet Protection Act (CIPA) as an example. This act was passed by Congress in 2000, mandating that public schools and libraries receiving E-Rate funding install filtering or blocking software on their computer networks, that they implement acceptable use policies (AUPs), and that they regulate minors' access to "inappropriate" materials while safeguarding information on minors (e.g., addresses, phone numbers, photographs). This law prompted L.A. Unified to update and enforce an AUP for all student use of the Internet and to undergo a series of gyrations over the practicality and legality of implementing a filtering system when none is foolproof but all are restrictive.

If adult students or the parents or guardians of minors do not sign AUPs and release forms, students are unable to use the Internet in any classes or in school libraries. Additionally, students must pass an "Internet test," mostly concerning issues of security and etiquette, before they are permitted to use computers. Students who leap through these legal and cultural hurdles are branded "authorized" to use computers and receive an indicating sticker on their IDs, a password to log in to the network, or some other indication of authorization. That said, if we can learn from other occasions where students must obtain parents' signatures, as with declarations of poverty that make students eligible for federally subsidized lunches, parents are often loath to sign *any* forms, especially if they are illegal or recent immigrants or otherwise skeptical of the intended uses of the forms.

While this situation could be read as an extension of existing practices of securing parental approval for field trips, health testing, or photographs, the difference lies in whether or not the outcome of failing to get parental approval is intimately tied to fundamental educational access. Taken to the extreme — for sake of clarifying the point — being deprived of an occasional field trip excursion is quite different from being denied instruction on a daily basis. It is worth noting here that education in the United States is not a constitutionally guaranteed "right." Based on the equal protection clause of the Fourteenth Amendment, however, states that do offer public education must ensure equal opportunity to attend those school systems (Spring 1998, 46). By contrast, The United Nations' Declaration on Human Rights does include the right to education.

The Children's Internet Protection Act propagated ripples of control that have spread throughout public schools. Waves of AUPs and release forms have penetrated educational practices in classrooms and splashed out into students' homes, holding parents and guardians responsible for school activities. Once policies are implemented, they acquire a tenacity that is not easily shaken. In this case, technology policies in conjunction with the law have remapped the educational terrain to accentuate legality over learning, thereby calling into question what is "public" about public education. This is not to say that there is no present value in creating nurturing and protected environments for students but instead to draw attention to how the rules governing public spaces — from boardrooms, to classrooms, to Internet chat rooms — are rigidly regulating or eliminating avenues for participation by or preservation of "the public."

Institutional Cultures

The previous sections have guided the argument for flexible governance across several interconnected fields. First, I noted how the location, time, and format of L.A. Board of Education meetings function to exclude meaningful public participation, and how the e-government version of these meetings, in turn, aggravates and obscures these exclusions rather than corrects them. Next, I drew parallels among the loss of space for participation in government policymaking, the loss of public space in urban settings, and the loss of the public domain with intellectual property and technology laws. This section tackles the way that institutional cultures refract these modalities of public exclusion and erosion, such that self-governance and self-adaptation to systemic rigidities become naturalized.

One can better understand the forces at work in the transformation of public spaces, and the rights within them, by breaking them down into three overlapping and reinforcing institutional cultures:

- *Audit culture* (Strathern 2000) refers to regimes of accountability, embraced by public and private organizations alike, as strategies for purportedly achieving global competitiveness. As Cris Shore and Susan Wright (2000) explain, audit culture compels both organizations and individuals within them to render their activities auditable, giving rise to new identities and subjectivities that are predicated upon self-policing and obsessive documentation. There are frequent audits in public education, but the cultural shift can more readily be seen in the production of acceptable use policies, mission statements, performance reports, release forms, curriculum benchmarks, and test scores. In a less apparent way, audit culture can be discerned in numerous activities of self- and community disciplining: individuals refusing to talk to researchers who fail to jump through the hurdles of LAUSD's "Program Evaluation and Research Branch"; teachers not using the Internet in classes, even with AUPs, for fear of lawsuits; administrators centralizing control of technology decisions out of what they claim to be fear of external audits and lawsuits for school-site noncompliance with contracts.
- *Regulation culture* (my term, with a nod toward Weber and Foucault) describes the many laws, formal and informal policies, standards, tests, and other social mechanisms that govern practices within public spaces. Many of these emerge out of audit culture, such as AUPs and Internet filters, but they also include things such as limitations upon participation time in board meetings, strict contracts governing teacher responsibilities, and prepackaged software-driven curricula in schools, such as "Open Court" reading software. Regulation culture might also explain material manifestations of social regulation, such as fences and walls that physically separate schools from communities, or the many cables, chains, bolts, and screws that ostensibly protect computer hardware but restrict mobility in and modification of classrooms.

- *Firewall culture* (a term used by my informants) indicates the many territorial reactions to these audit and regulation forces, and, by extension, reactions to globalization. With increases in documentation and restrictions on sanctioned activities, individuals seek to erect protective barriers ("firewalls") to prevent unwanted scrutiny and to secure their preferred modes of autonomous operation. Firewall culture is visible across the organization: in teachers shutting classroom doors, in board meetings going into strategically timed "closed sessions," and in technology administrators hiding the "bad news" of construction delays from policymakers and the public. Firewall culture may have both positive and negative effects, depending on the specific circumstances; but rather than pass judgment on each instance of it, it is more essential to note how firewall culture spreads out to insulate both audit and regulation cultures as well, shielding them from scrutiny or critique. Thus, as one of the only viable defenses from obsessive regulation, documentation, and compliance, firewall culture actually ensures the sustained vitality of these other institutional regimes.

As an approximation, this typology of institutional cultures should communicate an overall picture of practices that discipline organizations and individuals, that remove the instruments of discipline from scrutiny or critique, and that rezone public spaces and rights in the process. Just as with gated communities and IP laws, public institutions function within a paradox of succumbing to global pressures while denying responsibility for the unintentional social effects of their elected changes. Gated communities, IP laws, and institutional cultures, for instance, each delimit public spaces, domains, and rights within the exclusionary confines of physical and/or regulatory walls. As Teresa Caldeira (2000) and Setha Low (2003) observe, however, fortified enclaves not only aggravate social inequality and foreclose substantive democracy, but they also atrophy the social lives of those living within walls and behind gates. The same can be said of employees who live behind figurative firewalls as audit and regulatory apparatuses police their every move.

The implications for those living, working, and learning in public school systems are that actions are more controlled with every passing month, possibilities inside and outside of classrooms are more pro-grammed, and involvement in determining the structures that govern experiences (legal, spatial, or technical) is more restricted. This is not to say that individuals are becoming truly "docile bodies" (Foucault 1977, 1988) in the sense of internalizing discipline and sacrificing agency to the system, but even territorial tactics of subversion (e.g., firewall cultures) are prefigured and codified by the broad audit and regulation forces (or "governmentalities") to which they respond and with which they engage.

Conclusion: Toward Flexible Governance

This chapter has extended the focus on individual and structural flexibility within globalization to analyze some governance interfaces and institutional cultures in public education. I have argued that technological medi-ation in the form of e-government is contributing to the loss of public space for democratic interchange, legal frameworks governing technology and intellectual property within the United States are similarly eroding the public domain, and institutional cultures arising in this climate are perpet-uating social relations of disciplined self-governance. In combination, these developments engender an inflexible governance regime that closes down opportunities for meaningful public participation or alternative approaches to technology policy.

On the empirical and locally specific level of L.A. Unified, this chapter has considered issues of governance and technology by investigating the policy arena that is traditionally considered "public," typified by meetings of the L.A. Board of Education. The main risk here is that the myth of technological transparency, achieved through television or Internet access to such meetings, aggravates existing barriers to public involvement by pro-viding a false impression of openness. This phenomenon, as I see it, is part of a globalizing process that is acutely visible in urban metropolises: the elimination of public spaces, the erection of barriers between social classes, and the privatization of public entities and the public domain. The result is a technology-assisted disciplining of publics and diminishment of public rights.

One starting point for establishing flexible governance structures is to dispel the illusion of transparency with e-government. Because access to government through technological media provides a semblance of ready-made apolitical truths, and because this vision reduces opportunities for meaningful public participation, policymakers should be given incentives for being responsive to public opinion. Perhaps the best way to do that is by establishing a community context for open meetings (something that does occur infrequently): hold all meetings at times that individuals could attend and at locations, such as schools, that are not inaccessible and disassociated from the lives of those whom the institution serves. Web sites, e-mail, and television could be used to disseminate information about upcoming meetings, solicit agenda items for meetings, and provide background reports, editorials, and discussion boards for issues, but the presence of technology should not be interpreted in and of itself as an indication of real participation in government. In other words, technological media should supplement but never be a substitute for open debate, discussion, and input in policymaking.

Another step toward structural flexibility in governance would involve the demystification of technological networks to show them for the political and contingent structures that they are. If more people were aware that students' lives were positively or negatively altered depending on the design of networks and the choices made with hardware and software, it is conceivable that people would want to question the decisions made, if not provide input into the process itself. If more people knew how the range of possible learning environments was bound by territorial debates among district employees or by unnecessary stipulations on grants, they would likely contest design processes or grant stipulations. Public involvement of this kind could only be positive, given the current lack of conversation and awareness. What I am advocating here is a type of technological literacy on par with curriculum or school construction — a basic awareness that important decisions are being made that will affect students, that these decisions are costly and will have long-term ramifications, and that alternatives exist. This simple level of literacy would likely be sufficient to propel technology into the public policy arena, inviting a degree of conversation and critique that does not now exist because the setting of IT policies is relegated to administrators outside of public awareness or access.

As a third step, publicizing that the barriers to public access in policy-making processes stem in large part from a more general trend toward the eradication of public space and the public domain could serve as a beginning corrective to these conditions. Thus far, social workers, researchers, and legal scholars are well aware of these problems, but the next step is to communicate them in coherent form for others outside of these specialized realms so that the public could identify problem areas to act on.

Finally, the establishment of globalization regimes within public institutions (audit culture, regulatory culture, and firewall culture) threatens to dispatch individual autonomy and perhaps even the individual rights of those subjected to them. As a response to audit and regulatory cultures, firewall culture serves the same structural purpose as gated communities: it attempts to shield groups from perceived threats rather than contend with them, while it meanwhile isolates and polices those who try to shield themselves. One of the only ways I can envision to defuse this disciplinary cycle is by publicly calling attention to how these regimes detract from the mission of these institutions: *test scores do not equal learning; computers do not signal equity; audits do not create opportunity; accountability does not inspire innovation.*

Flexible governance seeks to create new spaces for legitimate participation in policymaking while safeguarding all avenues for contending with — without sanitizing — difference. Technology should be used as a supplement rather than a replacement for existing democratic forums, and the design of e-government interfaces or technology regulations should be seen as an opportunity for reevaluating existing mechanisms for community involvement. Flexible governance is an ethical challenge to keep conversations open, debates active, and politics present within all states of change, and to imbue the conditions of our lives with the promise of these potentialities.

7
FUTURE IMAGINARIES

The imagination is now central to all forms of agency, is itself a social fact, and is the key component of the new global order.

Arjun Appadurai 1996, 31

[T]o be among the ruins was to have your time-sense unsettled. You felt that your life and ambition had already been lived out for you and you were looking at the relics of that life. You were in a place where the future had come and gone.

V. S. Naipaul 1979, 27

V. S. Naipaul's novel *A Bend in the River* takes place in the interior of Africa in a remote town that is trapped in merciless flux between primitive and modern ways of life. A powerful river runs alongside the town, serving as an undeniable symbol of movement (if not progress) and profound interconnection with the outside world. Yet, propitiously located where the river bends, the town is also hidden from sight, and there is great fear that the benefits of modernization will pass inhabitants by or will enmesh them in violence beyond their control or understanding. It is a place, as the narrator says, where one could believe that "the future had come and gone," leaving only ruins and ruined hopes in its wake.

Surprisingly enough, students in the Los Angeles Unified School District offer almost identical interpretations of information technologies and the promised flows of electronic data in — and through — public education. In focus-group interviews, they say that they feel they are "falling behind their futures" and "falling behind society"; they say that computers might help them "catch up," but it is probably too late. Indeed, if the future has passed them by, as they perceive it to have done, then it might already be too late for catching up. Equally intriguing — if more disturbing — is students' impression that they have fallen behind society, that they are somehow outside of society, which has pulled ahead of them. Regardless of the veracity of these statements, how such beliefs shape the life trajectories of youth in public schools should be of concern to all of us.

This chapter takes the construction of future imaginaries about technology, like those articulated above, as its point of inquiry. Attending specifically to the shaping of technological rationalities, I first document how industry and vocational goals inculcate a mentality of "catching up" that often dictates restrictive approaches to the role of technology in public education. Second, I analyze the valuation of automated control mechanisms for data collection and data mining as examples of dominant technological imaginaries, and I question the types of futures these mechanisms promise to bring. Third, I investigate how imaginations for the use of technology are molded through professional industry conferences. Finally, I present some student classroom designs and vocalizations about the future to highlight the constraints that past and present experiences place on visions of the future, and, by extension, on future possibilities.

I understand the imagination to act as a cultural structure, delimiting a range of possible thoughts and presenting powerful but not necessarily overpowering obstacles to thinking otherwise. Under this rubric, flexible imaginaries are those that *encourage* nondominant and inclusive thoughts or actions rather than opposing or simply accommodating them. As with the forms of structural flexibility introduced in previous chapters, the cultivation of flexible imaginaries is an important condition for keeping the future open to surprise, possibility, and radical difference — a condition that can help safeguard against the exclusion of marginal social groups from meaningful and nonexploitative participation in the mapping of their own futures. Because all social systems and constructs create and are defined by states of marginality, arguing for flexible structures that afford greater participation in designing the conditions of one's life — whether in spatial, imaginary, or other domains — means advocating for greater democratic inclusion and acceptance of marginal positions in the ongoing reconstruction of social worlds through technological change. In this sense, structural flexibility is an idealized orientation toward the future, but one that must operate on the level of particularity rather than serving as a universal(izing) corrective for social inequalities.

"Catching Up" with Industry

At an April 2001 meeting of L.A. Unified's Instructional Technology Commission (ITC), held at a high school in South Central Los Angeles, technologists bemoaned what they perceived to be an administrative culture of opposition to information technology. One member compared the organizational structure of the district to a caste system, saying that long-standing divisions between administrators and teachers were preventing technology projects from getting off the ground and developing successfully. He concluded by saying that administrators must alter their perceptions of technology in order to "punch through and see the future," implying that unified support for technological change would help break persistent and pernicious patterns of group infighting in the district.

The metaphor of punching through some visual impediment to clear thinking is a provocative one, suggestive of Plato's parable of the cave. In the case of L.A. Unified, the enlightened philosophers would be the tech-nologists who have broken free of their intellectual shackles, have per-ceived a bright future unbound from organizational politics, and have returned to the shadowy cave of the school system to persuade others to follow. Undoubtedly, district technologists do have a vision of the future, which motivates them to engage in infrastructure-building projects, but how that vision is manufactured and sustained is something that resists critical investigation. This section analyzes dominant discourses in L.A. Unified of "catching up" with industry in order to begin probing the limi-tations of such an industry-oriented vision of technology and the future.

Three themes of relations among industry, education, and technology emerged from my interviews. The first and most expected was that wiring all public schools for Internet use would provide students with the technical skills that they would need for future employment. As one director of a school-within-a-school media academy explained to me, businesses want employees who are resourceful and creative, who can solve problems and innovate, and who can project a vision of the future and then meet goals to make that vision a reality. These are good requirements for business purposes, she continued, but also for learning, because the best way to achieve these goals is through integrated project-based assignments — an approach she saw as superior to rote learning, for instance. This vocational explanation (which I covered in greater detail in Chapter 2) stresses accelerating student performance to meet the flexible labor demands of globalizing industries. The following quote, from L.A. Unified's "Instructional Technology Plan," shows that in addition to following examples set by industry, the business ideology of emphasizing "outcomes" and devaluing "process" is also finding expression in technological rationalities for education:

> It is projected that workers will typically change professions as many as five times during their working careers. Some estimates indicate that workers in the 21st century will require one year of formal instruction for every seven years of employment. Businesses have increased their technology education programs in response to employee needs for continuous professional growth. It is critical that LAUSD follow this example. It has become increasingly more important to measure a person's potential by what he/she knows and can apply in real situations, rather than how many years of school are completed. This is a primary motivation to move toward standards-based education. New paradigms indicate a shift in educational requirements focusing on subject matter rather than seat time. This is reflected by the dramatic shift in global business towards outcomes, not process. (LAUSD 2002, 2)

An answer I received just as often to the question of "What is motivating technological change in public education?" was the need to bring public education up to industry levels of technology application. One Board of Education member, for example, told me with distress that public education was "light years" behind industry in the utilization of technology for everyday tasks. A high-level technology administrator expanded on this theme by saying that education was doomed to remain in the middle of the curve of technological progress, always several steps behind industry. When I asked him, "If industry is in the lead and education is in the middle, who's coming in last?" he floundered and then begrudgingly admitted that much of education was currently coming in last, too, but that they were quickly "catching up."

The final type of response, one not as often given voice, emphasized conditions of financial interdependency between industry and public education. Note this theme in the following passage taken from an interview with a policymaker in the governor's office of the secretary for education:

Isn't the push for technology in education predicated upon the belief that students will not only need this literacy in their lives or in their work but also that it will improve achievement?

I don't know that there's a lot of solid data about achievement. I think that it's one of the things that people in education technology say, but I don't know that policymakers believe it. I don't think the data's there. Quite candidly, if the question becomes — if the dynamic changes to [one where] we're only spending money on stuff that we can document improves student achievement, technology funding would drop really quickly. It's just not documentable.

That leaves me wondering why it's so popular.

Because everybody loves it! Kids like computers and video games and stuff, so people perceive they like it; parents like to walk into their kid's school and see computers — they actually feel better about it; politicians like it because they get to give computers to kids; and high-tech companies like it when politicians spend money on things that help their bottom line.

This passage acknowledges the political expediency of funding technology projects in public education — an expediency that transcends but does not preclude goals of student learning or performance. One of the dimensions of this expediency is financially supporting California's industries with equipment and construction contracts. "Catching up," in this instance, is a financially lucrative process for industries, to the tune of over $400 million a year in L.A. Unified alone (Konantz 2001) and nationally up to $2.25 billion a year from E-Rate alone (NYSL 2003).

If the guiding vision for educational technology is catching up with industry — in terms of preparing students for the labor market, integrating technologies into the daily practices of public education, and supplying industry with contracts — this begs the question of where industry is going and what the consequences will be if education goes on the same ride.

I have argued in previous chapters that the destination is toward a certain type of globalization that is structurally inflexible and that the consequences include solidifying exploitative, post-Fordist organizational models that compel human adaptation and perpetuate inequality. Not only were there no alternative visions in interviews to "catching up with industry," but those involved with technology in L.A. Unified did not outline for me any goals beyond that imperative. Evidently, because no one believed that education could ever catch up, the incessant chase was vision enough. However, an imagination governed by an obligation to follow may unduly restrict visions of what education is or could be (Monahan 2002c). The next section follows this technological chase into the domain of administrative data management to discern some of the future implications of importing industry models into public education.

Decision Support Systems: Automating Societies of Control

Early in my fieldwork, I became aware — through passing remarks at technology meetings — of a strange-sounding administrative project in public education: the development of "decision support systems." As with the rapid proliferation of many catch phrases, soon after my initial awareness, every time I would turn on public radio or open the newspaper, I came across references to emerging "decision systems," and not just for education but for all administrative realms.[1] I began to wonder what it meant that decisions were (and are) so in vogue and that decisions were something that individuals perceived the need of automated support systems to help them make. In terms of this chapter's focus on future imaginaries, this section questions the development of automated systems of data control and management and asks what these systems signify for relationships to the future. As an important caveat, I am not evaluating the merits or functionality of these systems, since they were not in place at the time of my fieldwork; instead, I am concerned with what kinds of approaches to the future (and understandings of future social relations) they engender.

In the domain of public education, decision support systems (DSS) represent mechanisms for collecting, coordinating, and mining data on students, teachers, and curriculum or training programs. The monthly magazine *Technology & Learning*, which is an industry publication

subscribed to and read by most technology coordinators, offers one explanation of these systems:

> Decision support systems are those tools and technologies that help
> administrators make efficient and informed decisions about critical issues
> such as student and employee performance or financial resource alloca-
> tion. While one common decision support system is the ordinary spread-
> sheet, more specialized information management tools can help educators
> easily make multidimensional queries (asking questions that span several
> variables, such as grade level, ethnicity, economic status, and test scores)
> with just a few clicks on a graph. (McIntire 2002, 20)

The idea behind such systems is to allow for flexible, specialized, and
rapid assessment, so that policy interventions can be made at earlier stages
of the educational process. As I will elaborate, there is also a disciplinary
valence to these systems, which is couched in the language of tracking
"employee performance" in the above quotation.

Similar to the domains covered in other chapters, the collective vision
of the kind of futures such decision systems will help shape is infused with
a flexible ideology of quick responses and adjustments, yet at the same
time, it is constrained by a Fordist conception of standardization, hierarchy, and control. One can perceive this ideological imbrication in articulations by administrators, where DSS is described as being potentially
empowering for teachers while being foremost a tool for administrators.
The following passage from an interview with a technology administrator
involved in the design of DSS in L.A. Unified reveals this post-Fordist
and Fordist ambiguity, which is manifested as ambivalence over providing
teachers with the tools of managers:

> The grand plan at some point in the future is to have things like this DSS
> available, on a selective basis, to teachers. Where teachers can see past
> records of their own students, you know, whatever, that sort of thing.
> So teachers, in a way, will have access to administrative applications as
> appropriate. That's kind of the grand plan.
>
> *What would it take to give teachers access to DSS?*
>
> Well, it would take some kind of ironclad security system because there
> are legal constraints on divulgence of student records. So, let's say we get

that down, and we have teacher name and password, and we make accounts for all the 45,000 teachers. Well, to do that, the system software and security staff would have to be expanded. . . . You know what happens now? The teacher does have access: they run it off on their local printer; they leave it on their desk, and another student comes up and sees somebody else's grade over the past six years. Not only is that illegal, it's poor practice and everything else. There are a lot of issues that need to be dealt with and they're not all technical issues, and we don't have a good model. New York's not doing it; Chicago's not doing it; Seattle's not doing it. I mean, no one else has done it yet either, that we know of.[2] So there are a lot of issues, and things that look like technical issues, the technical part turns out to be the easiest part of the whole thing.

If no one else has done this kind of project, what is motivating LAUSD to do it?

I really don't know, because it's not a technical issue — it's a user issue.

But you must have some ideas about what the purpose is?

The purpose is exactly what I told you: ultimately to give teachers a better handle on student performance, so that they can track it, and see it, and map it over time, and interact more effectively with individual students. That's the goal.

What do you think the word "decision" indicates in the system? Where are the decisions?

Well it depends on what level the user is compiling the data and building the quarry to answer what question. . . . [DSS] takes the data and turns it into information. When the day comes that teachers do have access to that kind of data, then they'll be trained and taught [about] student data integrity. If it becomes a new obligation, then teachers will be trained, and new teachers will be prepared.

This passage reveals a sense of heightened discomfort with providing teachers with what are clearly identified as "administrative applications." The interviewee implies that this process must be both regulated — "on a selective basis" and "as appropriate" — and postponed —"at some point in the future," "ultimately," and "when the day comes." The story of a teacher leaving confidential student information on his or her desk for anyone to see drives home the point of the necessity of controlling the social side of the system by training teachers to police themselves so as not to compromise data flow or "integrity." In the future, from this administrator's perspective, only by making data entry and management a "new obligation" for teachers will the system become reliable and robust. However, the potential problem of intensifying labor for teachers without releasing them from other tasks, which can be seen as a dimension of the neoliberal paradigm emphasizing worker flexibility, is not addressed in this particular call for more training.

My interviewee's use of the word *quarry* instead of *query* was intentional, and it is worth commenting on as another indication of how metaphors shape imaginaries and drive technology practices. People no longer analyze data — they mine it. And the more data there is to mine or quarry, so the thinking goes, the more valuable the information that can be extracted. Thus, in articles and at conferences, school administrators are advised to collect more data from as many different sources as possible:

> What additional data do you need to collect? Think creatively and go beyond the confines of your traditional transactional databases, which most often include student demographics, grades, test scores, and attendance. Explore what useful new information you could gather about students, teachers, parents, and programs that could help you design targeted service and support. (McIntire 2002, 24)

This data-mining paradigm justifies the administration of more surveys and tests and the generation of more reports as symbolic goods in and of themselves, regardless of the usefulness of the data, the time devoted to data generation, or the social effects of turning students and teachers into data producers. The market-based imaginary at work thereby emphasizes data accumulation over experience, increasing the potential for surveillance over all actors in the data loop (from students to administrators).

While most teachers revile administrative data collection projects such as tests and are quick to point out their faults (increasing depletion of classroom autonomy, control over curriculum, waste of time and resources, racist and classist biases, deleterious effects on students' educational experiences, etc.), the policymakers I interviewed embrace standardized testing data and, if anything, want more of it. This is not to say that policymakers are entirely blind to the problems of testing, but with the gradual privatization of public institutions, their jobs increasingly require data on performance (of students, teachers, principals, schools, local districts) in order to craft policy interventions. One board member told me outright that Stanford 9, the main evaluation test used in California, is likely racist, but that through the data derived from it, she is able to leverage the state for more money for schools with "underperforming" student populations. This high premium placed on data not only affects social relations in the classroom (by altering the curriculum and adding many hours of testing) but also compels even larger technological investments (in equipment, software, and personnel) to store and mine all the data; these investments, in turn, require increased *use* to justify their cost and existence.

In theory, DSS will be a device for helping individuals in the school system to do their jobs more efficiently and effectively. These anticipated outcomes rely on refashioning teachers, principals, and others as "decision makers" who have obligations not only to decide but also to act on their decisions and accept responsibility for the outcomes of those actions. Decision systems reorient individuals to the future and to the organization, based on individuals' capacity for producing and mobilizing data and for achieving measurable results (e.g., higher student test scores).

This vision for the use of DSS, however, neglects attention to existing power relations and the embedding of those relations into technology design. Specifically, the territoriality of L.A. Unified and ongoing battles over local or central control feed into the conceptualization of DSS, such that, as seen in the quotes above, administrators are reluctant to give teachers access to the system, perhaps because access implies empowerment. It seems more likely that DSS will be used to acquire documented proof on teachers' performance or lack of performance in the classroom, so that administrators can draw on the data to justify decisions to discipline underperforming teachers. The twist here is that noncompliance with data generation, or with what my interviewee called the preservation of "data integrity," can itself become a disciplinable action, or as the *Technology & Learning* article on DSS puts positively: "Assign ownership for each data element. . . . A clear chain of accountability, with appropriate checks, will result in greater data quality" (McIntire 2002, 26).

It should be pointed out that as an instrument for imagining future organizational compositions, DSS introduces an imaginary of flexible interventions predicated on recursive hierarchies: it positions students and teachers in structurally identical relationships to teachers and administrators. This is one place where ambiguity between flexible and mass production regimes emerges, because if teachers are dominated through the DSS system by administrators, then teachers, in turn, dominate students by compelling them to adopt subject positions of data producers. The flexible potential of data mining is therefore supported by organizational rigidities in data collection and the social relations of domination needed to hold those rigidities in place. As with the other domains of educational technology, however, one would expect many avenues for appropriation should the system become an actuality; certainly both students and teachers could voluntarily or selectively fail to comply with data collection, or they could publicly oppose it, as occasionally occurs with standardized testing in public education (see http://www.fairtest.org).

The implementation of decision support systems or automated curriculum software such as "Open Court" should be ripe territory for negotiations with teachers' unions. And the teachers' union in Los Angeles — United Teachers Los Angeles (UTLA) — is strong, yet it does not seem to be aware of the challenges to workplace autonomy or job security posed by emerging technological systems. Labor unions more generally have been notoriously slow to recognize threats brought about by IT and automation (Cherkasky 1999), but one would hope that teachers' unions would learn from the mistakes of others and bring these issues to the collective bargaining table before the systems of control are hardwired.

Seen as a mechanism for social control, DSS is a system of symbolic power that bodes to ossify the inflexibilities of fragmented centralization, allowing policymakers and administrators to control school programs and personnel from a distance while distributing responsibility for "performance" to those at school sites. One interpretation is that the resulting condition will yield what Gilles Deleuze (1992, 5) theorized as a "society of control," reducing social actors to systems components:

Indeed, just as the corporation replaces the factory, *perpetual training* tends to replace the *school*, and continuous control to replace the examination.

Which is the surest way of delivering the school over to the corporation. . . . The numerical language of control is made of codes that mark access to information, or reject it. We no longer find ourselves dealing with the mass/individual pair. Individuals have become "*dividuals*," and masses, samples, data, markets, or "*banks*."

Imaginations for future possibilities are confined to the metaphorical tunnels and mine shafts that plow under the experiences of those in public education. As teachers who oppose standardized testing in L.A. Unified and elsewhere often say, the implications of installing technical systems that ostensibly tell us *what is important* and *what to do* are dangerous when these systems disguise and contribute to the enforcement of unequal power relations and when they increasingly reduce the elements of every-day life to the status of data. Decision regimes, in other words, can construct rigid parameters for meaningful participation in the future while espousing flexible opportunities for systemic change. They embody the ideologies of Fordist and post-Fordist production, but in an admixture that dilutes opportunities for future change within societies of control.

"Imagineering" the Future: The CUE Conference

Thus far, this chapter's discussion of how imaginations for technology and education get shaped has focused mostly on metaphors, technical systems, and institutional cultures, with no incontrovertible link between public education and global industries. This section argues that the construction of technology-oriented metaphors, systems, and cultures is anything but haphazard or coincidental; it is instead a concentrated, strategic effort on the part of technology industries to cultivate a desire for the commodities and services they sell. The Walt Disney Company's term "imagineering" captures this process well, where *imagineering* means the intentional engi-neering of imaginary worlds that can substitute for or supplant reality. In Walt Disney's words, imagineering is "the blending of creative imagina-tion and technical know-how" (cited in Eisner 1996, 9), yet the capacity of imagineered worlds to substitute for or colonize reality is expressed in CEO Michael Eisner's direct allusions to the British Empire: "Since the sun never sets on a Disney theme park, someone is smiling, laughing, singing, learning, caring, uniting, even forgetting about their most serious of worldly cares, even as you read these words" (Eisner 1996, 9). In the context of this chapter, agency and intentionality are always involved in the process of imagineering, so stories about the natural evolutionary advancement of technology are really imagineered visions designed to serve the interests of technology industries (to sell goods and services) and global capital (to produce flexible workers and avid consumers). A trip that I took in May 2001 to the major national conference for technologists in education — Computer Using Educators (CUE) — opened my eyes to the extent to which such imagineering takes place.

After a several hour drive, I arrive in the afternoon at the enormous Anaheim Convention Center, located across the street from Disneyland's even more massive new California Adventure theme park.[3] My informants have been looking forward to this year's conference so that they could catch a glimpse of all the new technological gadgets and programs that are now (or will soon be) available for educators. The parking lot abuts the side of the Convention Center, and it is not clear how to locate the main entrance. So, hyper-aware that I have not registered and do not yet have a badge, I enter through a side door where attendees have gathered to steal their cigarette fixes. I cautiously evade a cadre of senior-citizen, part-time badge checkers who, decked out in red sports jackets, diligently patrol the perimeter of the conference hall. After finding the registration area and accepting my "package" of literature, receipts, and conference badge, I enter into a vast room spanning more than the length of a football field and reaching about four stories high.

Everywhere I look, I see what must be hundreds of people milling around booths displaying the latest wares or services: furniture, imaging software, technology camps for kids, video and audio software, "learning" software, "best practices" displays, student testimonials for technology curricula, antiplagiarism software, security systems, standards integration software, standardized testing on Palm Pilots, paper laminators, printers, projectors, digital Internet libraries, distance learning systems, and much more. This is an industry conference, and vendors call out to passers-by from their booths, offering "free" giveaways of T-shirts, Frisbees, and mugs, all with company logos and brands prominently displayed. Other vendors are raffling off bigger-ticket items such as printers, Palm Pilots, monitors, software, and furniture. Vendors at every booth want to place orders now, and they quickly size me up by glancing at my color-coded badge to see whether or not I am a potential buyer — my badge says I am.

Overwhelmed by stimuli, I quickly lose myself in the crowd and stumble across a demonstration and training session. The company organizing this session has secured an area at least twice the size of other booths, located on a "corner" space amid the partitioned aisles. Chairs have been set up for potential buyers to rest on while they are trained to use a software application by a charismatic woman equipped with a wireless headset microphone and a laser pointer. I pause for a moment, and a man whom I did not initially notice steps out from the periphery and quietly invites me to sit down. I decline and then navigate toward the back part of the room, trying to find a somewhat open space to quell my rising claustrophobia.

The vendors at this event seem agitated and frantic, desperately afraid of missing a big order. The crowd of educators and technologists, by contrast, emote an attitude of skeptical curiosity, eager to engage in conversation, ask questions, or participate in workshops but always self-aware and collected. Both groups are involved in a subtle dance of negotiation, governed by exchanges of feigned interest or noninterest, and the more eager the vendors are, it seems, the greater the indifference of the potential buyers.

An old acquaintance from high school — one whom I have not seen since then — spots me in the crowd and approaches, quickly explaining his presence at the conference: "I became a cop after we graduated, but after a few years decided that wasn't for me. So, I became a teacher." I have a more difficult time explaining that I am researching globalization and technological change in public education, but once I do, my friend volunteers his interpretation of the CUE conference. He explains that almost all schools have some technology budget, either from grants or discretionary funds, and that the principals of these schools turn to technology-minded teachers or technology coordinators to decide how to spend that money. Most of those attending the CUE conference do not have money to spend on software, for instance, but they can identify applications that they like and then request that their respective schools purchase licenses for that software. This is why vendors are so eager to make good impressions on the conference attendees, because they are hoping that those impressions will translate into sales in the near future.

In the evening, I accompany many of the conference participants to a reception and buffet-style dinner hosted by C-SMART (now called CalSAVE), which is an organization whose mission is to bring technology corporations and educators together and, reputedly, to leverage "the statewide buying power of California schools to secure the lowest possible price [on educational technologies]" (CalSAVE 2003). This is a raucous social event with two to three hundred people, a cash bar, vendor displays and personnel lining the walls, and a nonstop raffle for industry-donated products — the amplification of "winning" ticket numbers over the public address system mixes into the cacophony of conversation until soon it is barely noticed at all, and as a result, winners fail to claim and thus forfeit their prizes. Spinning tops, disposable cameras, and other toys adorn each of the dozens of round tables that people pit-stop at to eat, chat briefly, and then move on. Everywhere, people are caught up in the exuberant party atmosphere, giddy and drunk on the festivities made possible by the ongoing and well-fueled IT revolution.

The cultivation of an imagination for a technological future is not so difficult to locate in the event of this conference and its related celebrations. Now that local, state, and federal governments are subsidizing educational technologies, industries court educators in order to ensure that this revolution takes root; they target those in a position to effect change and then assist them in integrating technology into educational practices. Even I "won" a mug and ten site licenses for a program called Inspiration, which I dutifully signed over to my primary field site, in case they wanted to try the program. My thinking at the time was, "Why let this go to waste if someone could use it?" But this is exactly how everyone else at the conference was behaving also, and the net result is the insertion of products into schools and the measured development of a culture of technological dependency.

Educators are undoubtedly complicit in these changes, but they are certainly not puppets. Someone at my table during the C-SMART reception explained to me that because school districts are such territorial entities and seniority plays such a dominant role in determining control over territory, younger teachers are using technological literacy as a way to secure territory in the form of better rooms, course releases, and input into budget outlays. Technology industries explicitly cater to career interests by offering to pay these teachers $1,000 or more to train other teachers to use educational technologies (which was an offer being made at the CUE conference by www.teachtheteachers.org). Finally, this missionizing strategy is replicated across L.A. Unified (and most likely across other school districts): one computer teacher told me, for example, that he "implants his students with a hidden agenda," so that they demand that their other teachers use technologies, too. And a board member revealed to me that her strategy was to give laptop computers to teachers and administrators, encouraging them to become "covert revolutionaries" who enact technological (and institutional) change from the ground up.

The imagineering or intentional shaping of an educational culture dependent on externally provided technologies should not be read as some kind of grand conspiracy. This is how the capitalist market works: it adapts to specific organizational compositions, rationalities, and dynamics — like those in public education — to further capital accumulation. Teachers involve themselves in this process for their own interests, whether pedagogical or personal, and software vendors simply do their best to succeed in a very competitive market. It is the shaping of a dominant view of education as a "market" that I am calling into question here.

The CUE conference is one forum for imagineering, for the crafting of a certain vision of the future that may serve the interests of a select group of technology-minded educators, but it is a vision that seeks to (re)inscribe relations of interdependency and interconnection between public education and global technology industries. Once the demand for computers in public schools becomes an end in itself, as appears to be the case with state policies requiring specific student-to-computer ratios, then any vision of the future must operate within that dominant paradigm. This is not to say that educators, parents, policymakers, or others cannot think differently or cannot bring about alternative realities, only that visions for the future are constrained by cultural dominants, and the imagineered model of the commodification of public education and individual adaptation to global industries has become one such dominant.

Enabling Uncharted Futures

This chapter now turns to the more philosophical question of how to encourage imaginations (and thus possibilities) for alternative futures —

futures that are increasingly foreclosed by societies of control and imagineered visions of technological worlds. As a starting point, a key conceptual obstacle to imagining and achieving alternative futures lies in perceiving the present (or the "real") as a logical extension of the past (Grosz 2003). This construction of past-present causality helps us make sense of the world but simultaneously denies inquiry into past contingencies (or alternative present realities); neither does this causal approach to time afford critical investigation into the mechanisms by which immediate reality is projected back to produce *that which was possible*. Put otherwise, if we believe that we can unproblematically learn from history and thereby avoid repeating its errors, we are constructing a deterministic model of the present as a realization of the past, and this, in turn, implies a construction of the future that is bound to the logics and circumstances of the present — it proffers a teleology that defies agency and alterity.

One response to the dominance of *the present* over *the possible* is to substitute the concept of *duration* for time, where duration is seen as a recognition of "the indivisibility of movement and action" (Grosz 2003, 12), a moment of singularity with few constraints upon actualization, and an openness to unpredictable change and surprise. Duration accomplishes these goals — at least conceptually — by recognizing the simultaneity and the enfolding of the present and the past, such that the past acquires its meaning and implication through its immediate coexistence with the present. As with linguistic utterances, an understanding of futurity as embodied in duration — rather than in linear historical progression — relies on transient relationality for ascriptions of meaning and therefore does not shackle future possibility to the glaciation of the past.

This approach to futurity, which embraces particularity, movement, and radical change, resonates with my thesis of overcoming structural rigidities through flexible and mutable embodiments, but it is unclear what such alternative conceptualizations of the future would look like empirically. As I notably found in my interactions with students, dispositions to futurity become sedimented with experience, and, contrary to idealized narratives of identity selection within globalization, these dispositions cannot be cast off and reconstructed at will. For example, when students saw me sketching spatial layouts of rooms and the movement of people through those spaces, they would often, with encouragement, offer to draw their ideal visions of future technology learning spaces. Given the open-endedness and imaginative potential of this task, I was shocked to see students produce sketches of incredibly disciplinary spaces with marked similarity to their current learning environments.

Let me offer two quick examples. The first student sketch depicts a rectangular classroom with four rows and three columns of computer tables, with each table partitioned to accommodate three computer stations and three students (see Figure 7.1). The teacher's desk is located front and center, and each of the thirty-six students faces the teacher. The artist of this sketch, a 16-year-old male from Sri Lanka, has traced lines with arrows down each of the aisles to demonstrate routes of possible mobility, but aside from the slightly increased opportunities for movement and the implied presence of computers, nothing distinguishes this design from the Fordist layout of most rooms at this high school. In this instance, the student not only lives in spaces of standardization and discipline but has embodied these spatial logics through his everyday practices such that they exert a confining force on his vision of the future.

The second student sketch, by a 15-year-old Russian male, reveals a remarkably panoptic classroom in the shape of a triangle (see Figure 7.2). A teacher's perch sits in the middle of the triangle, and student computer stations line each of the three walls. Importantly, computer monitors face the center, so that students have their backs turned to the teacher at all times, yet students' work and movements are subjected to (the potential for) constant centralized surveillance. The key difference in this design from Bentham's panopticon is that students are unable to perceive their peers except through sideways glances or audible keyboard clicks. Students are atomized well beyond opportunities for developing a sense of a shared plight (or collective consciousness) and well beyond the internalization of peer-enforced discipline. Where the previous student's design replicated dominant and standardized spatial *forms*, this design translates and extends prevalent educational *concepts* of discipline and control into a disturbingly restraining projection of the future.

It occurred to me later that this classroom design is almost an exact homology of some Nazi concentration camps, such as the one at Sachsenhausen, just outside of Berlin (see Figure 7.3). Both employ a triangular layout with a somewhat centrally located observation station to maximize

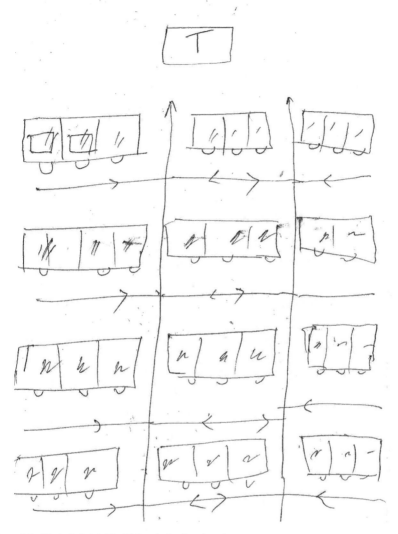

Figure 7.1 Student sketch (1) of future technology learning space.

visibility and control. Given the many other similarities of urban public schools to incarceration centers and the very real problems of controlling the occupants within these spaces, it should not be surprising that students (or others) would stumble across historically proven designs for efficient containment. By making this comparison, I am not arguing that the schools of the future will be like the concentration camps of the past; rather, I interpret this student's vision as an indication of how dominant

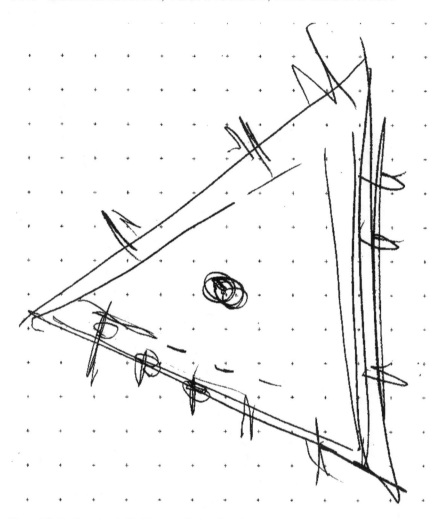

Figure 7.2 Student sketch (2) of future technology learning space.

rationalities can reproduce conceptual forms across space and time and as a warning sign for the continued, uninterrupted projection of the past into the future.

It is worth pointing out that all of the half-dozen or so student sketches I gathered of future technology learning spaces illustrated rooms with static walls and disciplinary controls, as opposed to flexible or polyvalent rooms with varied task stations (as described in Chapter 1), and certainly none portrayed outdoor learning environments. The implication for this chapter's

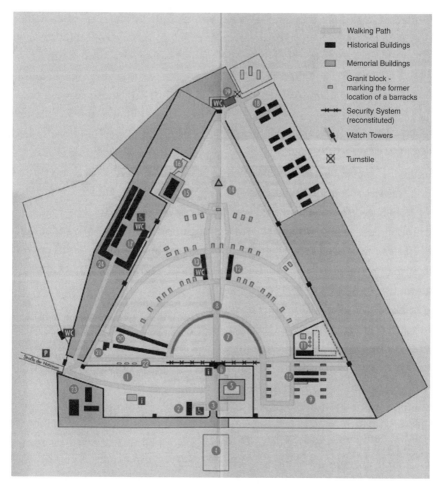

Figure 7.3 Map of concentration camp at Sachsenhausen, Germany.

focus on imaginaries is that what is perceived as possible is largely constrained by what is known and experienced routinely. Yet one cannot simply explain this pattern of reproducing dominant forms and concepts as resulting of students' limited educational or cultural experiences.

Indeed, many students at Concrete High have not been in the United States for that long, and they have had remarkably different educational experiences in other countries. One young woman of 17 from Guatemala, who had been in the United States for 4 years, stressed that school in Guatemala was dramatically different from and better than public education in the

United States: there they had few computers, much more individual attention, smaller classes, shorter days, and diverse and "important" subjects such as agriculture. Another student, a 17-year-old male youth from Bangladesh who had been in the United States for 2 years, said that they had few technologies in his home country but that individuals in Bangladesh seemed to be less dependent, more autonomous, and more respectful of authority because of this absence. Another 17-year-old female student from Russian who had been in the United States for 6 years posited that U.S. education encouraged individual materialism and instrumental friendships, whereas Russian education was less accepting of diversity but people were more genuine.

Granted, these students also told me stories of beatings by teachers, grueling tests for graduation, and lack of opportunity for advancement. So, I offer these counternarratives of alternate educational experiences not to romanticize non-U.S. education but instead to emphasize that exposure alone does not dictate perceptions of the future. Each of these students possessed comparative frames of reference that allowed them to criticize practices in their immediate environments, yet they were, at the same time, bound to the rationalities of U.S. public education. When pressed, each of them asserted that computers represented the future and that their past experiences were somehow backward because they did not prepare students for a computerized future. They additionally said that their previous education would not have prepared them for the service sector or creative jobs to which they now aspired: an airline reservations agent, computer programmer, and graphic designer, respectively.

Future imaginaries, then, not only emerge from experience and exposure but are also differentially shaped by which experiences are considered socially valuable, legitimate, and necessary. Because the U.S. public education system is perceived to be in a state of disciplinary and technological crisis (popularly mobilized under the rhetorics of "school violence" and "the digital divide"), social control and computers acquire greater symbolic weight for future developments than any other visions — they become emblems of educational modernity, especially if one can achieve social control *through* computerization (as the student sketches show).

In imagining the future, students seemingly draw only on past experiences that resonate with dominant visions of modernity, visions that speak to perceived needs for well-controlled and well-wired lives. The effect is the relegation of student experiences in other countries (such as Guatemala, Bangladesh, and Russia) to a decidedly non-modern and therefore non-legitimate past. As Appadurai (1996, 31) cautions, such discrimination in valuation Orientalizes others while rationalizing the status quo:

> [T]he apparent increasingly substitutability of whole periods and postures for one another, in the cultural styles of advanced capitalism, is tied to larger global forces, which have done much to show Americans that the past is usually another country. If your present is their future (as in much modernization theory and in many self-satisfied tourist fantasies), and their future is your past (as in the case of the Filipino virtuosos of American popular music), then your own past can be made to appear as simply a normalized modality of your present.

Edward Said (1978), Johannes Fabian (1983), and, more recently, Arturo Escobar (1995) have similarly criticized the methodological approach and the political ramifications of relegating cultures under study to other (non-present) temporal or spatial realities. I would add to this that the imagination operates as a cultural structure that is embedded in political economies and defined in conversation with others. So, studies of future imaginaries (and identity constructions) must attend to power and dominant cultural symbols to explain discriminatory selection processes of past materials for future worlds.

Returning to Grosz's concept of duration, freeing future imaginaries from the shackles of a selectively filtered past would require movement toward the leveling of power relations and the neutering of hegemonic cultural dominants. If imaginations are encumbered by past experiences that are considered "valuable," to the dismissal of other histories, then opportunities for multiplicity through duration are precluded. Life events in other countries or in other settings (like the street or the home) are seen as atavistic and irrelevant rather than as knowledge resources for imagining change. A flexible approach to the imagination must first recognize the artificiality of socially constructed symbolic dominants and then leverage duration and simultaneity to the fullest extent so that the multiplicity of the past can feed into the creation of the future. Put otherwise, experiences of and in developing or nonmainstream worlds should be placed on par with those in industrialized nations and institutions, so that countries such as the United States can begin to recognize and contend with the developing worlds within their borders, so that trajectories toward societies of control can be diverted, and so that the youth of the world do not perceive the future as something that has already left them behind.

Conclusion

This chapter has probed imaginations for future technological worlds, specifically in public education, has outlined some of the constraints placed upon future imaginaries, and has speculated on the outcomes that dominant visions of the future may produce. As with other aspects of technological change, politics color perceptions of the future in ways that often go undetected, such that circumscribed imaginaries become normalized through the production and circulation of symbolic cultural dominants like modernization, control, and technological imperatives. The restriction of "the possible" to dominant constructions of needs — networked, data-generating, and disciplinary environments, for instance — inflexibly condenses future imaginaries to the binary of success or failure in meeting those needs. One is either in the lead or catching up, succeeding or failing, compliant or unruly; and while levels of difference may be acknowledged between these extremes, opportunities for true diversity in vision are not.

This is not to say that alternate outcomes cannot or will not emerge or that individuals will not be able to appropriate future conditions. Still, imaginaries crisscross over all the other domains covered in this book, and restrictions placed on them have effects in the built world, organizational forms, policies, and so on. Even when labor conditions appear to embody other attributes of structural flexibility, such as the organizational fluidity found with individual contracting for high-tech jobs (or found in other sectors of the information economy), collective imaginations for and expectations about the nature of that work drive individuals to colonize all aspects of their personal lives with work-related demands (Jackson 1997; Ross 2000, 2003).

For these reasons, all the domains covered here should be thought of systemically as an assemblage of pressures, demands, and opportunities, yet not every element of this assemblage possesses equal power or weight. The more structural flexibility that occurs at each level, the greater the valence for democratic empowerment. But perhaps the imagination is the most crucial of all domains, because biopower can mobilize through it to negate the benefits of structural flexibility elsewhere. Myths of students being left behind, of technology as the future, of requisite data-management systems, of imagineered worlds, and of obligatory student discipline reverberate across the institution of public education, limiting alternative realities. Imaginations for flexible futures, by contrast, can flourish when the hidden politics of symbolic dominants are unearthed and when all experiences are placed on equal footing as legitimate material for imaginative acts.

8
NEOLIBERAL ORDERS

[N]eoliberalism has to be understood within a larger crisis of vision, meaning, education, and political agency.

Henry A. Giroux 2004, xv

Retrenching on its commitments to the social wage, the contemporary state has not reneged at all, of course, on its commitments to social order.

Cindi Katz 2001, 47

Privatization by other means: this is one outcome of the information revolution in public education. This result occurs, however, without the political backlash usually associated with proposals for outsourcing (e.g., through school vouchers) or dissolving public education altogether. Through publicly funded grants, billions of dollars for "educational technologies" flow yearly into the accounts of private technology companies and contractors. Meanwhile, the impoverished coffers of public education are increasingly committed to technology projects and personnel, leaving scant resources for long proven mechanisms for fostering student learning and achievement, such as smaller class sizes or more teacher preparation time. School districts turn to crisis-management techniques of hiring emergency credentialed teachers, establishing charter schools, or implementing year-round, multitrack schools in order to contend with shortages of qualified employees and adequate school spaces. And accountability regimes proliferate to keep a tally on the state of the crisis and assign responsibility for it, subsequently contorting the primary functions of school actors into those of data generation and management.

The transformations under way are not merely about the transfer of public resources to private industries; they indicate, instead, the widespread commodification of public education and the production of new forms of life. Neoliberalism, as the dominant expression of globalization in the public sector, colonizes public education with its rationalities and yokes the institution to global capital. When public education scales back its social or civic functions in order to accommodate global expectations and industry needs, it concurrently exerts greater social control on actors in these systems. This helps explain why flexible, multitasking, and enterprising students are desired by the system, and it also helps explain why less adaptive students are labeled as disciplinary problems and doomed to poverty, imprisonment, or both.

This story, however, extends beyond the production of students to encompass mutations across all domains of public education. As seen with the example of the Los Angeles Unified School District, relations among employees are shifting, so that decision-making authority is becoming more centralized while responsibility for centrally made decisions is becoming more widely distributed. These emerging organizational relations, which I call *fragmented centralization*, occur under the rubric of "decentralization" and are embedded in rituals of disclosure and discipline associated with new accountability regimes. While the semblance of direct accountability and local responsiveness may be a convincing façade, fragmented centralization undermines much of the democratic history and potential of public education. Through these developments, then, we can observe neoliberalism's slow neutering of democratic values, goals, and governance in the institution of public education.

It should be clear that neoliberalism as described here represents a cultural disposition (Comaroff & Comaroff 2000; Duggan 2003). It is a pervasive orientation to the world: one that views all public programs as suspect, all private appropriations of public goods as benign, and all critical inquiry into its operations as dangerously subversive and possibly terrorist. As a cultural shift, neoliberalism institutes new social and moral orders that normalize its assumptions as fundamental truths. Thus, even without a "smoking gun" of direct industry influence over politicians, for instance, this disposition performs to radically rescript all that is (or once was) considered "public."

Information technology (IT) provides neoliberal orders with both galvanizing rationales and structural support, in part by means of the intricate mythologies surrounding such technologies. First, they are perceived in deterministic terms as advancing in unidirectional evolutionary fashion. Next, they are seen paradoxically as neutral "tools" whose positive outcomes are somehow inherent and whose negative ones are unfortunate "side effects," most likely caused by social factors. Finally, information technologies are interpreted as universal correctives to social inequalities, as is apparent with the discursive force of "the digital divide." In combination, these myths deliver a clear message to those concerned with the plight of students in public education: there is only one path toward progress and it requires the incorporation of IT into public education. No need to address deeper social problems, the message implies, because they will be ameliorated in due course.

This book has shown the danger of these myths. In following technologists as they negotiate specifications, navigate organizational politics, and contend with spatial constraints, one quickly realizes that there is no single evolutionary course for technology to take; instead, there are many trajectories, some progressive and others regressive, but all are infused with politics. The politics of technologies manifest not only in organizational conflicts over who should be in charge but also in the social relations produced in classrooms, offices, and Board of Education meetings. The current trend in social relations, in spite of the democratic promise of information technologies, is toward increased discipline, control, and centralized power. The technologies being deployed both engender and hardwire these relations into school systems; meanwhile, by means of their purported neutrality, they deflect inquiry into emerging power differentials.

Concerning the situation described here, several important caveats are in order. First, actors in school systems do have agency to resist, appropriate, and modify technology design and technological politics. Many students use computers to unsettle disciplinary relations with teachers; teachers give computer assignments to students to momentarily escape oppressive workloads; technology coordinators select software, operating systems, and network designs to meet the particular needs of schools; groups of local technologists fight specifications set by central administrators; and central administrators cultivate technology dependency to ensure job security. Without a doubt, these actors demonstrate agency. This does not, however, much alter the overall trajectory toward fragmented centralization. And while many of these expressions of agency are reactionary rather than proactive, most of them are slowly being eliminated or attenuated, not just by administrators but by the unfolding of neoliberalism throughout public institutions and public life.

As a second caveat, the critique advanced here is not one of anti-technology. To say that technologies are political indicates that sometimes they enable democratic conditions and other times they impose authoritarian control; sometimes they afford open communication and other times they support one-way directives. Technologies are polyvalent and underdetermined, meaning that while they are not neutral, they are open to interpretation and selective application to varying degrees (Eglash et al. 2004). I have questioned the extent to which IT either adapts to a full range of human activities or forces individuals to adapt to it. In order to answer this question, I observed the development of technological systems and the kinds of social relations co-constructed by them. And throughout this text, I have documented structurally flexible alternatives to the dominant disciplinary role of IT in public education.

The theory of *structural flexibility* offers an idealized framework for evaluating and crafting technological systems and politics for democracy. The principles of structural flexibility are contexts that (1) afford alteration and modification; (2) enable multiple forms of individual action, interaction, and expression; and (3) motivate power equalization among actors in the system. In contrast with the neoliberal trends toward the elimination of the welfare state and the rise in social control, these principles suggest ways to tap the latent possibilities for democratic practices within globalization. While the shakeup of social ties and material conditions associated with globalization and technological change is undoubtedly destructive, the associated unsettling of sedimented dispositions affords moments for progressive intervention. If flexibility is valued rhetorically, then actors can mobilize this to try to leverage flexible workplace conditions or policies.

If "shop" classrooms are atavistic holdovers from an era of Fordist mass production, then teachers can transform them into open learning spaces that support student mobility and multiple activities. If large bureaucracies are being phased out in favor of smaller, supposedly autonomous districts, then more direct lines of communication can be established among community members, school-site personnel, and proximate administrators in the smaller districts. These are potentialities that arose, albeit infrequently, in the school district that I studied. I am not claiming that harnessing all these potentialities could radically redirect globalization in public education; instead, I am suggesting that they could draw attention to the magnitude of the changes under way and serve as a countervailing force that begins to correct systemic inequalities.

Any alternatives to globalization in public education must be grounded in specific localities. The emphasis here has been on the social worlds in L.A. Unified, a school system serving a large population of poor minority students in urban and suburban neighborhoods. Los Angeles may be a cosmopolitan "global city," yet the school system struggles to meet the basic needs of students: to provide them with opportunities to learn, with incentives to stay in school, and with promises of a better future. Likewise, the United States may be an industrialized superpower, but there are many developing worlds within its borders, and public schools offer a window into some of those worlds. As with other development narratives, the scenes behind the window betray a system seemingly more concerned with symbols of progress than with cultivating democratic conditions, fostering economic equality, or achieving social justice.

More studies of globalization on the ground are needed, and while remaining ever attentive to local mediations and productions of "the global," such research must be situated within larger fields of power. I chose to study organizational restructuring and the implementation of technological systems intended to facilitate or support learning, and I analyzed these developments not in isolation but as a whole, as local articulations of ideological conflicts and contradictions within emerging global orders.

Thus, in each institutional domain (space, pedagogy, organization, policy, governance, and imagination) I have tried to show how global forces feed back into the grounded materiality of lived experience, specifically at school sites and in classrooms. The resonances produced by these grounded forces then create a feedback loop that modulates the tonal frequency of globalization, compelling responses and readjustments that account for local differences. Whether the issue is organizational decentralization, curriculum benchmarks for technological literacy, policies for equipment purchases, or conceptions of world challenges facing youth — each domain and each concern tangibly affect the built environment and everyday experiences of individuals navigating those spaces. Each conflict, silent or voiced, changes the meaning of the institutional enterprise and its relationship to the state and to industry. It is through local demands and dependencies, through technological investments and commitments, that the project of globalization is rescripted, becoming something different, something that contains a piece of that which it affects. Globalization is refracted and redefined through its mediation on the plane of institutional particularity.

IT in public education, whether used for learning, management, or social control, tends to necessitate greater flexibility of students and workers in order for them to adapt to systems that are ever more rigid and controlling. Not coincidentally, the molding of flexible bodies accustomed to instability may be exactly what globalization requires. In the face of these emerging orders, intelligent tactical resistance is called for so as to redirect such imperatives to more socially just and equitable ends. This is globalization's immediate challenge and latent opportunity — it is an invitation that demands a response.

APPENDIX: ACRONYMS AND ABBREVIATIONS

AB 2882   California Assembly Bill 2882
AMSA   Applied Math and Science Academy
ANAT   Apple Network Administrative Toolkit
BFAT   Business, Finance, Audit, and Technology standing committee
          of the Board of Education in LAUSD
CIPA   Children's Internet Protection Act
CUE   Computer Using Educators
DHS   Digital High School
DSS   Decision Support System
E-Rate   Education Rate: the federal government's technology discount
          program
FY3   Funding Year Three for the federal government's E-Rate
          program
HVAC   Heating, Ventilation, and Air Conditioning systems in buildings
IASA   Federal Improving America's Schools Act
IP   Intellectual Property
IT   Information Technology
ITAF   Instructional Technology Applications Facilitator at "local
          districts" in LAUSD
ITB   Instructional Technology Branch of LAUSD
ITC   Instructional Technology Commission of LAUSD (informal
          organization run through Bell High School)
ITD   Information Technology Division of LAUSD
LA   Los Angeles

LAUSD   Los Angeles Unified School District
PDA   Personal Digital Assistants (e.g., "Palm Pilots")
PVC   Polyvinylchloride
SLD   School and Libraries Division of Federal Communications Commission's E-Rate program

NOTES

Foreword

1. R. Arnove and C. A. Torres, eds. *Comparative Education: The Dialectics of the Global and the Local.* Lanham, MD: Rowman and Littlefield, 1999. Second edition, 2003.

2. A detailed analysis of the contemporary trends in educational reform impacted by globalization and neoliberalism, with an emphasis on the discourse during the recent presidential campaigns, could be found in my article "NCLB: A Brainchild of Neoliberalism and American Politics" in the *New Politics.* A Journal of Socialist Thought symposium on public education in the US. (see http://www.newpol.org/). *New Politics*, no. 8, winter 2005.

3. Carlos Alberto Torres, "Expert Knowledge, External Assistance and Educational Reform in the Age of Neoliberalism: A Focus on the World Bank and Question of Moral Responsibilities in Third World Educational Reform." In Marilyn Gittell, Bernd Reiter, and Michael Sharpe, Editors, *Old and New Frontiers in Education Reform: Confronting Exclusion in the Democratic Tradition.* New York: Lexington Books, (in press).

Introduction

1. See Monahan (2002a) for a detailed overview of the "Los Angeles studies" literature.

Chapter 1

1. Saying that technologies contain traces of the values of their designers or of the ideologies of their design contexts and that technologies condition events through relational reenactments of these traces does not imply technological determinism, as some have argued (e.g., Pinch 1996), but instead a recognition of partial determination and the effects of value-laden

technological constraints on action and interpretation. Akrich (1992, 222) reaches a similar conclusion in talking about the "political strength" of technological objects, such as photoelectric lighting kits, to shape social relations and simultaneously obscure that shaping process.

2.   Valence suggests a molecular view of artifacts, implying that every technology is differentially "charged," either positively or negatively, for certain outcomes, and that outcomes or uses can be mapped with a fair degree of predictability (Bush 1997). The powerful insight of this concept is that no technologies are neutral, in spite of their openness to interpretation and innovation; when the molecular analogy is extrapolated out to the societal level, this observation about nonneutrality opens technologies up for critical evaluation of the values and ideologies embedded within them.

3.   A "built pedagogy" approach to the analysis of technological spaces merges the work of Michel Foucault (1977) and Michel de Certeau (1984), acknowledging not only architecturally reinforced and bodily internalized disciplinary states but also tactical opportunities for movement, emotion, and thought. Attention to space as a field of social operations allows for analyses of constraints and possibilities, adaptations and re-creations, politics and practices.

4.   The absence of women in this narrative is intentional. At this school, I witnessed only one woman working as part of the technology staff, and she served as a computer lab aide rather than as a participant in design. This observation is consistent with national U.S. studies indicating that women account for only 20 percent of IT professionals (AAUW 2000). At the same time, as one of my male interviewees pointed out, women now make up more than half of the users of the World Wide Web (Brown 2000). Differential access to technology design persists even as access to technology use opens up. [It should be said that the valuing of technical professions over social ones (such as teaching) reveals that gender inequities go way beyond issues of technology access.]

Still, my research findings show an anomaly in this trend of access to technology design: women do occupy many lead positions in L.A. Unified's technology coordination efforts—I would estimate about 30 to 40 percent. I attribute this to the first phase of an emerging IT occupational group that has drawn its personnel largely from its teaching staff. This group is gaining more control over school territories and displacing power held by teachers and administrators (see Chapter 3 for further elaboration). I predict that L.A. Unified will eventually invest in trained IT professionals from outside of educational fields, and then, unfortunately, this emergent IT group will likely adjust to reflect the gender inequities in industry.

5.   In reality, information technology industries are incredibly polluting, releasing chemicals, deionized water, hazardous and bulk gases, and much

more, besides consuming electricity and filling landfills (Silicon Valley Toxics Coalition. 1997; Smith. 1997).

6. Exceptions could be said to exist in the creation of transient spaces for individuals in large advertising agencies and consulting companies or of open spaces for collaborative work in government. However, in the first case, ownership of office space is seen as a liability, because "successful" employees are seldom stationary; instead they travel incessantly or use their mobile technologies (laptops, cell phones, pagers) to stay on call while they are in transit (Schwarz 2002). Such configurations can hardly be interpreted as "flexible spaces" that conform to individuals' personal needs, because they are flexible only to the degree that they facilitate employee adaptation and labor maximization through placelessness. In the second case, government employees, such as those in Mayor Bloomberg's offices in New York City, flee mandated open spaces whenever possible to preserve political territoriality and privacy to engage in virtual back-room deals, mostly over cell phones (Purnick 2002). Here again, labor is intensified, as individuals must adjust even more to spaces touted as flexible and enabling, because singular "open" spaces can become impediments when larger institutional systems remain closed.

7. These properties of flexible space could be labeled as fluidity, versatility, convertibility, scaleability, and modifiability (Monahan 2002b). It should go without saying that I am not advocating for multi-purpose rooms here, which architects often call "no-purpose rooms" because they do not suggest themselves to any particular uses or alterations. Multi-purpose rooms, in other words, require users to do all the cognitive and physical work to make the spaces support particular activities. For a compelling case study of a "fluid technology" in action, see Marianne de Laet and Annemarie Mol's analysis of the Zimbabwe Bush Pump (de Laet & Mol 2000).

Chapter 2

1. See Petrosky (1990) for an exploration of the elaborate systems of interrelated dependencies required to produce the "simple" artifact of a pencil.

2. Social practices create ties between individuals, technologies, and the world, so attending to them enables a perceptual shift that reveals the production and reproduction of cultural meanings across system levels (de Certeau 1984; Bourdieu 1977; Ortner 1994). Lave and Wenger (1991, 52) articulate this perceptual shift well in their treatment of learning:

> to insist on starting with social practice [instead of social structure], on taking participation to be the crucial process, and on including the social world at the core of the analysis . . . suggests a very explicit focus on the person, but as a person-in-the-world, as

a member of a sociocultural community. This focus in turn promotes a view of knowing as activity by specific people in specific circumstances.

Studying people-in-the-world this way pushes scholarship to account for how knowledge construction is simultaneously situated in a set of local practices and connected to larger social structures. I focus on practices to trace the relations and flows of meaning that link individuals to the world while enabling individuals to construct that world.

3. This chapter is a modified version of a previously published article (Monahan 2004a).

4. John Dewey's writing on the necessary material constraints of all learning experiences resonates with the concept of built pedagogy developed in Chapter 1. Dewey (1944, 18) says: "[I]n general it may be said that the things we take for granted without inquiry or reflection are just the things which determine our conscious thinking and decide our conclusions. And these habitudes which lie below the level of reflection are just those which have been formed in constant give and take of relationship with others."

Chapter 3

1. Many social scientists would question the independence of the managerial class and consequently its label as a "class" versus some other designation such as status group, occupational group, or stratum (e.g., Bell 1980). Following from Barbara and John Ehrenreich (1977), who posit the rise of a "Professional-Managerial Class" (PMC), I perceive information technology specialists as comprising a new occupational stratum within this growing PMC: regardless of the lack of unity among them, these specialists are collectively ushering in new forms of technological life. But, perhaps the classic Marxist definition of class as tied to economic determinants, such as relationship to ownership or means of production, is becoming less relevant in the post-Fordist era where people no longer perceive themselves as class members or act in class differentiated ways, and where other determinants such as race, gender, education, or religion continue to play major roles in structuring life chances. Of course, class should be studied and economic inequalities corrected, but such corrections would only be one step toward achieving a just society.

2. Passages from a previously published article (Monahan 2005) appear in this chapter.

3. I call this trend a "development" rather than a departure, because the key financial and assessment functions of the district have depended almost entirely on standardized, quantified information for some time. The figures for student "average daily attendance" determine the number of tax dollars allocated to the district for educational operations, and

the figures for student performance on the "Stanford 9" standardized test determine the ranking of schools on the "academic performance index," which is used to ascribe educational success or failure. Both of these functions are validated by a technological culture of information generating, processing, and storing.

4. Title I is the largest Federal aid program for education. It originated with the Elementary and Secondary Education Act of 1965 and was reauthorized with the Federal Improving America's Schools Act (IASA) of 1994. It is awarded to schools in high poverty areas (determined by number of students receiving subsidized meals or by other measures) to help meet the needs of those student populations.

Chapter 4

1. Passages from a previously published article (Monahan 2005) appear in this chapter.

2. One deleterious effect of this new accountability regime is that good teachers in schools serving poor neighborhoods have incentives to relocate to wealthier neighborhood schools rather than be held responsible for the substandard performance of needy students. This incentive structure is then replicated across school districts, as school superintendent Roy Romer (2001) explained, when credentialed teachers relocate to neighboring and better paying school districts, leaving L.A. Unified with 25 percent noncredentialed teachers.

3. As I was waiting for an interview in a local district office, one of the secretaries lamented to me that a year after restructuring, she must still redirect calls every day to central offices from people who incorrectly presume that all business is now managed by local districts. This is but one insight into the steep learning curve that frequent restructuring imposes upon employees in the district. An additional amazing fact was shared with me by student TAs at Concrete High who said that the thermostats for air conditioners at the high school were located in the downtown offices miles away, presenting serious cooling challenges for all the new technical hardware being installed. I was unable to verify this claim.

4. The influence of the teachers' union in negotiating territories, responsibilities, and rewards betrays a social justice side to territoriality in L.A. Unified. While as a whole the outcomes may be less than ideal, the organization lives by maintaining productive tensions that are not simply about individual or group recalcitrance.

5. Another way that L.A. Unified adapts to changing external pressures and educational mandates is through its creative expansion of time into space in the form of year-round, multi-track schools. As an example, when a school can only accommodate 2667 students but is required to serve 4000,

it can split the student population into three groups, known as "tracks," and then rotate the tracks throughout the year so that only 2 tracks are "on" at any given time. Teachers are then assigned to tracks just like students. This destroys any sense of shared vacation time for students and their families, but it does manage to expand the capacity of the school system without building more schools. Charter schools and school-university partnerships represent two other ways to contend with spatial and financial crises through the postponement strategy of outsourcing, and thereby decentralizing, responsibility.

6. Military conceptualizations of L.A. Unified's mission contribute to this obstacle of territoriality. As the media and policymakers describe it, L.A. Unified is engaged in a "war" on poor student achievement (Bai 2001), and many teachers perpetuate this military myth with metaphors of their classrooms as "battle zones" or "trenches." The military metaphor is reinforced in the disciplinary architecture of schools: barbed-wire, locked gates, weapons screening technologies, alarm systems, immovable desks, and so on. Finally, standardized testing, which was developed for military screening and ranking purposes to begin with (Carson 1993), is embraced, by administrators at least, as the primary diagnostic tool for assessing progress in this never-ending war. Until such conceptualizations begin to change, and their manifestations in architecture and policy change as well, efforts at decentralization will rub against the grain of the indefatigable mission impossible.

Chapter 5

1. This chapter is a modified version of a previously published article (Monahan 2004c).

2. For instance, in April 2001, participants in the Instructional Technology Commission (ITC) online discussion group criticized E-Rate network specifications set by IBM for L.A. schools. The conversation was quickly silenced by a central administrator who stated: "Since the list serve is open forum, I will state the network design was not from IBM or finalized by IBM."

3. One of the general arguments of this book is that publicly funded technology projects achieve privatization by other means, by transferring public money into the private sector. While E-Rate is technically funded by telecommunications companies, these companies simply pass the cost burden on to consumers through "universal service" surcharges on phone bills. Thus, in practice, E-Rate is a publicly funded program that funnels billions of dollars a year into the private sector with the ostensibly altruistic goal of overcoming "the digital divide." Recent investigations have revealed that telecommunications companies have routinely defrauded the program,

leading a House Oversight Committee to conclude that these companies view the program as "a big candy jar [of] free money" (Dillon 2004).

4. This problem framing by central and local social worlds is accurate on the surface but also reductive. Administrators do tend to encourage the completion of some school infrastructures before others, and this is likely due to a variety of reasons: strong collaborative ties with those schools, cooperative vendors assigned to those schools, fewer funding mismatches, etc. Likewise, school-site technology coordinators often assist other schools with grant writing, equipment selection, district purchasing procedures, and even wiring.

Chapter 6

1. At the time of this research, the Board of Education was clearly divided into two main camps: those generally hostile to teachers' unions and receptive to privatization, and those generally supportive of teachers' unions and skeptical of privatization. The alternative press in Los Angeles frequently ran stories on how the "business friendly" Mayor of Los Angeles at the time, Richard Riordan, heavily subsidized the election campaigns of antiunion Board members.

2. The establishment of ICANN is an important example because it illustrates some of the difficulties and pitfalls of governing public goods in an increasingly privatized sector. While initially intended to be a bottom-up organization with public representation, it has since become a top-down enforcer of corporate trademark interests. According to the organization Computer Professionals for Social Responsibility: "These trademark interests are currently pressing non-legislative expansion of rights for trademark holders, at the expense of free speech and expression . . . ICANN's claim of 'openness and transparency, based on Internet community consensus, bottom-up in its orientation and globally representative' is far from the reality of the situation. ICANN is the classic top-down organizational structure without accountability. When its bylaws are inconvenient, they are changed without discussion" (U.S. Senate 2001; see also Mueller 2002).

Chapter 7

1. For example, on June 22, 2001, I heard an underwriting advertisement on NPR for "decision assistance" by Lexis-Nexis. Furthermore, a quick search with the Google search engine on January 12, 2005, turned up 641,000 exact matches for "decision support system."

2. As might be expected, other school districts (as related by McIntire 2002) and many institutions of higher education do have such systems in place, but perhaps not on the same scale of L.A. Unified's DSS venture. And, in

higher education, such systems are becoming even more widespread and integrated to assist the federal government's Department of Homeland Security in tracking foreign students (Arnone 2003a, 2003b). Thus, fragmented centralization is occurring between federal and local levels (and recursively beyond), not just within organizations.

3.   A Disney Web page describes this theme park: "Designed by Walt Disney Imagineering in the tradition, fun and magic of classic Disney to capture the allure and beauty of Northern, Central and Southern California on 55 acres of attractions. Among the themed areas is an exciting California beachfront, a Hollywood-inspired district, and an area celebrating the state's natural beauty and diverse cultures" (Disney Online 2003). As an icon of imagineering, the California Adventure stands in as an amazingly sanitized simulacrum and substitute for any direct interaction with the state's terrains, attractions, or peoples.

REFERENCES

AAUW (American Association of University Women Educational Foundation). 2000. Tech-Savvy: Educating Girls in the New Computer Age [cited 2005], available from http://www.aauw.org/member_center/publications/TechSavvy/TechSavvy.pdf.

Abu-Lughod, J.L. 1999. *New York, Chicago, Los Angeles: America's Global Cities*, Minneapolis, MN: University of Minnesota Press.

Agre, P.E. 1997. Beyond the Mirror World: Privacy and the Representational Practices of Computing, in *Technology and Privacy: The New Landscape*, P.E. Agre and M. Rotenberg, Eds., Cambridge, MA: MIT Press, 29–61.

Akrich, M. 1992. The De-Scription of Technological Objects, in *Shaping Technology / Building Society: Studies in Sociotechnical Change*, W.E. Bijker and J. Law, Eds., Cambridge, MA: MIT Press, 205–224.

Alther, J. 2001. Local Area Data Networks: Monthly Progress Report, BFAT Committee, Los Angeles: Los Angeles Unified School District, available from http://www.lausd.k12.ca.us/lausd/committees/bfat/pdf/erate112901.pdf.

Amin, A. 1994. Post-Fordism: Models, Fantasies and Phantoms of Transition, in *Post-Fordism: A Reader*, A. Amin, Ed., Cambridge, MA: Blackwell Publishers, 1–39.

Anders, G. 1987 (1956). *The Obsolescence of Man (Die Antiquiertheit des Menschen: Über die Seele im Zeitalter der zweiten industriellen Revolution)*, J. Gaines and P. Keast, Trans., Munich: unpublished manuscript.

Anderson, R. and Sharrock, W. 1993. Can Organizations Afford Knowledge?, *Computer Supported Coop. Work* 1:143–161.

Appadurai, A. 1996. *Modernity at Large: Cultural Dimensions of Globalization*, Minneapolis, MN: University of Minnesota Press.

Apple, M.W. 2000. Between Neoliberalism and Neoconservatism: Education and Conservatism in a Global Context, in *Globalization and Education: Critical Perspectives*, N.C. Burbules and C.A. Torres, Eds., New York: Routledge, 57–77.

Apple, M.W. and Jungck, S. 1998. "You Don't Have to be a Teacher to Teach This Unit": Teaching, Technology, and Control in the Classroom, in *Education / Technology / Power: Educational Computing as a Social Practice*, H. Bromley and M.W. Apple, Eds., Albany, NY: State University of New York Press, 133–154.

Arnone, M. 2003a. Reorganization of U.S. Agencies Leaves Colleges Worried About How Foreign Students Will Be Treated, *Chron. of Higher Educ.* 49 (26):A28.

Arnone, M. 2003b. Database to Track Foreign Students Still is not Ready, Government Report Finds, *Chron. of Higher Educ.*, March 24, online.

Bai, M. 2001. A Cowboy Takes L.A. to School, *Newsweek*, July 23, 32–33.

Barrett, B. 2001. LAUSD's Online Bungle, *Los Angeles Daily News*, March 22, 1, 16.

Barthes, R. 1957. *Mythologies*, A. Lavers, Trans., New York: The Noonday Press.

Beare, H. and Slaughter, R. 1993. *Education for the Twenty-first Century*, New York: Routledge.

Becker, H.S. 1982. *Art Worlds*, Berkeley, CA: University of California Press.

Bell, D. 1980. The New Class: A Muddled Concept, in *The Winding Passage: Essays and Sociological Journeys 1960–1980*, D. Bell, Ed., Cambridge, MA: ABT Books, 144–164.

Bijker, W.E., Hughes, T., and Pinch, T. 1987. *The Social Construction of Technological Systems: New Directions in the Sociology and History of Technology*, Cambridge, MA: MIT Press.

Bijker, W.E. and Law, J. 1992. *Shaping Technology / Building Society: Studies in Sociotechnical Change*, Cambridge, MA: MIT Press.

Blackmore, J. 2000. Globalization: A Useful Concept for Feminists Rethinking Theory and Strategies in Education?, in *Globalization and Education: Critical Perspectives*, N.C. Burbules and Carlos Alberto Torres, Eds., New York: Routledge, 133–155.

Bourdieu, P. 1977. *Outline of a Theory of Practice*, R. Nice, Trans., Cambridge, UK: Cambridge University Press.

Bourdieu, P. 1998. *Acts of Resistance: Against the New Myths of Our Time*, Cambridge, UK: Polity Press.

Bowker, G. 1992. What's in a Patent?, in *Shaping Technology/Building Society: Studies in Sociotechnical Change*, W.E. Bijker and J. Law, Eds., Cambridge, MA: MIT Press, 53–74.

Bowker, G.C. and Star, S.L. 1999. *Sorting Things Out: Classification and Its Consequences*, Cambridge, MA: MIT Press.

Boyle, J. 1997. A Politics of Intellectual Property: Environmentalism for the Net?, available from http://www.law.duke.edu/boylesite/intprop.htm.

Bromley, H. 1998. Introduction: Data-Driven Democracy? Social Assessment of Educational Computing, in *Education / Technology / Power: Educational Computing as a Social Practice*, H. Bromley and M.W. Apple, Eds., Albany, NY: State University of New York Press, 1–25.

Brown, J. 2000. What Happened to the Women's Web?, Salon.com, August 25 [cited 2001], available from http://www.salon.com/tech/feature/2000/08/25/womens_web/index.html.

Brown, J. 1992. *The Definition of a Profession: The Authority of Metaphor in the History of Intelligence Testing, 1890–1930*, Princeton, NJ: Princeton University Press.

Brown, W. 1995. *States of Injury: Power and Freedom in Late Modernity*, Princeton, NJ: Princeton University Press.

Bucciarelli, L.L. 1994. *Designing Engineers*, Cambridge, MA: MIT Press.

Burbules, N.C. and Torres, C.A. 2000. *Globalization and Education: Critical Perspectives*, New York: Routledge.

Bush, C.G. 1997. Women and the Assessment of Technology, in *Technology and the Future*, 7th ed., A.H. Teich, Ed., New York: St. Martin's Press, 157–179.

Caldeira, T.P.R. 2000. *City of Walls: Crime, Segregation, and Citizenship in São Paulo*, Berkeley, CA: University of California Press.

California Department of Education. 2002. Update on Digital High School Funding.

CalSAVE. 2003. FAQs About CalSAVE. Monterey County Office of Education.

Carson, J. 1993. Army Alpha, Army Brass, and the Search for Army Intelligence, *Isis* 84:278–309.

Castells, M. 1996. *The Rise of the Network Society*, Cambridge, MA: Blackwell Publishers.

Chandler, A.D. 1977. *The Visible Hand: The Managerial Revolution in American Business*, Cambridge, MA: Belknap Press.

Chapman, P.D. 1988. *Schools as Sorters: Lewis M. Terman, Applied Psychology, and the Intelligence Testing Movement, 1890–1930*, New York: New York University Press.

Cherkasky, T.D. 1999. Design Style: A Method for Critical Analysis of Design Applied to Workplace Technologies, Doctoral dissertation, Science & Technology Studies, Rensselaer Polytechnic Institute, Troy, NY.

City of Los Angeles. 2003. City of Los Angeles 2003 Economic & Demographic Information [Web site], November 18 [cited August 1 2004], available from http://www.lacity.org/cao/econdemo.htm.

Clark, L. and Wasson, P. 2002. ALA Applauds Federal Court Ruling on the Children's Internet Protection Act [Web site]. American Library Association [cited June 11 2002], available from http://www.ala.org/cipa/cipatrial9.html.

Clarke, A. 1990. A Social Worlds Adventure: The Case of Reproductive Science, in *Theories of Science in Society*, S.E. Cozzens and T.F. Gieryn, Eds., Bloomington, IN: Indiana University Press, 15–42.

Clement, A. and Van den Besselaar, P. 1993. A Retrospective Look at PD Projects, *Commn. of the ACM* 36 (6):29–37.

Clifford, J. 1997. *Routes: Travel and Translation in the Late Twentieth Century*, Cambridge, MA: Harvard University Press.

Comaroff, J. and Comaroff, J.L. 2000. Millennial Capitalism: First Thoughts on a Second Coming, *Public Cult.* 12 (2):291–343.

Cuban, L. 1986. *Teachers and Machines: The Classroom Use of Technology Since 1920*, New York: Teachers College, Columbia University.

Davis, M. 1990. *City of Quartz: Excavating the Future in Los Angeles*, New York: Vintage Books.

Dear, M. 2000. *The Postmodern Urban Condition*, Oxford, UK: Blackwell Publishers.

Dear, M. 2002. Los Angeles and the Chicago School: Invitation to a Debate, *City & Community* 1 (1):5–32.

Dear, M. and Flusty, S. 1998. Postmodern Urbanism, *Ann. of the Assoc. of Am. Geographers* 88 (1):50–72.

de Certeau, M. 1984. *The Practice of Everyday Life*, S. Rendall, Trans., Berkeley, CA: University of California Press.

de Laet, M. and Mol, A. 2000. The Zimbabwe Bush Pump: Mechanics of a Fluid Technology. *Soc. Stud. of Science* 30 (2):225–63.

Deleuze, G. 1992. Postscript on the Societies of Control, *October* 59:3–7, available from http://www.nadir.org/nadir/archiv/netzkritik/societyof control.html.

Deloitte & Touche LLP. 2002. Los Angeles Unified School District Proposition BB Bond Program: A Review of Project and Program Management for the Proposition BB Bond Program, Los Angeles: Los Angeles Unified School District, available from http://www.lausd.k12.ca.us/lausd/offices/IG/PDFdocs/ReviewBBBond.pdf.

Dewey, J. 1944. *Democracy and Education: An Introduction to the Philosophy of Education*, New York: Free Press.

Diamond, D. 2002. One Nation, Overseas, *Wired Archive* 10 (6), available from http://www.wired.com/wired/archive/10.06/philippines.html.

Dillon, S. 2004. School Internet Program Lacks Oversight, Investigator Says, *The New York Times*, June 18.

Disney Online. 2003. Disneyland Resort: Disney's California Adventure, Disney [cited March 17 2003], available from http://disney.go.com/vacations/grandopening/press2.html.

Douglas, M. 1986. *How Institutions Think*, Syracuse, NY: Syracuse University Press.

Downey, G.L. and Dumit, J. 1997. *Cyborgs & Citadels: Anthropological Interventions in Emerging Sciences and Technologies*, Santa Fe, NM: School of American Research Press.

Drucker, P.F. 1999. *Management Challenges for the 21st Century*, New York: Harper Collins.

Duggan, L. 2003. *The Twilight of Equality?: Neoliberalism, Cultural Politics, and the Attack on Democracy*, Boston: Beacon Press.

Edelman, M. 1988. *Constructing the Political Spectacle*, Chicago: University of Chicago Press.

Edwards, P.N. 1996. *The Closed World: Computers and the Politics of Discourse in Cold War America*, Cambridge, MA: MIT Press.

Eglash, R. 1998. Cybernetics and American Youth Subculture, *Cult. Stud.* 12 (3):382–409.

Eglash, R., Croissant, J.L., Di Chiro, G., and Fouché, R. 2004. *Appropriating Technology: Vernacular Science and Social Power*, Minneapolis, MN: University of Minnesota Press.

Ehrenreich, B. and Ehrenreich, J. 1977. The Professional-managerial Class, *Radical America* Part 1 (11):7–31.

Eisner, M.D. 1996. Foreword, in *Walt Disney Imagineering: A Behind the Dreams Look at Making the Magic Real*, Imagineers (Group) and Walt Disney Company, Eds., New York: Hyperion, 9–10.

Escobar, A. 1995. *Encountering Development: The Making and Unmaking of the Third World*, Princeton, NJ: Princeton University Press.

ETS (Educational Testing Service). 1999. Does it Compute?: The Relationship between Educational Technology and Student Achievement in Mathematics, Princeton, NJ: Educational Testing Service, available from ftp://ftp.ets.org/pub/res/technolog.pdf.

Eubanks, V. 2004. Popular Technology: Citizenship and Inequality in the Information Economy, Doctoral dissertation, Science and Technology Studies, Rensselaer Polytechnic Institute, Troy, NY.

Fabian, J. 1983. *Time and the Other: How Anthropology Makes its Object*, New York: Columbia University Press.

Ferguson, J. 2002. Global Disconnect: Abjection and the Aftermath of Modernism, in *The Anthropology of Globalization: A Reader*, J.X. Inda and R. Rosaldo, Eds., Malden, MA: Blackwell Publishers, 136–153.

Fischer, M.M.J. 1999. Emergent Forms of Life: Anthropologies of Late or Postmodernities, *Annu. Review of Anthropology* 28:455–78.

Fisher, J.A. 2005. Pharmaceutical Paternalism and the Privatization of Clinical Trials, Doctoral dissertation, Science and Technology Studies, Rensselaer Polytechnic Institute, Troy, NY.

Flusty, S. 1994. *Building Paranoia: The Proliferation of Interdictory Spaces and the Erosion of Spatial Justice*, West Hollywood, CA: Los Angeles Forum for Architecture and Urban Design.

Fogelson, R.M. 1967. *The Fragmented Metropolis: Los Angeles, 1850–1930*, Berkeley, CA: University of California Press.

Fortun, K. 2001. *Advocacy after Bhopal: Environmentalism, Disaster, New Global Orders*, Chicago: University of Chicago Press.

Foucault, M. 1977. *Discipline & Punish: The Birth of the Prison*, New York: Vintage Books, Random House.

Foucault, M. 1986. Of Other Spaces (Des Espaces Autres), *Diacritics* 16:22–27.

Foucault, M. 1988. Technologies of the Self, in *Technologies of the Self: A Seminar with Michel Foucault*, L.H. Martin, H. Gutman, and P.H. Hutton, Eds., Amherst, MA: University of Massachusetts Press, 16–49.

Fraser, N. 1989. *Unruly Practices: Power, Discourse, and Gender in Contemporary Social Theory*, Minneapolis, MN: University of Minnesota Press.

Fujimura, J.H. 1987. Constructing Do-able Problems in Cancer Research: Articulating Alignment, *Soc. Stud. of Science* 17 (2):257–93.

Fujimura, J.H. 1992. Crafting Science: Standardized Packages, Boundary Objects, and "Translation," in *Science as Practice and Culture*, A. Pickering, Ed., Chicago: University of Chicago Press, 168–211.

Fulton, W. 1997. *The Reluctant Metropolis: The Politics of Urban Growth in Los Angeles*, Baltimore, MD: Johns Hopkins University Press.

Gell, M. and Cochrane, P. 1996. Learning and Education in an Information Society, in *Information and Communication Technologies: Visions and Realities*, W.H. Dutton and M. Peltu, Eds., New York: Oxford University Press, 249–264.

Giroux, H.A. 2004. *The Terror of Neoliberalism: Authoritarianism and the Eclipse of Democracy*, Boulder, CO: Paradigm Publishers.

Graham, S. and Marvin, S. 2001. *Splintering Urbanism: Networked Infrastructures, Technological Mobilities and the Urban Condition*, New York: Routledge.

Grosz, E. 2001. *Architecture from the Outside: Essays on Virtual and Real Space, Writing Architecture Series*, Cambridge, MA: MIT Press.

Grosz, E. 2003. Deleuze, Bergson and Uncharted Futures: Duration, the Virtual and History (unpublished manuscript).

Habermas, J. 1989. *The Structural Transformation of the Public Sphere: An Inquiry into a Category of Bourgeois Society*, Cambridge, MA: MIT Press.

Hakken, D. 1999. *Cyborgs@Cyberspace?: An Ethnographer Looks to the Future*, New York: Routledge.

Haraway, D.J. 1992. The Promises of Monsters: A Regenerative Politics for Inappropriate/d Others, in *The Promises of Monsters: A Regenerative Politics for Inappropriate/d Others*, L. Grossberg, C. Nelson, and P.A. Treichler, Eds., New York: Routledge, 295–337.

Haraway, D.J. 1997. *Modest_Witness@Second_Millennium.FemaleMan_Meets_OncoMouse: Feminism and Technoscience*, New York: Routledge.

Hardt, M. and Negri, A. 2000. *Empire*, Cambridge, MA: Harvard University Press.

Hartung, W.D. 2004. Outsourcing is Hell, *The Nation*, June 7.

Harvey, D. 1990. *The Condition of Postmodernity: An Enquiry into the Origins of Cultural Change*, Cambridge, MA: Blackwell Publishers.

Harvey, D. 1991. Flexibility: Threat or Opportunity?, *Socialist Review* 21 (1):65–77.

Hess, D.J. 1995. *Science & Technology in a Multicultural World: The Cultural Politics of Facts & Artifacts*, New York: Columbia University Press.

Illich, I. 1971. *Deschooling Society*, New York: Harper & Row.

Illich, I. 1973. *Tools for Conviviality*, New York: Harper & Row.

Inda, J.X. and Rosaldo, R. 2002. *The Anthropology of Globalization: A Reader*, Malden, MA: Blackwell Publishers.

Jackson, T. 1997. Working Cyberspace, *Bad Subjects: Political Education for Everyday Life* 32, available from http://eserver.org/bs/32/jackson.html.

Kaschadt, K. 2002. Jeremy Bentham: The Penitentiary Panopticon or Inspection House, in *CTRL [SPACE]: Rhetorics of Surveillance from Bentham to Big Brother*, T.Y. Levin, U. Frohne, and P. Weibel, Eds., Cambridge, MA: MIT Press, 114–119.

Katz, C. 2001. The State Goes Home: Local Hypervigilance of Children and the Global Retreat from Social Reproduction, *Soc. Justice* 28 (3):47–56.

Keil, R. 1998. *Los Angeles: Globalization, Urbanization and Social Struggles*, New York: John Wiley & Sons.

Klein, N M. 1997. *The History of Forgetting*, New York: Verso.

Konantz, J. 2001. Business, Finance, Audit & Technology Committee: Technology Projects Status Report, April 19, 2001, Los Angeles: Los Angeles Unified School District.

Korten, D.C. 1995. *When Corporations Rule the World*, West Hartford, CT: Kumarian Press.

Latour, B. 1987. *Science in Action: How to Follow Scientists and Engineers through Society*, Cambridge, MA: Harvard University Press.

Latour, B. 1992. Where Are the Missing Masses? The Sociology of a Few Mundane Artifacts, in *Shaping Technology / Building Society: Studies in Sociotechnical Change*, W.E. Bijker and J. Law, Eds., Cambridge, MA: MIT Press, 225–258.

Lave, J. and Wenger, E. 1991. *Situated Learning: Legitimate Peripheral Participation*, Cambridge, UK: Cambridge University Press.

Lefebvre, H. 1991. *The Production of Space*, D. Nicholson-Smith, Trans., Cambridge, MA: Blackwell Publishers.

Lessig, L. 1999. *Code: And Other Laws of Cyberspace*, New York: Basic Books.

Los Angeles Unified School District. 2001. News Release: LAUSD Makes Major Investment in Reading [Web site], Los Angeles Unified School District [cited June 1 2002], available from http://www.lausd.k12.ca.us/lausd/offices/Office_of_Communications/waterford.pdf.

Los Angeles Unified School District. 2002. Instructional Technology Plan [Web site], Los Angeles Unified School District [cited March 29 2003], available from http://www.lausd.k12.ca.us/lausd/techplan/LAU SDI TP 2K2.p df.

Los Angeles Unified School District. 2003. 5 Year Review LAUSD Ethnic Survey [Web site], Los Angeles Unified School District [cited January 21 2003], available from http://www.lausd.k12.ca.us/lausd/offices/bulletins/5_yr_review.html.

Los Angeles Unified School District. 2004. Fingertip Facts 2004–05, Los Angeles: Los Angeles Unified School District, available from http://www.lausd.k12.ca.us/lausd/offices/Office_of_Communications/Fingertip_Facts_2004_2005.pdf.

Low, S.M. 2003. *Behind the Gates: Life, Security and the Pursuit of Happiness in Fortress America*, New York: Routledge.

Lyon, D. 2001. *Surveillance Society: Monitoring Everyday Life*, Buckingham, UK: Open University.

Lyotard, J.-F. 1979. *The Postmodern Condition: A Report on Knowledge*, G. Bennington and B. Massumi, Trans., MN: University of Minnesota Press.

Madigan, N. 2004. $270 Million and School Could at Last Be Finished, *The New York Times*, June 28.

Marcus, G.E. 1995. Ethnography in/of the World System: The Emergence of Multi-sited Ethnography, *Annu. Review of Anthropology* 24:95–117.

Marcus, G.E. and Fischer, M.M.J. 1986. *Anthropology as Cultural Critique: An Experimental Moment in the Human Sciences*, Chicago: University of Chicago Press.

Martin, E. 1994. *Flexible Bodies: The Role of Immunity in American Culture from the Days of Polio to the Age of AIDS*, Boston: Beacon Press.

McCullough, M. 1996. *Abstracting Craft: The Practiced Digital Hand*, Cambridge, MA: MIT Press.

McIntire, T. 2002. Data-Driven Decision Making, *Technology & Learning*, June, 18–33.

Monahan, T. 2001. The Analog Divide: Technology Practices in Public Education, *Computers & Society* 31 (3):22–31, available from http://torin monahan.com/papers/analog.htm.

Monahan, T. 2002a. Los Angeles Studies: The Emergence of a Specialty Field, *City & Society* XIV (2):155–184, available from http://torinmona han.com/papers/LA_Studies.pdf.

Monahan, T. 2002b. Flexible Space & Built Pedagogy: Emerging IT Embodiments, *Inventio* 4 (1), available from http://www.torinmonahan.com/ papers/Inventio.html.

Monahan, T. 2002c. Hot Technologies on Every Pillow: The Discursive Development of Institutional Change, *Radical Pedagogy* 4 (1), available from http://radicalpedagogy.icaap.org/content/issue4_1/03_Monahan.html.

Monahan, T. 2004a. Just Another Tool? IT Pedagogy and the Commodification of Education, *The Urban Review* 36 (4): 271–292.

Monahan, T. 2004b. Digital Art Worlds: Technology and Productions of Value in Art Education, *Foundations in Art: Theory and Education in Review* 26:7–15, available from http://torinmonahan.com/papers/Digital_Art_ Worlds.htm.

Monahan, T. 2004c. Technology Policy as a Stealth Agent of Global Change, *Globalisation, Soc. and Educ.* 2 (3):355–376.

Monahan, T. 2005. The School System as a Post-Fordist Organization: Fragmented Centralization and the Emergence of IT Specialists, *Critical Sociology*, forthcoming.

Moore, S. 2002. L.A. Unified Brings Style to School Building Boom, *Los Angeles Times*, December 23, A1, A18.

Mueller, M. 2002. *Ruling the Root: Internet Governance and the Taming of Cyberspace*, Cambridge, MA: MIT Press.

Naipaul, V.S. 1979. *A Bend in the River*, 1st ed., New York: Knopf.

Nash, J. 1981. Ethnographic Aspects of the World Capitalist System, *Annu. Review of Anthropology* 10:393–423.

Negroponte, N. 1997. Negroponte, *Wired Archive* 5 (10), available from http:// www.wired.com/wired/archive/5.10/negroponte.html.

NYSL (New York State Library). 2003. E-Rate (Universal Services for Telecommunications Discounts Program), New York State Library [cited February 2003], available from http://www.nysl.nysed.gov/libdev/univsvc/.

Ong, A. 1991. The Gender and Labor Politics of Postmodernity, *Annu. Review of Anthropology* 20:279–309.

Ortner, S.B. 1994. Theory in Anthropology since the Sixties, in *Culture/Power/ History: A Reader in Contemporary Social Theory*, N.B. Dirks, G. Eley, and S.B. Ortner. Eds., Princeton, NJ: Princeton University Press, 372–411.

Osborne, D. and Gaebler, T. 1992. *Reinventing Government: How the Entrepreneurial Spirit is Transforming the Public Sector*, New York: Plume.

Peters, M., Marshall, J., and Fitzsimons, P. 2000. Managerialism and Educational Policy in a Global Context: Foucault, Neoliberalism, and the Doctrine of Self-Management, in *Globalization and Education: Critical Perspectives*, N.C. Burbules and C.A. Torres, Eds., New York: Routledge, 109–132.

Petroski, H. 1990. *The Pencil: A History of Design and Circumstance*, 1st ed., New York: Knopf.

Pfaffenberger, B. 1990. The Hindu Temple as a Machine, or, The Western Machine as a Temple, *Tech. et culture* 16:183–202.

Pfaffenberger, B. 1992. Technological Dramas, *Science, Technol., and Human Values* 17 (3):282–312.

Pinch, T. 1996. The Social Construction of Technology: A Review, in *Technological Change: Methods and Themes in the History of Technology*, R. Fox, Ed., Amsterdam, The Netherlands: Harwood Academic Publishers, 17–35.

Pinch, T.J. and Bijker, W.E. 1987. The Social Construction of Facts and Artifacts: Or How the Sociology of Science and the Sociology of Technology Might Benefit Each Other, in *The Social Construction of Technological Systems: New Directions in the Sociology and History of Technology*, W.E. Bijker, T.P. Hughes, and T. Pinch, Eds., Cambridge, MA: MIT Press, 17–50.

Piore, M.J. and Sabel, C.F. 1984. *The Second Industrial Divide: Possibilities for Prosperity*, New York: Basic Books.

Postigo, H.R. 2003. Copyright Law on the Internet: The Gap between the Law and the Individual, *Science, Technology and Society Nexus (Supplement)* 3 (2):14–17, available from http://sts.scu.edu/nexus/Issue3-2/Nexus3-2supplement.pdf.

Powers, R. 2000. *Plowing the Dark*, New York: Farrar, Straus, and Giroux.

Purnick, J. 2002. Overheard in the Bullpen: Not a Thing, *The New York Times*, June 17, B1.

Reich, R.B. 2000. *The Future of Success*, New York: A. Knopf.

Romer, R. 2001. Communication, February 27, LAUSD Board of Education Meeting, Los Angeles.

Ross, A. 2000. Silicon Valley as a Global Business Model (panel), paper read at Tulipomania Dotcom, Amsterdam, The Netherlands, available from http://absoluteone.ljudmila.org/25.php.

Ross, A. 2003. *No-Collar: The Humane Workplace and its Hidden Costs*, New York, NY: Basic Books.

Said, E.W. 1978. *Orientalism*, 1st ed., New York: Pantheon Books.

Sassen, S. 1991. *The Global City: New York, London, Tokyo*, Princeton, NJ: Princeton University Press.

Sassen, S. 2000. Lecture, paper read at Data, March 25, Rensselaer Polytechnic Institute, Troy, NY.

Schuler, D. and Namioka, A. 1993. *Participatory Design: Principles and Practices*, Hillsdale, NJ: Lawrence Erlbaum Associates.

Schwartz, J. 2003. Schools' Internet Subsidies are Called Fraud-Riddled, *The New York Times online*, January 10.

Schwarz, H.J. 2002. Techno-Territories: The Spatial, Technological and Social Reorganization of Office Work, Doctoral dissertation, Program in Science, Technology, and Society, Massachusetts Institute of Technology, Cambridge, MA.

Sclove, R.E. 1995. *Democracy and Technology*, New York: The Guilford Press.

Scott, A.J. 1996. High-Technology Industrial Development in the San Fernando Valley and Ventura County: Observations on Economic Growth and the Evolution of Urban Form, in *The City: Los Angeles and Urban Theory at the End of the Twentieth Century*, A.J. Scott and E.J. Soja, Eds., Berkeley, CA: University of California Press, 276–310.

Scott, A.J. and Soja, E.J. 1996. *The City: Los Angeles and Urban Theory at the End of the Twentieth Century*, Berkeley: University of California Press.

Scott W.R. 1995. *Institutions and Organizations*, Thousand Oaks, CA: Sage.

Scrapbookpages.com. 2003. Map of Sachsenhausen Camp [cited March 17 2003], available from http://www.scrapbookpages.com/Sachsenhausen/Map.html.

Shibutani, T. 1955. Reference Groups as Perspectives, *Am. J. of Sociol.* 60: 562–69.

Shore, C. and Wright, S. 2000. Coercive Accountability: The Rise of Audit Culture in Higher Education, in *Audit Cultures: Anthropological Studies in Accountability, Ethics, and the Academy*, M. Strathern, Ed., New York: Routledge, 57–89.

Silicon Valley Toxics Coalition. 1997. The Environmental Cost of Computers: Silicon Valley Toxics Coalition, available from http://www.corpwatch.org/article.php?id=3431.

Smith, D. 2000. 5 Blamed for Belmont Return to Jobs, *Los Angeles Times*, November 10, 2000, B1, B4.

Smith, T. 1997. The Dark Side of High-tech Development, *SVTC Action Archive*, Spring, available from http://www.svtc.org/resource/news_let/drkside.htm.

Sokal, M.M. 1987. *Psychological Testing and American Society: 1890–1930*, London: Rutgers University Press.

Spring, J. 1998. *Education and the Rise of the Global Economy*, Mahwah, NJ: Lawrence Erlbaum Associates.

Star, S.L. and Griesemer, J. 1989. Institutional Ecology, "Translations," and Boundary Objects, *Soc. Stud. of Science* 19 (3):387–420.

Starr, Paul. 1996. Computing Our Way to Educational Reform, *The Am. Prospect* 27:50–59.

Strathern, M. 2000. *Audit Cultures: Anthropological Studies in Accountability, Ethics, and the Academy*, New York: Routledge.

Thompson, F. 2003. *Fordism, Post-Fordism, and the Flexible System of Production* [cited April 1 2003], available from http://www.willamette.edu/~fthompso/MgmtCon/Fordism_&_Postfordism.html.

Trigg, R. and Clement, A. 2000. Participatory Design, Palo Alto, CA: Computer Professionals for Social Responsibility, available from http://www.cpsr.org/issues/pdf.

Tyack, D. 1990. "Restructuring" in Historical Perspective: Tinkering toward Utopia, *Teachers Coll. Rec.* 92 (2):170–191.

Uchida, D. with Cetron, M. and McKenzie, F. 1996. Preparing Students for the 21st Century, Washington, DC: American Association of School Administrators.

U.S. Senate. 2001. Committee on Commerce, Science, and Transportation, testimony of the Domain Name Rights Coalition and Computer Professionals for Social Responsibility, February 14, available from http://www.eff.org/Infrastructure/DNS_control/ICANN_IANA_IAHC/20010214_icann_sen_hearing/0214dnr.pdf.

Valle, V.M. and Torres, R.D. 2000. *Latino Metropolis*, Minneapolis, MN: University of Minnesota Press.

Wallerstein, I. 1990. Culture as the Ideological Battleground of the Modern World-system, *Theory, Cult. & Society* 7:31–55.

Weisman, L.K. 1992. *Discrimination by Design: A Feminist Critique of the Man-Made Environment*, Chicago: University of Illinois Press.

Winner, L. 1977. *Autonomous Technology: Technics-out-of-control as a Theme in Political Thought*, Cambridge, MA: MIT Press.

Winner, L. 1986. *The Whale and the Reactor: A Search for Limits in an Age of High Technology*, Chicago: University of Chicago Press.

Withrow, F. with Long, H. and Marx, G. 1998. Preparing Schools and School Systems for the 21st Century, Arlington, VA: American Association of School Administrators.

Wolch, J. 1996. The Rise of Homelessness in Los Angeles during the 1980s, in *The City: Los Angeles and Urban Theory at the End of the Twentieth Century*, A.J. Scott and E.J. Soja, Eds., Berkeley, CA: University of California Press, 390–425.

Woodhouse, E.J. and Nieusma, D. 2001. Democratic Expertise: Integrating Knowledge, Power, and Participation, in *Knowledge, Power, and Participation in Environmental Policy Analysis*, M. Hisschemöller, R. Hoppe, W.N. Dunn, and J.R. Ravetz, Eds., New Brunswick, NJ: Transaction Publishers, 73–96.

Zuboff, S. 1988. *In the Age of the Smart Machine: The Future of Work and Power*, New York: Basic Books.

INDEX